REVIVING
Evangelical
ETHICS

REVIVING
Evangelical
ETHICS

The Promises and Pitfalls
of Classic Models of Morality

WYNDY CORBIN
REUSCHLING

Brazos Press
Grand Rapids, Michigan

© 2008 by Wyndy Corbin Reuschling

Published by Brazos Press
a division of Baker Publishing Group
P.O. Box 6287, Grand Rapids, MI 49516–6287
www.brazospress.com

Printed in the United States of America

Library of Congress Cataloging-in-Publication Data
Reuschling, Wyndy Corbin.
    Reviving evangelical ethics : the promises and pitfalls of classic models of morality / Wyndy Corbin Reuschling.
        p.   cm.
    Includes bibliographical references and index.
    ISBN 978-1-58743-189-0 (pbk.)
    1. Ethics. 2. Christian ethics. 3. Religion and ethics. I. Title.
BJ37.R44 2008
241'.0404—dc22   2007029474

Contents

Acknowledgments

Throughout the research and writing of this book, I was constantly reminded of the gifts of time and space granted to those of us whose scholarly vocations are means of service to the church and various other communities. The opportunity and responsibility to think, reflect, and write are privileges I hope I never take for granted. It is appropriate to acknowledge the many individuals who made both the "time" and "space" possible for writing this book, and those who fostered my thinking, reflecting, and writing.

For the time it took to write this book, my thanks go to the Board of Trustees and the Administration of Ashland Theological Seminary for an approved study leave in the spring of 2006 in order to write the bulk of the manuscript. I am grateful for the space at Tyndale House in Cambridge, England, for the staff, and for the generous access to resources and living accommodations for three months in the spring and summer of 2006.

Those who have fostered my thinking, reflecting, and writing are many. My colleagues and friends at Ashland Theological Seminary continue to provide a rich environment for thinking and reflection on the ministry implications of our scholarly passions and teaching. A number of them have contributed in significant ways to my own thinking and are acknowledged at various places throughout the book. The members of the Evangelical Ethics Interest Group at the Society of Christian Ethics continue to meet together each year to think together on our common vocations and concerns. Two members in particular, Christine Pohl and Glen Stassen, provided helpful feedback to a paper I presented which is incorporated into chapter 2 on scripture and ethics.

The writing of this book was facilitated by the feedback, competency, and interests of the people at Brazos Press. Rodney Clapp saw potential in our preliminary conversations about the topic and was present as the conversation became a proposal, when the proposal became a manuscript, and when the manuscript became a book. His skill as an editor, his great insights, and his good humor made the process less intimidating and actually enjoyable. Rebecca Cooper, Lisa Ann Cockrel, Lisa Williams, and Jeremy Wells graciously lent their expertise in managing the nuts and bolts of getting this thing done and published.

Finally, my gratitude to my husband, Mike Reuschling, extends far beyond what he did during the writing of this book. He cooked most of (okay . . . all of!) the meals while we were on study leave; he cajoled when the days seemed too long; he comforted when we yearned for home; and he collaborated out of his deep passion for God and scripture. "You're a good man, Mike Reuschling . . ."

Introduction

Why Evangelical Ethics Needs Reviving

W hen people discover that I teach Christian ethics at a seminary, they typically ask three questions. The first question is, "What is Christian ethics?" This question may indicate a genuine interest in the subject matter of Christian ethics or some confusion as to how Christian ethics is different than "just plain old ethics." Another question typically posed is, "Isn't 'Christian ethics' an oxymoron?" This question indicates various degrees of cynicism and suspicion about ethics in general and Christian ethics in particular. The cynicism may be exacerbated by claims to the supremacy of Christian ethics simply because it *is* Christian and therefore "obvious." Perhaps the skepticism increases when the consistency between what we profess and how we actually live becomes apparent, thereby elevating the perception that Christian ethics is oxymoronic.

By far the most prevalent inquiry to my confession that I teach Christian ethics is a quick shift to a long-awaited debate on ethical issues, often started by the direct question, "Well then, what is your position on . . . ?" The topics of interest are myriad but somewhat predictable. They range from abortion to capital punishment, euthanasia to stem cell research, war to same-sex marriage, and Supreme Court nominations to school vouchers, just to name a few. The list could go on (and on), depending on the context in which the question "What is your position on . . . ?" is asked. This question reveals two common misconceptions about ethics. The first is the assumption that ethics is about one's position on ethical issues—to defend one's position is the "right" or ethical thing to do. This question may also expose the ways in which ethics is co-opted by contemporary sociopolitical issues and the call for Christians to "take a stand" on divisive issues that fall along the conservative or liberal divides in the "culture wars."[1] I suspect the question "So, what is your position on . . ." is posed to me because of the evangelical context in which I am located. This context appears, at least on the surface, to succumb more easily to the temptation to see ethics as merely decision making and taking right positions on right issues, given the historical and social context of evangelicalism and the side it has typically taken in the culture wars debate.

This book is an attempt to address the misconceptions on the topic of ethics in general and Christian ethics in particular. What is Christian ethics? What specifically is *Christian* about Christian ethics? Is Christian ethics just about taking "right positions" on selected issues? More specifically, this book is an attempt to speak about moral understandings and discourse in evangelical ethics and to speak into a tradition in which I live and work as helpful critic (I hope) and as constructive participant (I hope) for transformation in our moral horizons and ethical practices because of our commitments to the God revealed particularly in the person of Jesus Christ.

Promises and Pitfalls of Classic Models of Morality

I will start my exploration of moral formation in evangelical ethics by examining the three classic theories of ethics through the works of three philosophers who articulated a particular moral system. These theories are deontology, teleology, and virtue ethics. *Deontology* is the study of duty or obligation. *Teleology* is typically understood as the ascertaining and achievement of moral outcomes or ends by considering the consequences of decisions, for the good they achieve or the harm they minimize. *Virtue ethics* focuses on the character of the individual as shaped by and reflected in habits, dispositions, behavior, and decisions. I choose as representatives of these schools of thought Immanuel Kant, John Stuart Mill, and

1. See James Davison Hunter, *Culture Wars: The Struggle to Define America* (New York: Basic Books, 1991). Hunter's work describes the perceived culture wars between the orthodox, who locate binding moral authority in transcendence, and progressives, who situate moral authority within the realm of human experience. This divide, according to Hunter, has produced a culture war between political and religious conservatives and liberals where the battle is fought in the following arenas: family, education, media and the arts, law, and electoral politics. See chapter 7 of *Culture Wars*.

Aristotle, respectively. I use "classic" in the sense that these theories and their representatives are widely referenced in ethics and have been appropriated in a variety of ways by philosophers, political and social theorists, theologians, and applied ethicists. It is in this way I see these thinkers and their proposals as classic, in the fairly broad use and acceptance of these theories by various disciplines seeking to understand ethical theories and their application. By "classic" I do not mean a unilateral, uncritical, and unqualified acceptance of these theories as true, as givens, and as the only way for construing and articulating moral norms and claims. This would be not only a denial of the reality that epistemology is limited by social location, so that claims humans make about what is given and true are finite and influenced by the assumptions embedded within our own contexts, but an acceptance that would also be detrimental to the assumptions of the Christian faith that give preference to God as the One who truly knows what is real and the One who is all wise. I find the unilateral, uncritical, and unqualified acceptance of these theories particularly problematic in that it risks stripping Christian ethics of its uniqueness and particularity, a concern that will be addressed in this book.[2]

It is my desire to interact with these classic models of morality to explore their pitfalls and promises in ethics for two primary reasons. The first is to articulate the claims of these classic theories and the ways in which the contexts and stories that gave birth to Kant's understanding of duty, Mill's principle of utility, and Aristotle's view of virtue may conflict and diverge in significant ways from a Christian story that has its own context, its own assumptions, and its own claims on individuals and communities who profess to live by a Christian narrative for their moral lives. Second, it is my hope to look in depth at the particular forms that these classic theories have taken in evangelical morality and ethical practices. My hope is to critique the ways they constrain and limit our understanding of moral norms to just duty, to just what works, and to just personal

---

2. I am indebted to a number of works by Christian theologians, philosophers, and ethicists who utilize ethical theory in a critical way for the purpose of articulating the *distinctive* claims and particularity of Christian ethics. See Stanley Hauerwas, *The Peaceable Kingdom* (Notre Dame, IN: University of Notre Dame Press, 1983); *Virtues and Practices in the Christian Tradition,* edited by Nancey Murphy, Brad Kallenberg, and Mark Thiessen Nation (Notre Dame, IN: University of Notre Dame Press, 1997); Samuel Wells, *Improvisation: The Drama of Christian Ethics* (Grand Rapids: Brazos Press, 2004); Glen Stassen and David Gushee, *Kingdom Ethics: Following Jesus in Contemporary Context* (Downers Grove, IL: InterVarsity Press, 2003); Allen Verhey, *Remembering Jesus: Christian Community, Scripture and the Moral Life* (Grand Rapids: Eerdmans, 2002); and *The Blackwell Companion to Christian Ethics,* edited by Stanley Hauerwas and Samuel Wells (Malden, MA: Blackwell, 2004).

piety. My aim is not only deconstructive, since this approach can take us only so far. My intent is to provide a helpful reconstruction of ethics and moral formation for an evangelical context by broadening our horizons beyond the classics to use the sources and narratives of Christian ethics—such as scripture, the kingdom of God, and the Christian community—to help us develop capacities in moral agency, moral discernment, and the formation of conscience.

I limit my use of the classic theories to select works that contain the main premises of the ethical theories I explore here. I am not a philosopher, nor am I trained in the academic discipline of philosophy. While I recognize the significant and numerous intersections between philosophy, theology, and ethics that enable me to "dabble" periodically in philosophy, my primary areas of interest and reflection are in the relationship between theology and ethics, and the implementation of beliefs and commitments as practices for the purpose of moral formation in and social witness by the church. The second reason for limiting my use of the classic theories pertains to the purpose of this book. This book is not primarily concerned with ethics according to Kant, Mill, or Aristotle as normative for Christians, but ethics according to Jesus Christ and the church he formed and continues to form as normative for Christian ethics.

I use *The Groundwork of the Metaphysics of Morals* by Immanuel Kant to investigate his understanding of duty. By so doing I highlight salient aspects of Kant's universal deontology for its contribution to ethics but also to alert us to the dangers of duty as a sole criterion for fostering moral commitment and behavior, especially when applied to the role of the Bible in ethics. John Stuart Mill's *Utilitarianism* is the primary source through which I examine the context and the claims of utilitarianism for both its contribution to ethical discourse and its limitations for Christian ethics in an evangelical context when ethics takes on a decidedly pragmatic bent in an understanding of church growth and discipleship. By exploring Aristotle's classic work *Nicomachean Ethics*, I articulate the dimensions of virtue ethics as Aristotle proposed them, discerning their use in a Christian context but also looking for their pitfalls when virtues are co-opted by the ideology of individualism and a commitment to personal piety as a guarantee of moral competence. Forays into other works by Kant, Mill, and Aristotle will be made as needed, as well as into the works of other scholars whose insights help to illuminate the contexts and ideas of these classic thinkers.

Reviving Evangelical Ethics

In the remainder of this chapter, I explain why I locate my exploration of the appropriation of the classic theories to evangelical ethics. I attempt to move toward an explanation of how the theological commitments, historical trajectories, cultural responses, and social context of evangelicalism cohere with the three classic theories. My concern is to ascertain how this coherence impacts moral insight and practices. In chapter 1, I give attention to the three classic theorists by noting the influences and central ideas of duty, utility, and virtue. I limit my critique of the classic thinkers to the aspects and implications of their theories that I find most troubling from a Christian perspective. In chapters 2, 3, and 4 I examine the appropriation of these theories—deontology, teleology, and virtue, respectively—in evangelical moral commitments and practices. I am proposing that deontology is appropriated as "just obeying the Bible" as a universal system for morality, regardless of one's faith commitment. This way of viewing the Bible, I argue, actually limits scripture's rich role in moral formation, and hence its authority, severing the Bible from the church to which it belongs and has been given as a means to shape our moral lives consonant with its story. I examine the utilitarian nature of practices in evangelicalism when church growth is measured by the "greatest good for the greatest number," given the evangelistic impetus at the heart of evangelicalism. The greatest good seen as the greatest number "getting saved" works against the call to discipleship and the formation of Christ followers as the norm for Christian morality. This view also imbibes the ideology that effectiveness is measured by success, particularly as measured in numbers. For virtue ethics, I consider the ways virtue is constrained by a belief in personal piety as the ultimate mark and purpose of the moral life, especially deleterious in an evangelical context infused with individualism and a therapeutic milieu. This conflation may result in minimizing a larger moral vision of social justice and the social nature of Christian virtues.

I aim to offer a constructive appraisal for moral formation in an evangelical context, which is the focus of the final chapter. I present certain dimensions of the moral life, such as the development of capacities in moral reflection and discernment, and the development of conscience aided by scripture and the Christian community, as crucial dimensions of the Christian moral life. I conclude the book with some practical suggestions as to how pastors and leaders desiring to form and reform our communities of faith as ethical communities of Christ may utilize scripture and see the context of the church as key to Christian moral formation, the development of conscience, and growth in moral capacities.

It is important at this point to explain why the focus of this work is evangelicalism. The first reason is personal. I continue to self-identify as an evangelical, with all the numerous caveats that are needed for locating me in this work and in making this self-disclosure. As a child I was influenced by the Methodist church in which I grew up, with its warm piety and commitment to living out the Christian faith in the world in the spirit of Jesus Christ and in the tradition of John Wesley. I learned early on that "there is no holiness but social holiness." Involvement in youth groups and service projects, playing the piano for the choir, and other church-related activities instilled in me that faith must be lived out in the world through service to others. Another strong influence was the Baptist church that was the center of community life on my father's side of the family. This small church in a small town located on the Ohio River in northern Kentucky, where I spent the majority of my summers, also shaped my understanding of Christian faith. Each day at noon, and again at six o'clock in the evening, the church bells would chime with the programmed hymns of the faith. You could hear these hymns from any point in this town of eight hundred. I vividly remember these comforting reminders of the church's presence and hearing my grandmother and great-aunts sing the words by heart along with the chimes. This experience helped me to become interested in the Bible and the "everyday" reality of living with Jesus. Vacation Bible School each summer introduced me again to the stories of Jesus and the continual need for "telling the story of Jesus."

I spent one year at the University of Lancaster in England during my junior year in college. I was actively involved in the Christian Union on campus, which met on Friday nights. I also attended one of the Anglican churches in the city. This was a low Anglican church that was a part of the renewal movement influenced by the ministry of David Watson and St. Michaels le Belfry in York.[3] It was a church with a distinctively charismatic commitment to the freedom of the Spirit in worship. The evening service was usually packed with regular attendees and college students, and it sometimes lasted up to four hours. The praise songs of the Fisherfolk and Graham Kendrick filled our minds and spirits and kept

3. David Watson became the vicar of St. Michaels in 1965 and was instrumental in leading this church and other churches such as St. Thomas in Lancaster, England, where I attended in a reawakening to the charismatic gifts and spiritual renewal. The spiritual vibrancy, when coupled with the rich liturgical traditions of the Anglican church, is a wonderful example of the church always seeking reformation and renewal. David Watson died in 1984.

us coming back each week, eager to spend these hours in worship. Later in college and for a few years after graduation, I was involved in Young Life. My participation in this community increased my understanding of evangelism as reaching out to others on their terms and in ways that were readily more understandable. This venture influenced other choices before me as a commitment to full-time ministry was beginning to take shape in my life. These decisions ultimately led me to seminary, missionary service in Japan, pastoral ministry, and eventually to graduate school and to a faculty position at a seminary that identifies itself as evangelical with all of the necessary caveats.

What are the necessary caveats? What does *evangelicalism* mean and how is my understanding and use of this term related to the purpose of this book, which is to explore the particular shape of evangelical ethical practices and moral formation? My attempt to define and describe *evangelical* is not a new one. As church historian Timothy Weber notes, "defining evangelicalism has become one of the biggest problems in American religious historiography."[4] *Evangelical* is a contested term and subject to a number of interpretations given the variety of theological traditions that make some kind of claim to be evangelical.[5] Many of these traditions have influenced and formed my own faith experience: Wesleyan holiness, Anabaptist pietism, charismatic renewal, independent free churches, and parachurch evangelistic ministries.

Our understanding of evangelicalism is determined by the perspective from which we start. The definition of evangelicalism may differ if one starts from a theological or historical perspective, or from a cultural one, using sociological insights to describe the various evangelical subcultures. From a theological perspective, evangelicalism may be defined by its commitments to the authority of scripture, the unique and salvific work and claims of Jesus Christ, one's personal response to Christ through an act of conversion, and one's commitment to evangelizing mission and ministry in the world.[6] Gary Dorrien, in *The Remaking of Evangelical Theology*, offers four classifications for understanding American evangelicalism: clas-

4. Timothy Weber, "Premillennialism and the Branches of Evangelicalism," in *The Variety of American Evangelicalism*, edited by Donald W. Dayton and Robert K. Johnston (Downers Grove, IL: InterVarsity Press, 1991), 12.

5. See Robert E. Webber, *Common Roots: A Call to Evangelical Maturity* (Grand Rapids: Zondervan, 1978). Webber identifies an array of fourteen evangelical subgroups that have been formed along racial and class lines, historical particularity, and differing theological emphases, all which are in some way "evangelical."

6. Robert Booth Fowler, *A New Engagement: Evangelical Political Thought, 1966–1976* (Grand Rapids: Eerdmans, 1982), 2–3.

sical evangelicalism from the scholastic and Reformed traditions; pietistic evangelicalism from holiness and revivalistic traditions; fundamentalist evangelicalism, which emerged from the modernist/fundamentalist controversy of the late nineteenth and early twentieth centuries; and the postconservative evangelicalism of more progressive thinkers within evangelicalism who have broadened their sources, methods, and concerns in hermeneutics and theology.[7] All classifications have in common a commitment to the authority of scripture, the necessity of a vibrant, growing personal faith commitment to Jesus Christ, and a sense of purpose and mission in the world communicated in both word and deed. As summarized by Robert Johnston, "for all their variety and particularity, descriptions of contemporary American evangelicalism have a commonality centered on a threefold commitment: a dedication to the gospel that is expressed in personal faith in Christ as Lord, an understanding of the gospel as defined authoritatively by Scripture, and a desire to communicate the gospel both in evangelism and social reform. Evangelicals are those who believe the gospel is to be experienced personally, defined biblically, and communicated passionately."[8]

My second reason for addressing evangelicalism in this book is my interest in exploring the intersections among theological commitments, sociohistorical location, moral commitments, and ethical practices in evangelicalism to address the question, "What *really* shapes evangelical morality and ethical practices?" Theology as a culturally embedded pursuit both shapes and is shaped by history, social context, and cultural influences. Theological commitments have their own connections with social and historical contexts, and evangelical theology is no different. Evangelical theology does have its own particular concerns and forms, given the historical trajectories it has followed. Evangelicals are located in particular social and cultural contexts that influence our moral perceptions, commitments, and ethical practices. From this perspective, then, it is important to understand the historical influences, sociological dynamics, and cultural responses that have shaped evangelical theology, and the particular moral commitments and ethical practices that have developed from these influences. This is a critical task so that we can move closer to a constructive understanding of what *really* affects evangelical ethical commitments for the purpose of reconstruction.

---

7. Gary Dorrien, *The Remaking of Evangelical Theology* (Louisville: Westminster John Knox Press, 1998), 2–3.

8. Robert K. Johnston, "American Evangelicalism: An Extended Family," in *The Variety of American Evangelicalism* (Downers Grove, IL: InterVarsity Press, 1991), 261.

Evangelicalism has deep historical and social roots in the concept of "America" as a world of new possibilities. According to Nathan Hatch, certain segments of American Christianity took in the early ideologies of democracy as they took root in American soil, which became characteristic of the early impulses of evangelicalism as a more popular form of religious expression developed between the American Revolution and the mid-eighteenth century. In *The Democratization of American Christianity*, Hatch explores the emergence of five traditions that have both formed and have been formed by the democratizing influences of equality, the right to think for oneself, the leveling of distinctions between clergy and laity, and an emphasis on one's personal spiritual experience as the norm of genuine religious faith.[9] The five traditions that Hatch feels best express the democratization of American Christianity are the Christian movement (Disciples of Christ), Methodists, Baptists, black churches, and Mormonism, because in their own ways they each represented the religious affections of the common person and, "however diverse their theologies and church organizations, they all offered common people, especially the poor, compelling visions of individual self-respect and collective self-confidence."[10] Evangelical religious expression used the ideologies of individualism, marketing strategies in revivals, and the entrepreneurial spirit of competition to make religious appeals to the populace and to ensure results in the marketplace of religious ideas. These democratizing influences of individualism, open competition, and mass appeal still characterize and influence certain segments of evangelicalism, which, in turn, has an effect on the moral commitments and ethical practices as functionally utilitarian and heavily individualistic.[11] Strategies for evangelicalism are chosen based on the ends produced, strategies that enable the greatest level of appeal for the greatest number of persons.

Whereas Hatch locates the influences on American evangelicalism in the early democratization process of the eighteenth and mid-nineteenth

9. Nathan Hatch, *The Democratization of American Christianity* (New Haven: Yale University Press, 1989).

10. Ibid., 4.

11. Dennis Hollinger, in his study on individualism and social ethics in American evangelicalism, notes the ways in which individualism is sustained in evangelical theology and practice. According to Hollinger, the impulse of the Reformation continues to place primacy on individual conscience in matters of faith and practice. Pietism stresses an experiential, personal faith, coupled with the personal study and application of the Bible. The fundamentalist tendencies of evangelicalism fostered a suspicion of any kind of social reform that does not stress individual conversion as key to social change. See Dennis Hollinger, *American Individualism and Evangelical Social Ethics: A Study of Christianity Today, 1956–1976* (Ph.D. diss., Drew University, 1981).

centuries, George Marsden situates the historical emergence and ensuing commitments of contemporary American evangelicalism in the modernist/ fundamentalist controversy of the late nineteenth and early twentieth centuries. According to Marsden, fundamentalism was a response to three predominant challenges to American Protestantism from 1870 to 1930.[12] First, there were the intellectual challenges of Darwinism and the rise of the social sciences and higher criticism that leveled epistemological challenges to the Bible as the sole arbiter of truth. Second, rapid urbanization and immigration during this time period exposed the pluralities of religious belief, challenging the hegemony of white Protestantism in religious and civic life. The general secularization of modern culture prompted the third reaction of the fundamentalists. Not only were basic theological tenets such as the authority of scripture, the virgin birth, the resurrection, and the very ethos of a "Christian culture" (read: white Protestant) under attack, but understanding of nationhood and manifest destiny were also called into question. The response of the fundamentalists was both theological and cultural. As Marsden notes, "in the minds of most fundamentalists the theological crisis came to be inextricably wedded to the very survival of Christian civilization—by which they meant a Bible-based civilization."[13] Joel Carpenter qualifies the split between the modernists and the fundamentalists by reminding us of its location in Anglo-American elite denominations that saw themselves in the center of theological and religious power, who were battling from their respective positions of privilege. He writes that "fundamentalism, like other historic evangelical movements, has tended to attract Anglo-Americans and northern European immigrants of Protestant background who were part of the upwardly aspiring and 'respectable' sector of the working class, and of the lower middle class."[14] The split between the modernists and the fundamentalists exacerbated the growing alienation fundamentalists were experiencing: decreasing popular and ideological appeal, pessimism, and loss of respectability.[15] Their efforts to maintain influence in the sociopolitical and cultural arenas were part of the yearning for a "wider social expression of middle-class normalcy."[16] This desire to retrieve Protestant, and particularly evangelical,

12. George Marsden, *Understanding Fundamentalism and Evangelicalism* (Grand Rapids: Eerdmans, 1991). See chapter 1.
    13. Ibid., 207.
    14. Joel Carpenter, *Revive Us Again: The Reawakening of American Fundamentalism* (New York: Oxford University Press, 1997), 9.
    15. Ibid., 35–43.
    16. Marsden, *Understanding Fundamentalism and Evangelicalism*, 92.

authority in the larger culture became part of the fabric of evangelical moral commitments. The nation must be "saved," and Christian values must be reinstituted.

While retaining the theological commitments of their fundamentalist forefathers, "new evangelicals" emerged in the 1940s and attempted to reform aspects of fundamentalism out of a sense of mission that begged the need for a more robust engagement with American culture. These new evangelicals or neo-evangelicals differed in their interaction with the larger culture, because mission to the world implied and demanded engagement with the world for the sake of spreading the good news of the gospel. This sense of mission eschewed separation from society and other churches as counterproductive. About these new evangelicals and their "engaged orthodoxy," Christian Smith writes that, "by keeping with their nineteenth-century Protestant heritage, they [evangelicals] were fully committed to maintaining and promoting confidently traditional, orthodox Protestant theology and belief, *while at the same time* becoming confidently and more proactively engaged in the intellectual, cultural, social and political life of the nation."[17]

The moral commitments and ethics that emerged from this historical experience of evangelicalism out of fundamentalism continued to be fueled by a vision of a "Christian America." In *Christian America? What Evangelicals Really Want*, Christian Smith identifies five reasons why evangelicals believe that "America is a Christian nation," based on his interviews with self-identified evangelicals. Sixty percent of those interviewed believed that at one point America was a Christian nation, since it was founded on religious principles and a commitment to ensure religious freedom. It was also assumed by the interviewees that the majority of the early European colonists were Christians with a mission from God. Beliefs in the democratic principles that attempt to balance power are rooted in biblical warnings about human power "trumping" God's power. And finally, the interviewees noted the theistic beliefs of the founding fathers' intentions to found the nation on biblical principles.[18] As Randall Balmer notes, American evangelicalism has interpreted aspects of the American story as its own in noticeable ways, especially the democratic spirit of personal freedom and liberty as Christian values befitting a Christian nation. Evangelicalism grew up against the backdrop of a particular American

17. Christian Smith, *American Evangelicalism: Embattled and Thriving* (Chicago: University of Chicago Press, 1998), 10.

18. Christian Smith, *Christian America? What Evangelicals Really Want* (Berkeley: University of California Press, 2000). See chapter 1.

story, a story white fundamentalists felt they created and evangelicals feel they must maintain, since they have benefited from this story. According to Balmer, the story of America merges with the story of American evangelicalism, since "consistent with the American ethos, it offers a kind of spiritual upward mobility, a chance to improve your lot in the next world and also (according to the promises of some preachers) in this world as well."[19] The moral *telos* of an American evangelical social vision remains. It is a return to the Christian roots of the nation based on the assumption that the story of America is the same story of the scriptures and of evangelical Christians themselves.

What is the legacy of the historiography of American evangelism in its moral vision and social ethic? In other words, what *really* affects evangelical moral commitments and social practices? I propose the following legacies for consideration as ones that complement the theoretical and practical aspects of deontology, teleology, and virtue ethics. I explore these propositions in more detail in subsequent chapters, but I offer them here first as a way to explain why I am focusing on evangelical ethics.

The first legacy is a commitment to the Bible as a primary, if not sole, source for moral guidance. I argue in the next chapter that the use of the Bible in evangelical ethics tends to be deontological, which in many ways limits scripture's power in providing moral direction. The Bible contains rules and principles to follow, and in this way gives moral guidance for answering the question "What ought I to do?" The answer is, "I ought to obey what the Bible tells me." This is not a bad or unimportant moral criterion. What is noticeable about this commitment, however, in the context of evangelical faith and practice, are the authoritative expectations placed on the Bible to guide not just Christians, but non-Christians, and even nations such as the United States, to help them return to their biblical roots. The Bible is not just for Christians and the church. The Bible is for everyone to follow, regardless of their particular faith commitments, or lack thereof. The historiography of American evangelicalism contains a vision of a nation that "once was," a nation founded on biblical principles, regardless of the actual troubling, unbiblical practices of our nation, such as the treatment of American Indians, the land, the easy paths and excuses for war, slavery, etc. Granted, many evangelical traditions in the nineteenth century influenced people to reform these kinds of social practices because of their commitments to scripture. Evangelicals were known for their

19. Randall Balmer, *Blessed Assurance: A History of Evangelicalism in America* (Boston: Beacon Press, 1999), 11.

participation in the abolitionist movement, for promoting equal rights for women, for addressing the causes of poverty, and for peacemaking.[20] Working for social change because of our commitment to the God described in scripture is not a new commitment for evangelicals.

However, it appears tempting in our culture wars of the later twentieth and now early twenty-first century to ignore these reforming tendencies that once addressed class, racial, and gender injustices. Much of our reforming impetus today appears focused on "us" and the desire in these complex times to resolidify our racial, class, and gender privileges. Evangelicals attempt to do so by again appealing to the Bible. Social ills can be solved with a simple turning back to the Bible as a source of authoritative moral guidance. Perhaps this commitment is best captured by the efforts of Judge Roy Moore, former Supreme Court Justice in Alabama, to display the Ten Commandments in the courthouse. For Judge Moore, this fight was and is a moral battle to return God to the public arena, particularly the judicial system, as a reminder of not just the Christian, but the *biblical* roots of the nation, as noted on the Web site for the Foundation for the Moral Law.[21] This picture provides a window into an attitude toward the Bible in certain segments of evangelicalism, and fundamentalism, that sees it as a rule book, filled with prescriptions that ought to be obeyed by everyone.[22] If the Ten Commandments can *just* be displayed in public places, like courthouses and schools, there may be a semblance of order and morality as we are reminded of what rules to follow. Not only does this strike me as not taking sin very seriously—a bit ironic given evangelicalism's pessimism about human nature as sinful—but it is also naive about the nature of faith and moral development. This view also ignores the narrative and covenantal context of the "rules" of scripture, such as the Decalogue, the contexts that give them their meaning and purpose for the covenantal community of faith to whom they were

20. Donald Dayton, *Discovering an Evangelical Heritage* (Peabody, MA: Hendrickson, 1976).

21. The Web site for the Foundation for the Moral Law is www.morallaw.org. Two of the aims of the Foundation for the Moral Law are to "educate the public about the U.S. Constitution and the Godly foundation of the United States of America" and to "promote public policy through appropriate legislation and other government actions. In other words, to assist in reestablishing society with good morals and values as set forth in the Holy Bible."

22. I am using the case in Alabama simply for illustrative purposes, because in my view it captures on a popular level a common understanding of how the Bible's authority should be brought to bear on public life. I acknowledge that many evangelicals have a more nuanced and richer understanding of the Bible's role in the moral life. Gary Dorrien acknowledges this in *The Remaking of Evangelical Theology* in his discussion of postconservative evangelicalism.

originally delivered, and how the commandments fit in the overall story of the Christian tradition and faith. I will argue that this deontological view of the Bible as a universal rule book, something that simply ought to be obeyed, actually minimizes scripture's role and the myriad ways in which it forms the moral life of Christians.

The second legacy of the historiography of American evangelicalism is the commitment to the conversion of individuals as the greatest good to be pursued. This legacy flows right from the center of evangelical identity and commitment: that the gospel is good news that ought to be shared, and that a person's greatest need is to make a decision to accept Christ as one's *personal* Savior. The call to conversion and revivalism is at the heart of evangelical faith and practice, with many church traditions still holding revivals as part of their evangelistic efforts to save souls and reignite spiritual and evangelistic fervor. The focus on individual conversion, or "getting saved," tends to be seen as the ultimate *telos,* or end of one's life. This has a number of deleterious effects on evangelical morality and ethical practice. First, the means by which converts are "won" may be put beyond question, especially if they actually produce the good fruit of many conversions. The end may justify any means of evangelism, regardless of the ways in which people are viewed as "objects" of conversion to be manipulated for a desired response. Second, the actual cost of discipleship may be a hidden one to be sprung as an "Oh, by the way . . ." once the bargain is sealed, especially if the greatest good is simply "getting saved" as opposed to being and becoming a disciple of Jesus Christ as the norm of the Christian life. Third, viewing "getting saved" as the ultimate *telos* of one's life creates all sorts of bifurcations that are detrimental to Christian faith and morality. Getting saved as the ultimate goal of one's life actually results in a truncated, and even commodified, understanding of salvation as a simple transaction of receiving forgiveness because of Christ's death on the cross. Ethics has little to do with salvation. One can be justified before God without living a just and righteous life; one can acknowledge Jesus as Savior from sin without a commitment to Christ's lordship, something utterly foreign to the scriptures evangelicals purport to follow; and one's personal decision for Christ may have nothing to do with entrance into and belonging to an actual Christian community.[23] Finally, this quantitative view of the church as the greatest number getting saved as the mark of effectiveness ignores the qualitative aspect of the church as a morally

23. See Tod E. Bolsinger, *It Takes a Church to Raise a Christian: How the Community of God Transforms Lives* (Grand Rapids: Brazos Press, 2004).

forming community for Christians who are growing into the image of Jesus Christ as the norm, and cost, of the Christian life. The church itself is now seen through a utilitarian lens. It exists to meet the greatest needs of the greatest number and so structures its life to meet the demands of its religious consumers in the pursuit of their own good happiness.

The final legacy of the historiography of American evangelicalism is its emphasis on personal piety as an assurance of moral goodness. If the greatest good of one's life is getting "right with God" through conversion, then personal piety may be viewed as the guarantor of morality, minimizing the need for growth in discernment and Christian conscience in an evangelical context. This may explain why many evangelicals think political leaders who are Christian should be elected and are better leaders simply *because* they are Christians, and why we place such an emphasis on personal behavior, particularly in sexual ethics, as the barometer for one's level of morality.[24] Michael Emerson and Christian Smith note in their book *Divided by Faith: Evangelical Religion and the Problem of Race in America* the personalizing tendencies of evangelical perspectives on individual and social moral issues, particularly on the issue of race. Social issues like racism are filtered through a lens of individualism. Social problems are the extensions of one's personal moral failures, such as being racist, so the solutions to complex social ethical issues tend to be focused on individual solutions, not structural necessities to work toward more just social arrangements. Emerson and Smith identify this as the "personal influence strategy" based on the "tools" of freewill individualism and relationalism employed by many white evangelicals in their approach to social issues.[25]

The well-known mantra is "Changed people change society," while disregarding the ways changed societies can also change people. When we ignore the communal dimension of virtue formation, and particularly the church as a "society" that fosters the moral formation of its members, Christian virtues become unmoored from a larger narrative context informed by scripture and the Christian faith in favor of a perspective

24. This is the argument I made in my paper presented at the American Academy of Religion in November 1999: "Moral Selectivity—Picking and Choosing Sex as the Barometer of Moral Decline in the Culture Wars" (unpublished). I was interested in exploring the religious rhetoric surrounding the impeachment proceedings of President Clinton in the aftermath of his affair with Monica Lewinsky, the ways in which sexual morality was understood, and its connection with the "well-being of the nation."

25. Michael Emerson and Christian Smith, *Divided by Faith: Evangelical Religion and the Problem of Race in America* (New York: Oxford University Press, 2000), 118.

that collapses virtue into one's personal piety as all that matters in the moral life. Virtue formation becomes highly personalized and attached to the narrative context of individualism and the growing, if not already entrenched, narrative context of the therapeutic in American culture.[26]

The argument I am making is that evangelical understandings of morality and ethical practices, given the legacies of evangelicalism's historiography, dovetail with certain aspects of the three classic theories I explore here. The result is an easy acceptance and use of these theories *as Christian morality* because of commitments and experiences already in the fabric of evangelical identity, epistemology, moral understanding, and ethical practices. What are these common commitments and experiences?

In *Improvisation: The Drama of Christian Ethics*, Samuel Wells proposes that theories, such as deontology and teleology, take priority in Christian ethics when they are detached from the theological frameworks for ethics and the moral life. In other words, when Christian ethical commitments are severed from our theology and tradition, all we have left are these theories, as opposed to theology and practices, to describe the moral life. When Christian ethics is viewed as *just* individual decision making or *just* ensuring successful outcomes of our individual decisions, the epistemological frameworks are no different than the ones informing deontology and teleology. *Just* anyone can make a good decision if all of the options are present, and *just* anyone can follow a rule or a principle. It does not matter "who" the person may be, the source of his or her moral vision, or the reasons for choosing to act one way as opposed to another. Wells writes, "If the center of ethics is the choosing individual, the theories that will prove reasonable and useful are those that make no distinction between persons and treat circumstances and issues regardless of the identities and characters of the people facing them, regardless of notions of overarching providence or everlasting destiny, regardless of the habitual activities of those involved."[27] These theories that prove to be reasonable and useful, such as deontology and teleology, complement the ideologies

26. See Robert Bellah, Richard Madsen, William Sullivan, Ann Swidler, and Steve Tipton (New York: Harper and Row, 1985), *Habits of the Heart,* for an important sociological assessment of the therapeutic strand of contemporary American culture and its impact on the expression of religious faith. I also refer to the work of Wade Clark Roof in *The Spiritual Marketplace: Baby Boomers and the Remaking of American Religion* (Princeton, NJ: Princeton University Press, 1999), for a fresh way to understand the relationships among self-fulfillment, self-expression in religious faith, and the therapeutic "bent" of evangelical religious expression in the spiritual marketplace.

27. Samuel Wells, *Improvisation: The Drama of Christian Ethics* (Grand Rapids: Brazos Press, 2004), 27–28.

that have informed much of evangelical identity and ethical practices, ideologies such as individualism's autonomous decision maker who takes his or her own position or stands his or her own ground. If the aim of Christian ethics is to universalize morality, then the acceptance of these classic theories makes the nature of Christian morality far less complex, since we are not dealing with the character and habits of communities and individuals and the particular stories that give shape to a particular understanding of Christian morality. This also reflects the assumptions of much of evangelical ethical practice, to enable everyone to accept and abide by a universal ethic that is called "Christian" without attention to its own particularity and unique claims based on the narrative of scripture. As Wells also notes:

> These two approaches, the intrinsic (deontological) and the extrinsic (or consequential), are the two principal forms of ethical argument today. They are the contemporary "establishment," the norm in references to which any other approach must define itself. The former could be called "ethics for anyone," since it sees the individual as a universal category, the principles of whose actions could apply to anyone, anywhere at any time. The latter could be called "ethics for everyone," since it has a more democratic impulse, looking for outcomes that suit the most people in the most circumstances.[28]

While Wells is less critical of the ways in which virtue ethics has been appropriated in Christian ethics, he is concerned to articulate the ways in which Christian ethics unhinged from its biblical, theological, and ecclesial contexts is maladapted by what he calls the "sectarian temptation of Gnosticism,"[29] a critique I find especially appropriate for an understanding of virtue in an evangelical context. Wells suggests three temptations when Christian ethics is separated from its narrative context informed by scripture, theology, and the church, temptations inherent when the narrative contexts of individualism and autonomy in deontology, teleology, and virtue ethics are accepted as normative for Christian ethics.[30] The first temptation, according to Wells, is to confuse the church and the world, whereby Christians want to make the world the church, which undermines the distinctive narrative and nature of Christian ethics and the church, for the sake of acceptability. The second temptation is the opposite of the first. Whereas the first collapses the church into the world, the second, sectarianism, removes the church from the world and sees the church as

28. Ibid., 28.
29. Ibid., 40.
30. Ibid., 39–40.

the *only* way God works in the world. This second temptation leads to the third, one I find particularly tempting for evangelicals. This is Gnosticism, where "the spiritual quest is an individual matter," and human community is valuable only as it serves the needs of the individual.[31] Wells goes on to explain:

> Within the second, "sectarian" temptation, Gnosticism underwrites a sense of superiority over the faithless, perhaps evil, world. The church becomes a group of people who have special knowledge, or an access to a special experience, that the world cannot have. . . . Gnosticism tends to exist as an emphasis on personal piety, perhaps together with an emphasis on doctrinal purity. Thus Christians may engage in the most damaging public practices while still assuming that thinking "the right things" about salvation or having a "close personal relationship" with God ensures that righteousness remains with them.[32]

Wells's critique is an important one, given the assumptions that personal piety and doctrinal correctness function as moral benchmarks and guarantees in an evangelical context; being right in doctrine and "being right with God" means being right about everything else. Might Wells's insights be useful for seeing why evangelical morality and ethics gravitate to an understanding of virtue as simply personal piety, as well as to an understanding of ethics as the duty to make right decisions and ensure universal morality? I think Wells's observations do help to answer the question I raised earlier: What are the epistemological frameworks and common commitments within the fabric of evangelicalism that explain the easy use and acceptance of the classic theories of ethics? Or what *really* shapes evangelical morality and ethical practices? The next chapter explores in more detail the ways in which the epistemological and narrative frameworks of the classic theories complement the epistemological and ideological assumptions in evangelical ethical practice.

Conclusion

I gave two reasons why I am locating this work in an evangelical context and explained how I will be using the classic theories of ethics to deconstruct understandings of morality and the nature of evangelical ethical practices. The work is motivated by my own location within various streams

31. Ibid., 40.
32. Ibid.

of evangelicalism, and by the question "What *really* shapes evangelical ethical practices given evangelicalism's historiography and social context?" There is a final reason, one connected to the first, for directing my attention to Christian morality and ethics in and for an evangelical context. I write this as a Christian social ethicist who is making both evangelical and feminist claims about the nature of Christian morality.

I remain rooted in an evangelical context, with all of the noted caveats, as active participant and hopefully as helpful critic for change because of my active participation, but also somewhat from and on "the boundary."[33] This "boundary position" provides freedom but also fosters a degree of vulnerability. There is freedom because of the long years I have spent living and working in evangelical traditions, some of them considered "on the boundaries" of evangelicalism. This position enables me to understand the language, the commitments, the communities, and especially the moral and spiritual practices valued in evangelicalism. This "insider" position affirms my convictions that faith in God matters, that one's response to Christ ought to be life-changing, that the scriptures ought to be received as a gift, that the church has the potential to be truly countercultural, and that all people matter to God. However, from the inside, there is much that is troubling to me as an ethicist with evangelical commitments and feminist sensitivities, which when critiqued risks placing me in a vulnerable position on the "outside." I am concerned with a number of moral and spiritual practices valued within evangelicalism. The quick alliance with conservative political and social ideologies by naming them as "Christian" troubles me, because the church has never fared well with this kind of alliance, plus it shields the ways in which religious faith is co-opted and used for political legitimacy, which intentionally dulls the radical claims of the gospel. I am disturbed by the sense that a person's spiritual needs are privileged and viewed as the most important aspects of one's life at the expense of the concrete material existence of people's lives, which places social justice on the "back burner" or relegates it to a secondary, utilitarian form of evangelism in order to convert people. I believe that

---

33. See Nicola Hoggard Creegan and Christine D. Pohl, *Living on the Boundaries: Evangelical Women, Feminism, and the Theological Academy* (Downers Grove, IL: InterVarsity Press, 2005). Creegan and Pohl have written a powerful and provocative book on the experiences of evangelical women living on the boundaries between evangelical commitments and feminism. This book is an important resource for giving voice to the varied experiences, stories, and commitments of women who are attempting to live with integrity (and sanity) with their faith claims as evangelicals and their callings as academics who are negotiating many boundaries, such as feminism, in their lives, work, families, and communities.

Christian ethics is not the same thing as lobbing our personal moralisms from pulpits and podiums onto complex social issues. While I embrace the renewed commitment to spiritual formation as a normative aspect of Christian faith, I am concerned to name the ways in which spiritual formation is hijacked by a therapeutic context that equates spiritual formation with self-actualization, as opposed to moral formation, character, and commitments to just practices in the world. I am a woman called to ministry who has been both supported and demonized in evangelicalism. To name the patriarchical assumptions in much of evangelicalism is an important one for ethics, which must take seriously the nature of class, racial, and gender hierarchies. I have experienced them from the "inside" and critique them "on the boundary" for the ways in which patriarchical "givenness" denies the agency, giftedness, call, and importance of women, as well as others who do not fit the mold of evangelical acceptability in responding to the claims that the gospel makes on individuals and communities.

It is for these reasons, and many more, that I write this book. This work is an attempt to articulate the essential aspects of Christian faith for how they shape our lives by calling us to take even *more* seriously the authority of Jesus Christ, the scriptures that shape and guide us in a multitude of ways, and the Christian community as a morally forming one. My hope is that this work will contribute in some way to a renewed and expanded moral vision, building on the strengths of our common evangelical understandings, and challenging us to embody our moral commitments in practices consonant with the gospel of Jesus Christ.

1

Classic Models of Morality

Immanuel Kant on Duty, John Stuart Mill on Utility, and Aristotle on Virtue

In this chapter, I provide descriptions of three classic theories in ethics: deontology, teleology, and virtue ethics. In short, deontology is the study of duty or obligation, where the weight of moral focus is on the rule or prescription that enables a person to answer the question "What ought I to do?" The answer is, "I ought to obey the rules or prescriptions that tell me what I ought to do." Teleology is an understanding of ethics that places the moral burden on the outcome of a decision. Teleology encompasses related theories such as utilitarianism, negative utilitarianism, and consequentialism. Teleology emphasizes the outcome of decisions, and it attempts to answer "What kinds of outcome will this decision produce, or what desired end will this achieve?" Teleology as a moral criterion sets one upon a course of action that achieves a desired result, however this is defined, to produce the greatest good for the greatest number of people, or in reverse, to minimize harm for the minimal number of people. Virtue ethics relates the moral character of moral agents in that the kind of person we are will be reflected in the kinds of decisions we make and behaviors we exhibit. Virtue ethics concentrates on the question "What kind of moral character is needed, and what kind of moral character will be shaped by my actions and behaviors?"

To explore the primary claims of these classic theories, I will use selected works by Immanuel Kant, John Stuart Mill, and Aristotle to provide a focus for my descriptions of deontology, teleology, and virtue ethics. I use the term *classic* as a way of indicating the enduring value and influence these theorists and their works have in social, ethical, and political thought and practices, primarily in Western thought. I do not mean to use the term *classic* to indicate that these theories contain evident truths and are the unquestioned ways in which we should understand the nature of the moral life. As will be evident in subsequent chapters, an unquestioning and uncritical acceptance of these theories as normative for Christian ethics is a direct challenge to the very claims and uniqueness of Christian ethics as *Christian*.

My work in this chapter is both selective and descriptive. I describe selected salient points of these theories. As suggested in the introduction, certain aspects of these theories may hold an appeal for evangelical ethics, given some shared epistemologies and ideologies that I hope are evident in my interaction with these ethical theories in light of certain evangelical ethical practices. It is also important for me to acknowledge the limits of my descriptions in this chapter. I cannot cover the totality of the works by Kant, Mill, and Aristotle, or all of the implications and influences their ideas have in ethics and related fields such as political theory. I also am conscious that each of them attends to other moral theories and concerns as well. For example, Immanuel Kant does acknowledge teleology, and there is a virtue ethic in his deontological scheme. John Stuart Mill tries to combine all three aspects of morality into his principle of utility. One can approach Aristotle from a teleological perspective as well as through the lens of virtue ethics. I have chosen for the purposes of this book to articulate what I perceive to be the main foci of their moral schemes, recognizing that how I have grouped them is too tidy, but it is a grouping that makes the work of this chapter more manageable.

I also acknowledge that Kant, Mill, and Aristotle have their own historical, social, and class locations that help to illuminate and explain the ideas and claims of their theories. I provide brief biographical and historical descriptions as needed but focus primarily on the articulation of their theories in the works I have elected to explore. I realize, then, the limitations and selectivity of my descriptions in this chapter. That said, I illustrate the relevant points of their theories that have contributed to and have been appropriated in evangelical ethics in unique ways, both for good and for ill.

I proceed in the following way. First, I describe key aspects of Immanuel Kant's theory of ethics in *Groundwork of the Metaphysics of Morals*. Next, I focus on *Utilitarianism* by John Stuart Mill. Finally, by looking at Aristotle's *Nicomachean Ethics*, I describe relevant aspects of his understanding of virtue. I provide a brief summary at the end of each section on certain aspects of these moral theories and the ways they may appeal to evangelicals in our attempts to articulate the dimensions of the moral life and ethical decision making.

Immanuel Kant and Deontology

Immanuel Kant (1724–1804) in many ways is the quintessential representative of Enlightenment thought, with its elevation of reason and the exercise of human rationality as foundational epistemological assumptions. Kant's aim was to find a mediating position for morality, his own "metaphysics," one that could be unhinged from religion as a source of moral authority, but also one that would avoid the subjectivity and acceptance of self-interest, personal experience, and desire as normative criteria for moral decisions and behavior. Kant was not irreligious or an atheist. He grew up in a pietistic home in Königsberg, East Prussia. According to Roger Sullivan, the influence of pietism can be seen in Kant's concern to show the everyday, practical aspects of morality, indicative of a pietistic concern with obedience and the practice of religious faith.[1] Kant, however, did not believe that religion qua religion could be the source of morality. He writes at the end of *The Metaphysics of Morals*, "*So religion as the doctrine of duties to God lies entirely beyond the bounds of purely philosophical ethics*, and this serves to justify the author of the present ethical work for not having followed the usual practice of bringing religion, conceived in that sense, into ethics, in order to make it complete" (*M.M.* 6:488).[2] While morality might lead one to acknowledge God's

1. Roger Sullivan, *Immanuel Kant's Moral Theory* (Cambridge: Cambridge University Press, 1989), 6–7.

2. I am using Kant's *Groundwork of the Metaphysics of Morals,* edited by Mary Gregor (Cambridge: Cambridge University Press, 1998), as my primary source. At certain points, I will also reference Kant's *The Metaphysics of Morals,* edited by Mary Gregor (Cambridge: Cambridge University Press, 1996). I will use the standard academic method for quoting Kant's work by designating the work as *Gr.* (*Groundwork*) or *M.M.* (*Metaphysics*), followed by the section number.

part in moral affections and even induce a divine sense of awe about the promise of human moral goodness, one's belief in God would not ensure morality. In other words, morality could not be assured by one's belief in God, since faith is beyond the scope of pure reason.

Contrary to prevailing Enlightenment thought, however, the answer to the limitations and decline of religion's power as moral authority was not its opposite for Kant. Moral authority could not be grounded in enlightened self-interest and individual desire as a source either, since this would undermine morality's universality, making it contingent upon an individual's subjective experience, wishes, and desires. If morality was to be a morality for everyone, which for Kant was the essence of making moral claims, then the source of morality needed to be located in what all persons have in common. It must be found in and by pure practical reason.

According to Roger Sullivan, Kant aimed "to show how morality can be universally and necessarily true for all human beings for all time, and indeed in its most fundamental outlines, for all rational beings as well, if there are any besides us."[3] For Kant, ethics is one branch of philosophy that focuses on aspects of human rationality that has its essential expression in the exercise of a human being's will (*Gr.* 4:388). The primary aim of Kant's moral philosophy was to provide a "metaphysics of morals" or an explanation of the ultimate and "supreme principle of morality" (*Gr.* 4:392). The supreme principle of morality, what Kant understands as the categorical imperative, is accessible by human reason. It will determine what a person ought to do, guiding not just an individual's behavior but also the decisions and actions of all persons. In *Groundwork of the Metaphysics of Morals*, Kant notes his purpose in pursing this supreme moral principle. He writes:

> Since my aim here is directed properly to moral philosophy, I limit the question proposed only to this: is it not thought to be of the utmost necessity to work out for once a pure moral philosophy, completely cleansed of everything that may be empirical and that belongs to anthropology? For, that there must be such a philosophy is clear of itself from the common idea of duty and of moral laws. Everyone must grant that a law, if it is to hold morally, that it, as a ground of an obligation, must carry with it absolute necessity . . . therefore the ground of obligation must not be sought in the nature of the human being or in the circumstances of the world in which he is placed, but a priori simply in concepts of pure reason. . . . (*Gr.* 4:389)

3. Sullivan, *Immanuel Kant's Moral Theory,* 7.

Kant's assumption is that pure reason exists a priori in the human intellect and is something that must be assumed as essential for morality. The metaphysics of morals is the ascertaining of moral obligation, common to all persons, by the use of reason through a deductive method of logic.[4] In spite of his sophisticated and somewhat abstract thought, Kant was not interested in what he described as theoretical reason or speculative foundations for morality. Instead, he was interested in focusing on the very practical aspects of human life that were essentially moral in nature. He was more concerned with answering "What ought we to do?" than "Why ought we to do this?" As Sullivan comments, "the purpose of this entire analysis, after all, has been to define and defend our ability and obligation to act morally—not to understand or explain that power."[5] Theoretical or speculative reason, while important for philosophy, was not very helpful in the pursuit of morality, according to Kant. Theoretical reason was the concern to prove or establish the authoritative foundations for morality, which for Kant were both improvable and beside the point since humanity cannot avoid moral judgments, regardless of any theoretical understanding or justification of them. Humans must *make* moral decisions in everyday life; therefore, the reasons and ways to make moral decisions must be obvious, comprehensible, and accessible to all. As Alasdair MacIntyre observes, Kant assumed a moral universe and took for granted a person's desire and willingness to act morally. MacIntyre writes: "It is the moral consciousness of this ordinary human nature which provides the philosopher [Kant] with an object for analysis; as in the theory of knowledge, the philosopher's task is not to seek for a basis or a vindication, but to ask what character our moral concepts and precepts must have to make morality as it is possible."[6]

For Kant, the aim of moral philosophy is not to provide a theoretical or speculative foundation for moral claims but to provide the practical means by which we, ordinary human beings who live in a moral world,

4. Kant's method of deduction is important to his moral theory and is in sharp contrast to John Stuart Mill's principle of induction, which I discuss in the next section. Deductive reasoning starts with a "given" known fact or general principle and then takes one down a course to its implications for more particular situations. For Kant, the "givens" are the a priori assumptions of the capabilities of human reason and the universal nature of morality, which leads one down the path to deduce the ways in which morality is understood via the categorical imperative and applied to particular situations.

5. Sullivan, *Immanuel Kant's Moral Theory,* 94.

6. Alasdair MacIntyre, *A Short History of Ethics: A History of Moral Philosophy from the Homeric Age to the Twentieth Century,* 2nd ed. (Notre Dame, IN: University of Notre Dame Press, 1998), 191.

understand and enact moral duties based on the use of pure reason as a guide for the will *(Gr.* 4:404*).* Reason, according to Kant, is the human ability to move beyond the realm of the senses, or empiricism, to the realm of understanding where we can ascertain the laws of nature and their meaning, and so order our wills in accordance with what is reasonable and therefore moral *(Gr.* 4:452). In other words, humans, because we, a priori, possess reason, are capable of moving beyond our senses and experiences to an objective understanding of morality, which provides us with compulsory moral duties that instruct us in what we ought to do, what we are obligated to do, regardless of our experiences, inclinations, motives, or character. Even though these aspects of morality factor into Kant's moral philosophy to various degrees, they are of lesser concern in his moral theory, since it favors morality as purely objective, free from heteronomous influences such as experiences, desires, and even religion. Pure practical reason, therefore, must be the source of morality, since this is what humans have in common, unlike religious faith, experience, personal interests, and desires.

Reason, when purely and practically exercised in answering the question "What ought I to do?" will guide our wills to the knowledge of morality. Kant posits that reason is the governor of our will in a way that makes reason synonymous with the essence of what it means to be human. We possess a will that is rational, and the practical use of this rationality is the essence of morality *(Gr.* 4:395). He writes, "Everything in nature works in accordance with laws. Only a rational being has the capacity to act *in accordance with the representation* of laws, that is, in accordance with principles, or has a *will*. Since *reason* is required for the derivation of actions from laws, the will is nothing other than practical reason" *(Gr.* 4:412). What kind of moral guide does the use of pure practical reason lend to humanity? Since morality and the human will are intricately bound together in Kant's philosophy, and if reason is what ultimately provides moral guidance to the will, to what is our reason led and what provides moral guidance to our reason governing our will? It is the *categorical imperative.*

The categorical imperative, the centerpiece of Kant's moral philosophy, is what guides our reason and will by minimizing the conflict between what we may want to do and what we ought to do. The categorical imperative relieves a person of the contingencies of ethical decision making by focusing on the supreme principle of duty or obedience, which is the categorical imperative. The categorical imperative is a command that unconditionally obliges a person, and all people, to obey it. The categorical imperative is not determined by the end result it produces, the inclinations and desires of humans, or the intentions of the decision maker. It is unconditional and categorically obligatory because "if the action is represented as *in itself* good, hence as necessary in a will in itself conforming to reason, as its principle, *then it is categorical*" (*Gr.* 4:414). The categorical imperative is a good to pursue in itself, and the virtuous person is one who does his duty to the categorical imperative *for the sake* of the duty itself. It is an unconditioned demand to act morally accordingly to rules that must be required for all.

The first and primary expression of Kant's categorical imperative is its first formula: "Act only in accordance with that maxim through which you can at the same time will that it become a universal law" (*Gr.* 4:421). Kant understands a maxim to be a principle or rule for action. Therefore, principles of morality informing actions must be able to be universalized as maxims or rules that can apply to all persons, thereby making them universal laws. The claims that humans make about what one ought to do must be claims that can be made by and for everyone.

The most cited example of Kantian morality is the duty to tell the truth. Kant posed the question, "May I, when hard pressed, make a promise with the intention not to keep it?" (*Gr.* 4:402). The answer is more fully elaborated in *The Metaphysics of Morals* (*M.M.* 6:429). The answer would be no, since the question focuses on the result that the action, that is, making a false promise, may produce, an outcome that is not guaranteed. It also violates the ability to become a universal maxim, since it would make void the action of telling the truth and leave open the possibility that any person could then break a promise, making truth telling and promise keeping meaningless and hence irrational. As Kant also notes,

> A human being who does not himself believe what he tells another . . . has even less worth than if he were a mere thing; for a thing, because it is something real and given, has the property of being serviceable so that another can put it to some use. But communication of one's thoughts to someone through words that yet (intentionally) contain the contrary to what the speaker thinks on the subject is an end that is directly opposed to the natural purposiveness of the speaker's capacity to communicate his thoughts, and is thus a renunciation by the speaker of his personality, and such a speaker is a mere captive appearance of a human being, not a human being himself. (*M.M.* 6:429)

To lie is an irrational act and therefore an immoral one. It violates the intention of speaking, which is to communicate truthful information about one's thoughts. To do otherwise, such as making false promises, strips communication of its meaning and humanity of our moral nature. There is no guarantee that one's lies and false promises secure the desired outcome, no matter how noble one's motive may be.

A morality that applies to one person and not to another is illogical and irrational, something that violates the essence of our humanity, which is the need and potential for coherence and reason. It is only by adhering to the categorical imperative and the duty to obey that becomes incumbent upon us as rational beings that we can avoid a morality driven by competing self-interests and subjective experiences. In many ways, then, morality becomes a far simpler and more practical enterprise. We need not wrestle with issues of conscience, mediating between competing moral goods and claims, or rely on the virtuous dispositions of ethical decision makers. Of course, the classic Kantian dilemma is the quandary of wondering if it is ever right to lie in order to protect innocent persons or save individuals from violence. The categorical imperative removes these difficulties from ethical deliberation and leads us to understand what we ought to do. We ought not to lie, regardless of the circumstances or outcomes. We ought to obey categorical imperatives that all reasonable persons can understand, accept, and obey.

The second formulation of Kant's categorical imperative is "so act that you use humanity, whether in your person or in the person of any other, always at the same time as an end, never merely as a means" (*Gr.* 4:429). At the heart of this formulation is Kant's anthropology: the belief that "autonomy is therefore the ground of the dignity of human nature and of every rational nature" (*Gr.* 4:436). Roger Sullivan observes, "The imperative that we should act only on maxims capable of being universal laws, Kant writes, inevitably, 'will lead to' our recognizing that we must respect every human person as having objective and intrinsic worth or dignity . . . consequently, Kant also holds that the two formulas are otherwise 'at bottom the same' and the second formula is but a different way to 'represent' the original ultimate moral Law of Autonomy."[7] Kant writes that "autonomy of the will is the property of the will by which it is a law to itself (independent of any property of the objects of volition). The principle of autonomy is, therefore: choose only in such a way that the maxims of your choice are also included as universal in the same volition" *(Gr.* 4:440). Autonomy is synonymous with freedom, and both are necessary for a will (i.e., a person) to act

7. Sullivan, *Immanuel Kant's Moral Theory,* 193.

as its own "causality in accordance with immutable laws," since "*will* is a kind of causality of living beings insofar as they are rational, and *freedom* would be that property of such causality that it can be efficient independently of alien causes *determining* it . . ." (*Gr.* 4:446). Kant goes on to ask rhetorically, "What, then, can freedom of the will be other than autonomy, that is, the will's property of being a law to itself?" (*Gr.* 4:447). The mature moral agent is one who acts not from coercion, external influences, self-interest, or mixed inclinations, but one who is free to act autonomously according to duty for the sake of duty alone. Therefore, the affording of dignity to persons commanded in the second formulation of the categorical imperative is part of the duty owed to others, who are also free, and ought to be free as rational beings as both means and ends in themselves to act as causal agents for themselves. In his summary of the categorical imperative in *The Metaphysics of Morals*, Kant writes:

> A *person* is a subject whose actions can be *imputed* to him. *Moral* personality is therefore nothing other than the freedom of a rational being under moral laws (whereas psychological personality is merely the ability to be conscious of one's identity in different conditions of one's existence). From this it follows that a person is subject to no other laws than those he gives to himself (either alone or at least along with others). (*M.M.* 6:222)

Kant's commitment to autonomy and freedom as crucial aspects of the respect for rational beings as ends in themselves can be better understood when contrasted to his criticisms of heteronomy. Heteronomy is the subjection of a person to laws not of his or her own making, those that are extrinsic to the will and may hinder the will in the exercise of pure practical reason as the grounds for morality. The heteronomy of the will is described by Kant as the will that looks elsewhere, or "anywhere else than in the fitness of its maxims for its own giving of universal law" by "going beyond itself" in looking for external sources or validation for determining what one ought to do (*Gr.* 4:441). The implications for understanding religious beliefs as the source of morality should be obvious. Kant views them as "alien sources" of morality, ones that would impede the human use of pure practical reason for the ascertaining of universal maxims (*Gr.* 4:442). In what perhaps can be interpreted as a polemic reaction to the abuses of religious authority and power in Western Europe during his time, Kant rejects the derivation of morality from religion, which offers hope of reward or fear of punishment as the motivation for human behavior. This kind of manipulation perverts morality by undermining its rational grounding. It also presents the danger of using persons as means for ends not of their own choosing, whether political, religious, or personal. Kant writes,

> Among the *rational* grounds of morality or those based on reason, the ontological concept of *perfection* . . . is nevertheless better than the theological concept, which derives morality from a divine, all-perfect will; it is better not merely because we cannot intuit the perfection of this will but can only derive it from our concepts, among which that of morality is foremost, but because if we do not do this . . . the concept of his will still left to us, made up of the attributes of desire for glory and dominion combined with dreadful representations of power and vengefulness, would have to be the foundation for a system of morals that would be directly opposed to morality." (*Gr.* 4:443)[8]

According to Roger Sullivan, "Kant gives us metaphysical claim to the place inhabited by God in both theological and philosophical systems. By virtue of our supersensible freedom, *we* are not only the first causes of our own moral actions but also the *only* first causes available to serve as the objective ground for the final end of the universe."[9]

The first and second formulae of Kant's categorical imperative are related to the third and bring us full circle in his moral theory. The third formula is "the idea of the will of every rational being as a will giving universal law" (*Gr.* 4:431). The third formula encompasses the claims of the first two in the following ways. The aim of Kant's moral theory is consistency. What is true for one must be true for all. Morality, by its very nature, must be capable of becoming a universal law. The universal law is a discovered product of the free use of pure practical reason by rational beings who are both the means of discovery and the ends that the moral quest serves. Humans therefore must be treated as both means and ends due to the dignity afforded them as free, autonomous, and self-contained persons. Even though the focus of Kant's moral theory was on the individual freely pursuing pure practical reason, Kant did have a social ethic in mind. What one individual espouses as a categorical imperative is validated by its ability

8. Kant's philosophy of religion is a topic in and of itself to explore, which goes beyond my primary purposes in this book. However, it is clear that his philosophy of religion has profound implications for his moral theory. As noted before, Kant was not irreligious but believed that religion should be subject to the bounds of reason. It is no accident that his primary work on the philosophy of religion is *Religion within the Limits of Reason Alone,* as opposed to "Reason within the Limits of Religion Alone." See Nicholas Wolterstorff, *Reason within the Bounds of Religion* (Grand Rapids: Eerdmans, 1976).

9. Sullivan, *Immanuel Kant's Moral Theory,* 107.

to become universal and acted on by an aggregate of individuals. Kant refers to this as the "kingdom of ends" (*Gr.* 4:433). Kant understands the "kingdom of ends" as the "systematic union of various rational beings through common laws" (*Gr.* 4:433). Kant goes on to say:

> For, all rational beings stand under the *law* that each of them is to treat himself and all others *never merely as means* but always *at the same time as ends in themselves*. But from this there arises a systematic union of rational beings through common objective laws, that is, a kingdom, which can be called a kingdom of ends (admittedly only an ideal) because what these laws have as their purpose is just the relation of these beings to one another as ends and means. A rational being belongs as a *member* to the kingdom of ends when he gives universal laws in it but is also himself subject to these laws. He belongs to it *as sovereign* when, as lawgiving, he is not subject to the will of any other. (*Gr.* 4:433)

Common objective laws, both created and obeyed by rational agents, are what give rise to Kant's concept of duty. Kant's definition of duty is "practical necessitation," or the "necessity of action" in accordance with objective laws and principles (*Gr.* 4:434). Once one knows what one what ought to, practical necessity and reason dictate one must do it, regardless of inclinations and outcomes. It is duty that mediates conflicting desires and interests. Duty, therefore, is virtue in Kant's moral theory. Duty quells the "impulses of nature" that obstruct our desires to fulfill our duties (*M.M.* 6:380). "An action from duty is to put aside entirely the influence of inclination and with it every object of the will; hence there is left for the will nothing that could determine it except objectively *the law* and subjectively *pure respect* for this practical law, and so, the maxim of complying with such a law even if it infringes upon my inclinations" (*Gr.* 4:401). To obey the categorical imperative for the sake of duty itself is the rational (read: virtuous) course to pursue. We are obligated to obey, and obeying is the right thing to do.

What might immediately come to mind is Kant's own German context and the roots of the Holocaust, which is the archetypal example of the duty to authority and the repression of individual inclination to act in ways that would resist the duty to obey unjust and evil commands. According to Jonathan Glover in *Humanity: A Moral History of the Twentieth Century*, Kant has been unfairly used to explain such atrocities as the Holocaust and the predominant role that obedience to authority played in the various complicities of the Holocaust horrors. Glover, though, does acknowledge the dangers that Kantian duty presents to the role of the human inclination to disobey when what one is asked to do is fundamentally unjust and evil. The representative example often given is Adolf Eichmann's response during his interrogation at Nuremberg that he was just following orders. Glover writes that

> Kant, who believed that people are to be treated as ends in themselves and not merely as means, would have been appalled by this particular Kantian. But there is a side to Kant to which the Nazis could claim a sort of adherence: the emphasis on obedience to rules for their own sake. Kantian rules are supposed to be generated purely rationally, in a way independent of their impact on people. And they should be obeyed out of pure duty, rather than out of any sympathy for people. For Kant, to act out of feelings of sympathy for others is to act on a mere inclination rather than out of duty, and so to do something without moral worth. The Nazis produced a grim variant of this austere, self-enclosed morality.[10]

Appeal and Appropriations of Kantian Deontology

On the surface, what are the appealing aspects of Kant's moral theory, especially as they may be appropriated by evangelicals in their understanding of moral claims and duties? First, a Kantian morality is appealing to those who espouse that morality, by its very nature, must be universal and binding for everyone. Kantian morality provides a buffer, a response to the dread of postmodern relativism and the subjection of ethics to personal wishes and desires. It provides us with moral givens, a conception of morality that is universal and obligatory for all, with clearly desired delineations between right and wrong. Second, there is a "Golden Rule" kind of feel to Kant's second formula: "So act that you use humanity, whether in your own person or in the person of any other, always at the same time as an end, never merely as a means." It may be easy for some to equate Kant's dictum with Jesus's teaching in the Sermon on the Mount, "in everything, do to others what you would have them do to you, for this sums up the Law and the Prophets" (Matt. 7:12, NIV) as a universal moral code, regardless of the scriptural context in which Jesus is speaking and regardless of Kant's own objections to this way of interpreting his second formula.[11] Third, Kant's concept of duty provides a straightforward and simplistic understanding of ethics

10. Jonathan Glover, *Humanity: A Moral History of the Twentieth Century* (New Haven: Yale University Press, 1999), 356–57.

11. Sullivan, *Kant's Moral Theory*, 204. According to Roger Sullivan, Kant objects to a Golden Rule interpretation of his second formula, given that the Golden Rule is nonspecific about what

and fits with an understanding of ethics as decision making, following rules, and acting on objective, "given" principles about the moral life. Morality therefore need not rely on the messy, contested, and various dispositions of moral agents, and competing visions of the moral life. One's moral obligation is to obey, regardless of personal dispositions and outcomes. Fourth, Kant's anthropology shares assumptions with certain theological anthropologies in evangelicalism as it has also been shaped by Enlightenment assumptions of what it means to be human. The fundamental nature of humanity is often cast as essentially rational, essentially individual, and essentially autonomous. Therefore, this essentially rational and autonomous person does not need a narrative for his or her life, even though the narrative of the Enlightenment "tells the story" of the free, unencumbered person liberated from the influences of community as the predominant narrative for much of Western ethics. And finally, for those who view the Bible as the timeless, universal depository of truth that ought to be obeyed by everyone, regardless of religious persuasion, Kant's moral theory provides a way to view the Bible and select teachings as simply a bunch of rules to be obeyed. I provide a more sustained critique in the following chapter of how evangelical ethics may appropriate a Kantian morality in certain areas, with particular attention given to the ways the Bible is co-opted by the principle of duty at the expense of its authoritative role in the various ways it forms the moral lives of believers and Christian communities.

John Stuart Mill and the Principle of Utility

John Stuart Mill (1806–74) was a British philosopher and politician whose insights, building on the work of Jeremy Bentham, appealed to the revolutionary spirit of equality and democracy emerging in the American colonies, which had taken root in Western Europe vis-à-vis the French Revolution. The prevalent view of the social order was shifting from its more medieval ethos of central communities hierarchically organized around parishes, towns, and feudal patronage that shared a common outlook, even if often imposed, to a view that societies were "collections of individuals" with their own aspirations and ideas that needed to be unleashed for both individual and collective good.[12] The freedom of the

---

kind of duties are owed to ourselves and to others. See Kant's 4:430n in *The Groundwork of the Metaphysics of Morals*.

12. MacIntyre, *Short History of Ethics*, 232.

individual to pursue his or her own destiny was one of the prevailing ideologies of the day, which would come to shape the political and social thought of emerging nations such as the United States. An ethical theory was needed to provide moral guidance in societies where communal consensus was eroding. It could no longer be assumed that a collection of individuals could share a moral consensus; neither were they expected to do so. The Utilitarians, such as Jeremy Bentham and later John Stuart Mill, put forth the moral criterion of utilitarianism, or the principle of utility, as a way to navigate through some new moral mazes. Utilitarianism was a way to achieve a semblance of harmony in contexts where individuals were free to determine their own conception of happiness as the goal of their lives. The principle of utility is this: "The creed which accepts as the foundation of morals, Utility, or the Greatest Happiness Principle, holds that actions are right in proportion as they tend to promote happiness, wrong as they tend to produce the reverse of happiness."[13] In common parlance, utilitarianism is maximizing the greatest good or happiness for the greatest number of persons. The moral emphasis is placed on the consequences of decisions and actions as they are needed for achieving a desired end.

There are a number of aspects of Mill's theory of utilitarianism to be explored. First, for Mill, "it is the business of ethics to tell us what are our duties, or by what test we may know them; but no system of ethics requires that the sole motive of all we do shall be a feeling of duty; on the contrary, ninety-nine hundredths of all our actions are done from other motives, and rightly so done, if the rule of duty does not condemn them."[14] Utilitarianism, according to Mill, is a superior principle by which to act, since it is able to measure the results of an action as opposed to the unknowable intents and motivations of fallible decision makers. Mill is clearly arguing against Kant in that duty cannot be the sole criterion of moral action. Mill uses the example of a drowning person to illustrate that it is the result of an action, not duty, that reflects the moral worth and significance of an action. It is right to save a person from drowning, regardless of whether we think it is our duty to do so or if we are to be rewarded for this deed.[15] What is morally right is the outcome that a life was saved, regardless of the lifesaver's personal inclination or sense of duty in performing this action.

13. John Stuart Mill, *Utilitarianism,* in *The Basic Writings of John Stuart Mill* (New York: Modern Library, 2002), 239.
14. Ibid., 251.
15. Ibid.

Second, Mill's moral theory is derived through the process of induction.[16] Mill was an empiricist who believed that the single principle of utility is obvious and observable based on the senses and human experience. Mill writes, "According to the other doctrine [inductive school of ethics], right and wrong, as well as truth and falsehood, are questions of observations and experience."[17] Since Mill represents what he calls the "inductive school of ethics," we must rely on the particulars of the human senses and experiences from which we then induce and draw general conclusions. This is opposite to deduction, of which Kant is representative according to Mill, which starts with a general principle that then draws us to its application to particular circumstances, a method, Mill purports, that does not take seriously actual human experience as a moral arena. For Mill, two things are observable about humans: we desire to maximize pleasure, and we seek to avoid pain. In *Morality: Does God Make a Difference?* Wayne Johnson comments on Mill's ethic: "Mill's principle of utility is not grounded in some revealed truth; instead he claims it is a logical consequence of the natural human desire for happiness."[18] Therefore, actions that maximize pleasure and avoid pain are actions of moral worth, since this is what we can see that humans desire and pursue. The principle of utility is able to provide a measuring stick by which we can calculate what actions bring about the greatest good for the greatest number of people or minimize pain for the smallest number.

Third, because Mill was an empiricist, the world of senses, feeling, and experience is to be accepted. It is for this reason that Mill assumed that the maximization of the human desire for pleasure and happiness was a moral good to pursue and why he eschewed moral claims based on a priori principles of right and wrong as articulated by Kant. For Mill, what is pleasurable is obvious and is evidenced by the fact that people do order their lives according to what they desire and what brings them pleasure. He therefore draws the conclusion from these observations that efforts to maximize happiness are at the core of morality. Mill writes in *Utilitarianism* that

---

16. As explained above, Kant's method in ethics was deductive. Mill identifies this type of method as "intuitionism," whereby "the principles of morals are evident *a priori,* requiring nothing to command assent, except that the meaning of the terms be understood." Mill has a lengthy argument against deductionism or intuitionism in this section of *Utilitarianism.* See pages 234–36 in *Utilitarianism.*

17. Mill, *Utilitarianism*, 235.

18. Wayne G. Johnson, *Morality: Does God Make a Difference?* (Lanham, MD: University Press of America, 2005), 77.

The only proof capable of being given that an object is visible is that people actually see it. The only proof that a sound is audible is that people hear it: and so of the other sources of our experience. In like manner, I apprehend, the sole evidence it is possible to produce that anything is desirable, is that people do actually desire it. If the end which the utilitarian doctrine proposes to itself were not, in theory and in practice, acknowledged to be an end, nothing could ever convince any person that it was so. No reason can be given why the general happiness is desirable, except that each person, so far as he believes it to be attainable, desires his own happiness. This, however, being a fact, we have not only all the proof which the case admits of, but all which it is possible to require, that happiness is a good: that each person's happiness is a good to that person, and the general happiness, therefore, a good to the aggregate of all persons.[19]

According to Mill, people cannot act from any principle other than the principle of pleasure, because it is impossible for people to not act according to what brings happiness and what avoids pain.[20] Mill is not very precise in defining what he means by happiness or pleasure. Since they are givens of human experience, evidenced by observations, they are accepted as what ought to be as the ends of morality. What Mill may mean by happiness and pleasure can be inferred in his argument. According to Mill, we know what pleasure and pain are because we both see and experience them. Mill was careful to distinguish his form of utilitarianism from hedonism and from crasser forms of utilitarianism that tended to measure happiness in materialistic and quantitative ways.[21] Wayne Johnson attributes this softer form of utilitarianism to Mill's movement away from his predecessors like Jeremy Bentham. Johnson writes:

Mill followed Bentham in generally equating happiness with pleasure, but he introduced a qualitative distinction between pleasures which Bentham denied. This charge of "pig philosophy" had been leveled at Bentham's utilitarianism since Bentham had argued that all pleasures are equal, that "pushpin is as good as poetry" if it results in pleasure. . . . Mill, on the other hand, argued that qualitative distinctions between pleasures could and should be made, and that "it is better to be a human being dissatisfied than a pig satisfied."[22]

There is a qualitative dimension to Mill's understanding of happiness, since he recognizes that "some *kinds* of pleasures are more desirable and

19. Mill, *Utilitarianism*, 270.
20. Ibid., 274.
21. Ibid., 240.
22. Johnson, *Morality*, 77.

more valuable than others" and that "it would be absurd that while, in estimating all other things, quality is considered as well as quantity, the estimation of pleasures should be supposed to depend on quantity alone."[23] For example, one might desire the pleasure of food detrimental to one's health. However, the effect of this satiation would be poor health, which is not an outcome that produces individual happiness or a good for the greatest number of people. Quality of ends is an important consideration in determining various degrees of happiness and how best to achieve them. When deciding what kinds of pleasures to pursue and how to measure the qualitative differences in pleasures, Mill resorts to his empirical method. "Of two pleasures, if there be one to which all or almost all who have experience of both give a decided preference, irrespective of any feeling of moral obligation to prefer it, that is the more desirable pleasure."[24] We know, therefore, what are desired ends because of what human experience reveals as to what we desire. This is Mill's criterion for determining the moral nature of the aspirations and ends of human existence.

What might be the *kinds* of pleasures that we ought to pursue as ends? What are the dimensions of happiness that bring the greatest good for the greatest number? For Mill, activities that involve our higher faculties are the kinds of activities that bring happiness and pleasure to individuals and contribute to the greatest good for the greatest number of persons. Mill is vague on the exact nature of the higher faculties, but there are glimpses in *Utilitarianism* that he equates higher faculties with such things as intellectual pursuits and "mental cultivation." Mill writes that, "Next to selfishness, the principal cause which makes life unsatisfactory, is want of mental cultivation. A cultivated mind—I do not mean that of a philosopher, but any mind to which the fountains of knowledge have been opened, and which has been taught, in any tolerable degree, to exercise its faculties—finds sources of inexhaustible interest in all that surrounds it, in the objects of nature, the achievements of art, the imaginations of poetry, the incidents of history, the ways of mankind past and present, and their prospects in the future."[25] It is important to note that while there is an elitist perspective in Mill's ethic that privileges "mental cultivation," he did see implications for reversing the "subjection of women" and for addressing social inequities and injustices.[26] He used his understanding of

23. Mill, *Utilitarianism*, 241.
24. Ibid.
25. Ibid., 247.
26. See John Stuart Mill, *The Subjection of Women*, in *The Basic Writings of John Stuart Mill* (New York: Modern Library, 2002).

utilitarianism in his argument for the dignity and worth of women. Women were to be free to pursue their own individuality and development, for the good of themselves as well as for the common good. A good society, inclusive of women and men, that focuses on the greatest good for the greatest number of people will be a society where individual selfishness is ameliorated by good education, nobility of character, and attention to the relationship between one's own happiness and the happiness of others.

Mill consistently repeats that utilitarianism is not about the satisfaction of one's personal desires. His does not purport to be an ethic of hedonism. According to Mill, people can move beyond their egotistical perspectives and enlarge their capacities to understand the whole of society, where their own well-being is intricately linked to the happiness of others. At the same time, Mill recognizes that what an individual desires (and needs) will likely represent what the greatest number desire and need, so that pursuing one's self-interest will, in fact, benefit others. In a lengthy section, Mill explains the relationship between the individual, the good of society, and the nature of happiness in this regard.

> Genuine private affections, and a sincere interest in the public good, are possible, though in unequal degrees, to every rightly brought up human being. In a world in which there is so much to interest, so much to enjoy, and so much also to correct and improve, every one who has this moderate amount of moral and intellectual requisites is capable of an existence which may be called enviable; and unless such a person, through bad laws or subjection to the will of others, is denied the liberty to use the sources of happiness within his reach, he will not fail to find this enviable existence, if he escapes the positive evils of life, the great sources of physical and mental suffering—such as indigence, disease, and the unkindness, worthlessness, or premature loss of objects of affection. . . . All of the grand sources, in short, of human suffering are in a great degree, many of them almost entirely, conquerable by human care and effort . . . every mind sufficiently intelligent and generous to bear a part, however, small and unconspicuous, in the endeavor, will draw a noble enjoyment from the contest itself, which he would not for any bribe in the form of selfish indulgence consent to be without.[27]

Goods and pleasures, which are obvious in that they are valued by persons, include such things as freedom from poverty, disease, and harm, and other forms of human suffering. These freedoms need to be secured in order for humans to pursue happiness. The provisions of these securities of life are the aim and work of justice. In the final chapter of *Utilitarianism*, Mill

---

27. Mill, *Utilitarianism,* 247–48.

connects the principle of utility with his conception of justice. In response to critics who feared the demise of justice if ethics was to be grounded in human happiness, Mill responds by arguing that justice is the highest form of social utility that serves the greatest number of people. Humans empirically see justice as ensuring that wrongs are punished and that one's rights, such as rights to safety and security, are not violated. Human happiness cannot be obtained without human security. For Mill, justice is the establishment and protection of human security so that happiness may be achieved.

Mill believed that people understand instinctively that their well-being is joined to the collective well-being of all persons. Mill writes that since humans have higher mental faculties, we are able to distinguish between self-regarding and sympathetic sentiments. In other words, we are able to assess happiness in a social sense that puts us in sympathy with others, which is a characteristic required for justice. He goes on to write, "By virtue of his superior intelligence, even apart from his superior range of sympathy, a human being is capable of apprehending a community of interest between himself and the human society of which he forms a part, such that any conduct which threatens the security of the society generally, is threatening to his own, and calls for his instinct (if instinct it be) of self-defence."[28] Mill argues that even Kant would have to admit to being a utilitarian, since the categorical imperative acknowledges the collective interest of humankind in the formula "So act, that thy rule of conduct might be adopted as a law by all rational beings."[29] Justice, then, is the ultimate norm of social utilitarianism, since "the moral rules which forbid mankind to hurt one another (in which we must never forget to include wrongful interference with each other's freedom) are more vital to human well-being than any maxims . . . thus the moralities which protect every individual from being harmed by others, either directly or by being hindered in his freedom of pursuing his own good, are at once those which he himself has most at heart."[30]

Throughout *Utilitarianism*, Mill responds to objections that utilitarianism enshrines selfishness and is hedonistic, godless, and expedient.[31] Like

28. Ibid., 288.
29. Ibid., 289. In many places in *Utilitarianism,* Mill is explicitly and implicitly arguing with Kant. For Mill, utilitarianism encompasses both duties and virtues; we are obligated to maximize happiness for the greatest number of people, and it is virtuous to do so since "the multiplication of happiness is, according to utilitarian ethics, the object of virtue." See pages 252–54 for a more extended critique of virtue and deontology from Mill's perspective.
30. Ibid., 296.
31. In my view, this is one of the major differences between Kant's *Groundwork of the Metaphysics of Morals* and Mill's *Utilitarianism*. Kant was working to establish a metaphysics

Kant, Mill believed that God is unnecessary for morality, though morality may lead one to the acknowledgment of God behind moral aspirations. Mill was far less concerned than Kant with articulating a philosophy of religion and its relationship to morality. Mill's view of religion was fairly cynical, since religion had been used by all sorts of moralists to justify wrongdoing as well as to promote good. A utilitarian, like any other moralist, according to Mill, can use the Deity to bolster his or her position, depending on what *kind* of moral character they attribute to God, and if this is the way to appeal to religionists, so be it. Mill provides two defenses to those who charge utilitarianism as antireligious. His responses are consonant with the growing humanization of religion that focused on human experience, Enlightenment deism, and the Jesus of history who provides us with the supreme moral example. First, Jesus of Nazareth represents the best there is of the doctrine of utility codified in the Golden Rule and provides us with the ultimate norm of the utilitarian doctrine. Mill writes:

> I must again repeat, what the assailants of utilitarianism seldom have the justice to acknowledge, that the happiness which forms the utilitarian standard of what is right in conduct, is not the agent's own happiness, but that of all concerned. As between his own happiness and that of others, utilitarianism requires him to be as strictly impartial as a disinterested and benevolent spectator. In the golden rule of Jesus of Nazareth, we read the complete spirit of the ethics of utility. To do as one would be done by, and to love one's neighbour as oneself, constitute the ideal perfection of utilitarian morality.[32]

Mill's second justification is that God's own raison d'être is to ensure human happiness. He puts forward that God's own moral character depends on human happiness. In other words, what God desires for humans is our happiness. Mill writes, "If it be a true belief that God desires, above all things, the happiness of his creatures, and that this was his purpose in their creation, utility is not only not a godless doctrine, but more profoundly religious than any other."[33]

While these two claims may satisfy Mill's critics, they in no way ensure that people will, in fact, act morally. Religious affections and an appeal to a transcendent sense of duty are both inadequate, since neither can

---

of morals. Mill's work reads as a justification of the principle of utility in response to its critics, which takes up a good deal of space in the book. Mill works from his own a priori assumption that humans will pursue an altruistic kind of happiness for themselves and for others. He assumes this as a given, and it is one of his assumptions on which his own theory is based.

32. Mill, *Utilitarianism*, 250.
33. Ibid., 255.

guarantee that a good outcome will result from decisions informed by these orientations. This is why, for Mill, the principle of utility is the superior principle. It encompasses both duty and virtue by focusing on the virtuous actions and the obligation to maximize the happiness of the greatest number for the greatest good. The principle of utility acts as an umpire between competing duties and mixed personal dispositions and inclinations. The principle of utility is the criterion that mediates between conflicting obligations and competing concepts of human happiness. Mill writes:

> There exists no moral system under which there do not arise unequivocal cases of conflicting obligation. There are the real difficulties, the knotty points both in the theory of ethics, and in the conscientious guidance of personal conduct. . . . If utility is the ultimate source of moral obligations, utility may be invoked to decide between them when their demands are incompatible. Though the application of the standard may be difficult, it is better than none at all: while in other systems, the moral laws all claiming independent authority, there is no common umpire entitled to interfere between them; their claims to precedence one over another rest on little better than sophistry, and unless determined, as they generally are, by the unacknowledged influence of considerations of utility, afford a free scope of the action of personal desires and partialities.[34]

Appeal and Appropriations of Mill's Principle of Utility

Why might Mill's principle of utility hold appeal, and in what ways might it harmonize and be acceptable to an understanding of the nature of moral claims given the ideological and epistemological assumptions in evangelicalism? First, the assumptions of utilitarianism reflect some of the ideological and epistemological assumptions in evangelicalism. The belief that individuals are imbued with rights to happiness, safety, and security represents the sociopolitical milieu of much of American political thought that has been appropriated by evangelicals. It is this kind of thinking that conflates the Constitution and its Bill of Rights with Christian principles and maintains the vision of a Christian America. Second, the belief that societies and communities, and even churches, are no more than a collection of individuals reflects the personalized ways evangelicals view human societies. Mill's ethic may be appealing for a third reason. It provides a way to define "happiness" howsoever a

34. Ibid., 258–59.

person or communities desire, with little frame of reference beyond their own ideas and experiences as to what actually constitutes happiness. In many of the white, middle-class contexts of American evangelicalism, "happiness" is now substituted for the pursuit of self-fulfillment and the satisfaction of consumer desires in our privileged enclaves.[35] God's own *telos* and ultimate desire is believed to be focused on human happiness however we choose to describe it, given the ambiguous and open nature of "happiness." In other words, above all other things God desires our happiness as Mill affirmed and as we tend to believe. Fourth, since communities and even churches are typically viewed as little more than a collection of individuals, utilitarianism is a useful way to make moral claims in a context where each is free to pursue his or her own individual conscience with little expectation that there may be some sense of or need for a common moral consensus. In contexts where moral consensus is not expected or desired, utilitarianism is a handy way to understand what is valued in ethical decision making by focusing on what works as the mark of moral effectiveness. Fifth, and related to the previous point, utilitarianism appeals to the pragmatic bent of much of American church life, which values what works, what is efficient, and what produces desired results. When moral decisions are focused on the outcome, the task of assessing the nature of what one actually does and one's identity and character is minimized in favor of what is perceived to actually work. Therefore, means can be justified by the ends that they produce, even though the means themselves are morally questionable and dubious. And finally, as with Kant, there is a "Golden Rule" kind of feel to utilitarianism that may appeal to persons who understand ethics in the terms that Mill proposes. This would be an "ethic for everyone," regardless of the unique claims of Jesus and the narrative context of his Golden Rule teaching in the Sermon on the Mount.

That Mill's ethic is appealing is obvious, given his influence on our understanding of "majority rule," the pursuit of human happiness and liberty as inherent rights, and the lack of moral consensus in favor of whatever actions maximize human happiness, as we so define it. The majority of us, according to Mill, are functional utilitarians regardless of the moral claims we might actually make. The points of divergence with Christian ethics I explore in chapter 3, where I investigate the subversion

35. See Robert Bellah, Richard Madsen, William Sullivan, Ann Swidler, and Steve Tipton, *Habits of the Heart* (New York: Harper and Row, 1985), and Wade Clark Roof, *The Spiritual Marketplace* (Princeton, NJ: Princeton University Press, 1999), for helpful insights on expressive forms of religious faith that I think are applicable to American evangelicalism.

of Christian ethics by a form of utilitarianism that focuses on the "greatest good as the greatest number getting saved."

Aristotle and Virtue Ethics

Aristotle (384–322 BCE) is one of the preeminent Greek philosophers. Schooled in Plato's Academy, he tutored the future Alexander the Great and eventually founded his own school, the Lyceum outside of Athens. Aristotle modeled his philosophy of education through his *peripatetic* method, or "walking around" while teaching and conversing with students as a means for demonstrating the ongoing, forward-moving nature of education. Education was to be participatory and practical. Hence, Aristotle's method of teaching was focused on the learner, who was to be actively engaged in conversation, learning, research, and discovery, so that students also adopted the habit of walking around as they learned. Aristotle's moral philosophy, the development of virtue, is related to his pedagogy. The purpose of education was to form moral character, particularly the moral character of those who influence and control society, which in Aristotle's case were Greek males, rulers, academicians, and political leaders. The foci of Aristotle's education were the elite members of society. Even though Aristotle saw educated persons as crucial for the well-being of society, he was not an equalitarian in his view of the social order. Education was reserved for upper-class men, which continued to reinforce the strong hierarchical, gendered, and class dimensions of ancient Greek society.

Building on platonic thought, while also diverging in significant ways, "Aristotle . . . believed that acting like a human being is tantamount to acting like a rational human being, and acting like a rational human being is the same thing as acting as a good human being."[36] Reason therefore must be educated, since it is reason that ultimately controls the passions and dispositions of humans. The intellect is seen as the seat of the virtues and the means by which we control variant passions and desires by making choices and developing habits, a central part of character formation in Aristotelian ethics.

36. Aristotle, *Nicomachean Ethics,* translated by Martin Ostwald (Indianapolis: Bobbs-Merrill, 1962), xiii–iv. When citing directly from Aristotle's *Nicomachean Ethics,* I will use the standard method for citing his work by noting the cited section in parenthetical references. See 1096a10 for Aristotle's own critique of Plato's conception of Forms, which is the main area in which Aristotle diverged from Plato.

A large portion of Aristotle's moral philosophy is found in *Nicomachean Ethics*, a collection of lecture notes and writings that was organized and edited by his son, Nicomachus. In this work Aristotle expounds on crucial dimensions of his understanding of ethics. Ethics is concerned with discovering the highest good of human existence, and the highest good of human existence is the development and exercise of virtues necessary to achieve the highest good, which is happiness or well-being. In other words, virtues are intrinsic goods and hold the keys to a life of happiness, the ultimate extrinsic good. Aristotle uses the word *eudaimonia* to describe the highest good of human life. *Eudaimonia* can be understood as blessedness, well-being, happiness, and prosperity, or having a good spirit. In *After Virtue* Alasdair MacIntyre interprets Aristotle's *eudaimonia* to be "the state of being well and doing well in being well, of a man's being well-favored himself and in relation to the divine."[37] According to W. D. Ross in his important interpretation of Aristotle's work, the kind of life that brings satisfaction or well-being is a life in which one uses the higher faculties that direct one toward happiness. It is a life of activity, one that is vigorously pursuing the ends of happiness according to the proper function of humanity; it must be a life in accordance with virtues; and it must not be manifested in short bursts of virtuous endeavors, but sustained over one's lifetime.[38] In Aristotelian ethics, this is how virtuous character is formed. For Aristotle, then, ethics is the "study of character" and the attempts to "ascertain the proper function of man" as it relates to becoming good and achieving a life of well-being (1097b24).[39] Virtue and the concept of well-being and happiness are fundamental for understanding the proper function of humanity, which is to be excellent and to pursue excellence for its own sake. This makes us good, is a good, and will result in good. The development and exercise of virtue are critical to Aristotle's teleological view of the proper function and ends of humanity. *When* we act according to virtue, we are acting in conformity with what is excellent and with what eventually will bring about human well-being, which is the goal of ethics. He writes:

> The proper function of man, then, consists in an activity of the soul in conformity with a rational principle or, at least not without it. In speaking

37. Alasdair MacIntyre, *After Virtue* (Notre Dame, IN: University of Notre Dame Press, 1984), 148. It is important to note that Aristotle's conception of the divine was not the same thing as the monotheism of Judaism and later Christianity.

38. W. D. Ross, *Aristotle* (London: Methuen, 1949), 191.

39. Ibid., 187.

of the proper function of a given individual we mean that it is the same in kind as the function of an individual who sets high standards for himself . . . on these assumptions, if we take the proper function of man to be a certain kind of life, and if this kind of life is an activity of the soul and consists in actions performed in conjunction with the rational element, and if a man of high standards is he who performs these actions well and properly, and if a function is well performed when it is performed in accordance with the excellence appropriate to it; we reach the conclusion that the good of man is an activity of the soul in conformity with excellence or virtue, and if there are several virtues, in conformity with the best and most complete. (1098a7)

Aristotle has in mind the symbiotic relationship between who one is, or one's character, and the choices and activities one pursues with excellence in fulfilling one's proper function as the mark of the moral life.[40] While teleology is a significant aspect of Aristotle's ethic, I will concentrate on describing his understanding of virtue, since virtue ethics has experienced a renaissance and renewed attention in Christian ethics.[41] Key concepts of Aristotle's moral theory for consideration are his understanding of the virtues, the ways in which virtues are developed and exercised, and the role of friendship in the formation of moral character.

What is virtue? Virtue can be understood as a possession, a trait, a characteristic that is valued and revered as good. For Aristotle, there are

40. The aristocratic bent of Aristotle's philosophy is reflected in his understanding of one's proper function. As noted by MacIntyre in chapters 10 and 11 of *After Virtue,* the Homeric society that Aristotle inherited was hierarchical and patrician. One's proper function was the fulfillment of the duties and obligations inherent in one's social location; therefore, the good slave was the slave who fulfilled his obligations as a slave. As MacIntyre notes, Aristotle shared this thinking. He writes, "It is crucial to the structure of Aristotle's extended argument that the virtues are unavailable to slaves or to barbarians and so therefore is the good for man . . . what is likely to affront us—and rightly—is Aristotle's writing off of non-Greeks, barbarians and slaves, as not merely possessing political relationships, but as incapable of them. With this we may couple his view that only the affluent and those of high status can achieve certain key virtues, those of munificence and of magnanimity; craftsmen and tradesmen constitute an inferior class, even if they are not slaves. Hence the peculiar excellences of the exercise of craft skill and manual labor are invisible from the standpoint of Aristotle's catalogue of the virtues." See pages 158–59 in *After Virtue.*

41. Alasdair MacIntyre's work in *After Virtue,* while written from a philosophical perspective, has been influential in the renewal of interest in virtue in Christian ethics. See the following works: Stanley Hauerwas, *A Community of Character: Toward a Constructive Christian Ethic* (Notre Dame, IN: University of Notre Dame Press, 1981); Stanley Hauerwas and Charles Pinches, *Christians among the Virtues: Theological Conversations with Ancient and Modern Ethics* (Notre Dame, IN: University of Notre Dame Press, 1997); Joseph Kotva, *The Christian Case for Virtue Ethics* (Washington, DC: Georgetown University Press, 1996); and *Virtues and Practices in the Christian Traditions: Christian Ethics after MacIntyre* (Harrisburg, PA: Trinity Press International, 1997), edited by Nancey Murphy, Brad Kallenberg, and Mark Thiessen Nation.

two kinds of virtues. They are intellectual and moral virtues. He writes, "We call some virtues 'intellectual' and others 'moral': theoretical wisdom, understanding, and practical wisdom are intellectual virtues, generosity and self-control moral virtues. In speaking of a man's character we do not describe him as wise or understanding, but as gentle or self-controlled; but we praise the wise man, too, for his characteristics, and praiseworthy characteristics are what we call virtues" (1103a5). Virtues are characteristics and qualities of human behavior and intentions that moderate and direct the other two aspects of our being, which are our emotions and capacities or wills (1105b20). The emotions are the seat of our appetites and desires. They are the feelings that are aroused by our desire for pleasure and the need to avoid pain. We are affected by emotions and compelled to act in certain ways based on what we will to do. Aristotle understands capacities to be our potential to respond to emotions, thereby acting in ways to fulfill desire or to avoid displeasure by directing our wills according to virtue. Virtues are those characteristics that enable a person to avoid the extremes of excess and deficiency in emotions by directing our capacities to act virtuously, aiming at what is good. John Stuart Mill may seem to bear a resemblance to Aristotle in reference to maximizing pleasure and avoiding pain. Mill accepted the maximization of pleasure and the avoidance of pain as evident, with little moral criteria as to the natures of the pleasures we are to pursue and the types of pain we are to avoid; they are simply what humans are observed to pursue. Aristotle, on the other hand, believed that virtues are what direct our passions to the pursuit of higher goods *because* they are inherently good as opposed to utilitarian. Evidentiary pleasures and pains may be crude and fleeting forms of "good." Therefore, the virtues are those characteristics that define what inherent goods we ought to pursue.

Virtues assist us in finding the median between the extremes of excess and deficiency through the use of the intellectual virtue of practical wisdom (1107a). Aristotle illustrates the principle of the mean by exploring various characteristics he lists as virtues: courage, self-control, generosity, self-respect, gentleness, truthfulness, humor, friendliness, modesty, and righteous indignation (1107a32). For example, the virtue of courage moderates the extremes of cowardice (deficiency) and fearlessness (excess). Generosity is the virtue that is the median between stinginess (deficiency) and extravagance (excess). Righteous indignation is the virtuous means, moderating our excessive envy at someone else's success and our deficiency in feeling pain or empathy when someone suffers unjustly. Even though Aristotle believed that most humans have the capacity to be and become virtuous, the actual task of becoming good is a difficult one, for "not everyone can find the middle of a circle, but only a man who has the proper knowledge" (1109a25). The moral and intellectual virtues are intricately related in Aristotle's understanding of virtue even though he describes them as two sets of virtuous activity. It is the intellectual virtues of understanding and practical wisdom that enable a person to discern the means by which we live in order to avoid excesses and deficiencies in character. MacIntyre observes of Aristotle's virtue ethics that

> the exercise of intelligence is what makes the crucial difference between a natural disposition of a certain kind and the corresponding virtue. Conversely, the exercise of practical intelligence requires the presence of the virtues of character; otherwise it degenerates into or remains from the outset merely a certain cunning capacity for linking means to any end rather than to those ends which are genuine goods for man.[42]

The capacity to choose right ends for the right reasons relies on the pursuit and practice of intellectual and moral virtues. In Aristotle's theory, they are bound together. One cannot be morally virtuous without the use of practical wisdom, since "virtue or excellence is not only a characteristic which is guided by right reason, but also a characteristic which is united with right reason; and right reason in moral matters is practical wisdom" (1144b25). We may know the right thing to do. "Right reason" may enable us to craft well-developed arguments for why certain goods are more worthy of pursuit than others. However, right knowledge, according to Aristotle, will not guarantee right behavior. We may know the right thing to do and still fail to do it. It is practical wisdom and the development of the virtues that flow from "right reason" into rightly practiced behavior.

How does one go about the task of developing moral and intellectual virtues? We develop virtues in three ways, according to Aristotle. Virtues are cultivated through habits, choices, and friendship. First, virtues are developed through habits. Aristotle writes, "the virtues are implanted in us neither by nature nor contrary to nature: we are by nature equipped with the ability to receive them, and habit brings this ability to completion and fulfillment" (1103a24). To illustrate his point Aristotle uses examples from various professions. The harpist learns to be an excellent harpist by practice. If one's function is to be an excellent harpist, then the good one must pursue is playing with excellence. A builder learns to build

42. MacIntyre, *After Virtue*, 154.

houses by building them, with the goal of building them with excellence, which will bring happiness to both the builder and the inhabitant of the house. So it is with the virtues, according to Aristotle. "Similarly, we become just by the practice of just actions, self-controlled by exercising self-control, and courageous by performing acts of courage" (1103b). However, these are not simply routine, mimetic acts or singular performances. Acting virtuously one time is no guarantee that one will act with virtue the next. The person who desires to become virtuous must do so for the right reasons and in the right way over the long haul. Aristotle is clear that what makes someone virtuous is not the result of his or her niceties or personal characteristics. It is not the act itself that is virtuous. It is the person performing the act, and doing so for the right reasons, that makes it virtuous. Aristotle explains: "But in the case of the virtues an act is not performed justly or with self-control if the act itself is of a certain kind, but only if in addition the agent has certain characteristics as he performs it: first of all, he must know what he is doing; secondly, he must choose to act the way he does, and he must choose it for its own sake; and in the third place, the act must spring from a firm and unchangeable character" (1105a30).

Second, we learn virtue by making choices that are free and voluntary. Choice is a complement of habit, which trains us to pursue and choose virtues and act accordingly. Aristotle makes a distinction between voluntary and involuntary choices. Voluntary choices made by the moral agent and chosen as ends in themselves are superior to involuntary choices. They are superior "because the initiative in moving the parts of the body which act as instruments rests with the agent himself; and where the source of motion is within oneself, it is in one's power to act or not to act" (1110a15). Chosen ends are superior to involuntary ones. Those chosen under constraint are inferior because their initiative and intention are extrinsic to the moral agent; they contribute little or nothing to the development of one's moral character because they are not freely chosen (1110b17). In other words, this capacity and need to make voluntary choices about the kind of character we want to have is important for making morality intrinsic to us by our own choices and habits. It is ours because we have pursued it as ours. For Aristotle, an extrinsically driven morality is really no morality at all, since what is not freely chosen cannot direct our wills and emotions toward virtue.

It is choosing to be and become virtuous that demands the use of practical wisdom, since "the exercise of the virtues requires a capacity to judge and to do the right thing in the right place at the right time," according to

MacIntyre's interpretation of Aristotle.[43] This is why Aristotle is so harsh with those who act out of ignorance. Here he makes a distinction between one who acts *due to* ignorance and one who acts *in* ignorance. It is the one who acts in ignorance whom he finds morally heinous. In fact, Aristotle calls him wicked (1110b32). Why? The person who acts in ignorance has no regard for the nature of his moral agency, the import and impact of his actions, the ways in which he acts, and the overall result of his actions (1111a3). He violates everything that makes a human a moral agent with the capacity to reason correctly and choose rightly. Ignorance, according to Aristotle, is no excuse for bad behavior and dreadful deeds.

It is here that we see Aristotle's emphasis on reason and intellect as important components of his virtue ethic as it relates to our humanity. It is speculative but possible to illustrate Aristotelian ethics related to debates on "nature versus nurture." Where does Aristotle locate the origins of wrongdoing? Do we do wrong things because it is in our nature to do so? Or do we do the wrong thing because we have not been taught what is right? Aristotle may have answered yes to both questions. We learn what is right through education and moral training. Without this, we act due to ignorance, since we have not been nurtured properly to value and pursue the right things. Aristotle, however, seems to place greater moral culpability on nature. It is still within human capacity to understand the right thing through reason, and given the fact that no human being ever really exists alone. Even without proper nurture we are still responsible to understand what is right and even have the capacity to do so because of human reason and our observations of the virtues that others pursue. It is our willful remaining in ignorance about moral goods, and our failure to control unbridled and misdirected passions, ignoring their ill effects, that bears greater moral scrutiny from Aristotle. In ignorance, *we* deny what is fundamental about our humanity, *our* responsibility to know right from wrong and to act according to what we do know. Aristotle would have little patience with an explanation of bad behavior that starts with "I didn't know," or "The devil made me do it," or "I had no choice."

Aristotle's understanding of choice is where we see moral and intellectual virtues come together, since it is by our choices, informed by reason, that we reflect our character and enable others to see what really matters to us and who we are. We are known by our actions. It is a deliberate choice to act with virtue or to avoid acting in an unvirtuous way that shapes our character on an ongoing basis. Choice is not the same thing as freedom to

43. Ibid., 150.

choose and pursue what we want when we want. Choice is different because it involves reason and deliberation, aspects of our humanity that direct appetites, desires, wishes, and opinions toward good ends. For Aristotle, an important part of moral agency is the use of deliberation, since deliberation reinforces voluntary choices made by one's power and reason. He writes, "Since then, the object of choice is something within our power which we desire as a result of deliberation, we may define choice as a deliberate desire for things that are within our power: we arrive at a decision on the basis of deliberation, and then let the deliberation guide our desire" (1113a10).

To alleviate the burden that every act requires deliberation, Aristotle limits the need for deliberation to the areas of life "that hold good as a general rule, but whose outcome is unpredictable, and in cases in which an indeterminate element is involved" (1112b7). Deliberation that is focused, thoughtful, concerned with clarity, and allows itself the time to follow a process of thorough investigation will enable a person to understand the "indeterminate" elements, and by practical wisdom, sort through them, to arrive at a decision or pursue an action consonant with the good desired. According to W. D. Ross, Aristotle's conception of practical wisdom "is the power of good deliberation, not about how particular things are to be made . . . but about 'things good for oneself,' i.e., about how a whole state of being which will satisfy us is to be brought into existence."[44] Ross goes on to observe that in Aristotle's moral theory, ethics cannot be complete without practical reason, "since practical wisdom implies that a man does not follow his instinctive tendencies such as they may happen to be—some good, others bad—but directs his whole life towards the chief good, it is incompatible with a one-sided moral development."[45] Aristotle's conception of virtue ethics is not a "one-sided moral development" concerned only with virtue as virtue. The possession of virtue is not the end of morality. His is a theory where practical wisdom is a necessary ingredient for understanding *how* to be and act virtuous through the process of deliberation since "virtue in the full sense cannot be attained without practical wisdom" (1144b17). One who has the ability to deliberate is capable of being and acting virtuously through the use of practical wisdom. Knowing, being, *and* doing the right things provides the complete picture of virtue ethics.

Becoming morally virtuous relies on the use of intellectual virtues, like reason and deliberation, so that we might recognize by what means we

44. Ross, *Aristotle*, 217.
45. Ibid., 221.

ought to act according to practical wisdom. An action must be voluntary and within our power in order for it to be an act of moral agency, and one that can be called "good." However, the development of the virtues is not an individual endeavor, neither is the development of good character an end in itself. Even in the process of deliberation, we ought to be aware of our need for help. Aristotle writes, "When great issues are at stake, we distrust our own abilities as insufficient to decide the matter and call in others to join us in our deliberations" (1112b10). In other words, we need our friends. According to Nancy Sherman, this is an important aspect of Aristotelian ethics, not to be overlooked. She writes in *The Fabric of Character* that "unlike the Kantian, Aristotle does not merely permit attachment within a theory of morality constituted primarily by impartiality. Rather, he makes attachment essential to the expression of virtue, and living with friends a structural feature of good living."[46]

The development of moral virtue requires that we understand the relationship between our own moral integrity and the morality of the communities we inhabit and the "friends we keep." It is here that we see the relationship between the individual and the community that she or he inhabits in Aristotle's philosophy. We are essentially social beings and can thrive only in relationships vital to our well-being. Aristotle's ethic is essentially a political ethic, according to Ross, since "he [Aristotle] does not forget in the *Ethics* that the individual man is a member of society, nor in the *Politics* that the good life of the state exists only in the good lives of its citizens."[47] *Political* need not be construed in its narrower sense of the formal mechanisms and apparatus of governmental and state systems or electoral procedures. *Political* can mean in a fuller sense the ways in which a community organizes its life together according to common values and concerns based on their own identity and the ways in which members are socialized to embody the ethos of their given communities.[48] An inherent aspect of community life is the presence of "friends," which is the third means in Aristotle's ethics, along with habit and voluntary choice, for moral formation in the virtues. Since we are essentially social beings, the presence of others in friendship is crucial to our well-being and hence to theirs. For Aristotle, the interaction with a community of friends was not

46. Nancy Sherman, *The Fabric of Character: Aristotle's Theory of Virtue* (New York: Oxford University Press, 1989), 124.

47. Ross, *Aristotle,* 187.

48. See John Howard Yoder, *The Politics of Jesus,* 2nd ed. (Grand Rapids: Eerdmans, 1994), for an expanded sense of "political."

just a means to learn virtue. This interaction and "being in community" is a virtue, an inherent good that also makes us good.

Aristotle uses the word *philia* to describe his conception of friendship.[49] This word may draw us to certain images of love found in scripture, either *philia* or *agapao*. As I will discuss later in chapter 4, Aristotle's conception of "brotherly love" is in sharp contrast to a scriptural conception of love. Aristotle's *philia* carries the connotation of friends in relationships, committed to mutual sharing and the support of one another. "*Philia* constitutes the bond that holds the members of any association together, regardless of whether the association is the family, the state, a club, a business partnership, or even the business relation between buyer and seller."[50] These are the types of bonds in various communities that Aristotle has in mind when referring to the human need for friendship and community as a human good for its own sake. Friendship is "indispensable for life. No one would choose to live without friends even if he had all other goods" (1155a1).

Aristotle distinguishes between three kinds of friendship. First, there are friendships based on usefulness (1156a10). Friendships formed out of utility are not based on affection or on an inherent interest in another's good but instead "in terms of the good accruing to each other from the other" (1156a12). The second kind of friendship is created around pleasure, whereby "we love witty people not for what they are, but for the pleasure they give us" (1156a1l3). The most excellent of friendships, the third kind, is what Aristotle calls "the perfect form of friendship . . . between good men who are alike in excellence or virtue" (1156b6). These kinds of friendships may include aspects of the first two in that they are useful to us and we derive pleasure from their company. However, the third kind of friendship is complete friendship. It is more perfect because it is formed among people, men in Aristotle's view, who share excellence in virtue and who wish for the other a life of excellence and well-being. In these friendships, the good of the other and affection are sought as the proper virtue, ensuring excellence for both the receiver and giver of affection (1159a35). They are enduring and consistent compared to the fleeting nature of friendships based on convenience and entertainment, friendships that can easily be dissolved once their usefulness or amusement wanes.

What does Aristotle have to say about these kinds of bonds, their importance to human well-being, and the ways in which they function as

---

49. Aristotle, *Nicomachean Ethics,* 214n.
50. Ibid.

the context for formation in the virtues? Aristotle's prevailing assumption is that friendship is both a characteristic (i.e., a good) *and* an activity. Friendship itself is a virtue, the activity of "living in each other's company" (1157b2), whereby we are able to become good. Friends help us avoid error and give us opportunity to learn and perform good deeds for the welfare of others (1155a12). "Friends enhance our ability to think and to act" (1155a16). Assuming we recognize our limitations in practical wisdom and understanding the "indeterminate elements" of various actions and decisions, we are drawn to rely on friendships to help us think more cogently about given matters. Deliberating with wise and seasoned friends is one way to increase our capacities for understanding as they think alongside us and spur us on to good decisions and actions, consonant with the virtues and the goods to which we aspire. In friendship, we learn how to meet the needs of others by serving others, in poverty, infirmity, hardship, and trouble. Friendship provides the opportunity for us to do "good works" (1155a8). Good works done habitually are the primary means of learning to be virtuous. Friends correct us and keep us from going astray. Aristotle aptly sums up his ethic of friendship as it relates to one's own goodness and well-being:

> Thus, the friendship of base people becomes wicked, because unsteady as they are, they share in base pursuits, and by becoming like one another they become wicked. But the friendship of good men is good, and it increases [with the frequency of] their meetings. Also, it seems, they become better as they are active together and correct one another: from the mould of the other each takes the imprint of the traits he likes, whence the saying: "Noble things from noble people" (1172a10).

Appeal and Appropriations of Aristotelian Ethics

There is much in Aristotle's ethic that is attractive to the concerns of Christian ethics, thereby providing various points of connection and appeal. First, virtues can be found in scripture as the fruit of the Spirit, the product of salvation and sanctification, and characteristics that please God and serve others. However, what Aristotle understands as the classic Greek virtues, with their emphasis on human strength and intellect, vary significantly from the virtues associated with the Sermon on the Mount (Matt. 5:1–12), such as humility, peacemaking, mercy, and suffering for the sake of righteousness. These virtues likely would be viewed with disdain and ridicule in the rough-and-tumble world of Aristotle's *polis*. Second, with the renaissance of virtue ethics in Christian morality, Aristotle's ethic is appealing because of its emphasis on the importance of community and relationships and their influence on who we are and the moral commitments we make. However, the community of equals composed of individuals who are like one another in gender, race, and social class is a picture different from the *ekklesia* as the moral-forming community for the people of God that cuts across the barriers that divide us, barriers that Aristotle felt it was right (read: ethical) to maintain. Third, like Mill, Aristotle's conception of happiness is open to interpretation, so it can easily be appropriated by individualism and the therapeutic. What Aristotle conceived of as happiness can easily be interpreted to mean "my own personal happiness and well-being," even though this would be a misinterpretation. Fourth, Aristotle's ethic may hold appeal for evangelical traditions that emphasize the need for integrity and character, especially among pastors and leaders. Given the privileging of personal piety or "being right with God," virtue ethics may be narrowly construed, missing the essential components of the ways it is formed in community, through choices, and nurtured by practical wisdom and moral deliberation. Moral character is not guaranteed by one's right relationship with God or by one's sense of personal piety. Virtues are learned, nurtured, talked about, and embodied in social contexts.

Conclusion

In this very brief foray into moral philosophy, I focused on three ways of construing ethics through three representatives. This exploration was not meant to be exhaustive, but descriptive and illustrative for identifying points of convergence and divergence among these theories, and their use and appropriation in Christian ethics primarily in an evangelical context. Immanuel Kant's concept of deontology may appeal to those who understand Christian ethics as the search for and imposition of universal moral axioms by rational autonomous agents that can be codified in rules and commands. John Stuart Mill's principle of utility may be used in contexts where little or no moral consensus is required, where morality is seen as the purview of the individual, and the "best we can do" is ensure the greatest happiness for the greatest number of persons. This form of utilitarianism may appeal to those who value "what works" and what is effective as an indicator of moral worth. Perhaps Aristotle's notion of virtue complements a view that Christian morality is the same as personal piety and a compilation of characteristics and qualities that are pleasing to God.

I am not contending that duties, outcomes, and virtues have no place in Christian morality. They have an important place within the framework of understanding morality from a Christian perspective. It is to a more prolonged engagement with these theories and how they may be manifested in evangelical ethical practices that I now turn.

2

Trust and Obey?

Another Way for Scripture and Ethics

Attending church regularly as I was growing up, I imbibed the words of the hymn "Trust and Obey."[1] It was a standard hymn in many of the churches where I worshiped, often placed at the end of a service as a response to the words of the sermon. The response to hearing the written or spoken Word of God was to "trust and obey, for there's no other way to be happy in Jesus, but to trust and obey." This hymn made the Christian life sound so uncomplicated. After all, I was told that the message of the Bible itself was plain and straightforward. God loves me and has provided a way for me to return to this divine relationship through Christ, and the scriptures reveal to me how reconciliation with God is possible. I learned that the true Christian life was based on biblical foundations and that most personal and social problems were failures to obey the Bible. The essence of right living was living in obedience to the Bible. This seems fairly uncomplicated when applied to biblical texts that appear to offer rather direct commands. But how do we ascertain rules and principles from the narrative material of scripture? What do

1. "When We Walk with the Lord." Hymn by John H. Sammis (1846–1919), in *Hymns for Praise and Worship* (Nappanee, IN: Evangel Press, 1984), 422.

65

we do with the occasional Pauline epistles written to address specific issues and problems in various churches during the early formative years
of Christianity? What kind of moral claims do the imprecatory Psalms
place on us as they call down violent judgment on enemies? What do we
do with the Revelation of John, with its heavy symbolism and apocalyptic
material? How do we assess the legal material, and the reality that we
have already picked and chosen which cultic and moral laws to obey and
what to disregard based on cultural context? Given the needed sensitivity to these various genres, it is clear that the jump from various texts to
determining "what I ought to do" is not as simple as it seems. Singing
"trust and obey" is one thing. Exercising trust and discerning the means
and purposes of obedience when reading scripture in all of its intricacy
and richness is quite another.

In this chapter I will begin to explore the limitations of reducing
Christian morality, particularly when it comes to using the Bible in
ethics, to obedience to rules. I will return briefly to my description of
Immanuel Kant's metaphysics of morals and the principle of deontology as a starting point. I proposed in the previous chapter that Kant's
categorical imperative and the duty to obey may hold an appeal for
those who conceive of the moral life as one in which universal rules are
determined and obeyed by rational agents, regardless of our various
inclinations and dispositions. In the introduction I presented the possibility that evangelicals tend to see the Bible as the reservoir of timeless truths and principles, given a tradition that has been influenced by
the Reformation commitment to accessibility of the scriptures and the
particular sociohistorical trajectories of American evangelicalism as a
subculture that coalesced around "battles for the Bible." The result is
perhaps a conviction that the *summum bonum* of the moral life, for both
Christians and non-Christians, is to "trust and obey" the Bible and the
apparently clear-cut rules it presents.

In my view, this kind of deontological approach to scripture essentially
serves to undermine the numerous ways in which we are to *really* follow
the scriptures by living its story as our own. By *story* I do not mean some
fabricated fairy tale of how I wish life would be, or something I am free
to make up based on my own relativistic perceptions. Neither do I equate
story with myth. By *story* I mean what Alasdair MacIntyre refers to as a
"lived narrative" that recognizes "we live out our lives, both individually
and in our relationships with each other, in the light of certain conceptions
of a possible shared future, a future in which certain possibilities beckon us

forward and others repel us."[2] Scripture provides us with a living narrative through which the living God "beckons us" in numerous ways to live out the many possibilities presented to us in texts that shape our moral lives in abundant ways. We are summoned to live the Bible through rules, paradigms, poetic imagination, metaphor, stories, and prophetic ministry. I will mention briefly some of the many constructive possibilities and implications for how scripture forms our moral lives beyond the limitations of deontology, but I leave the bulk of this task until chapter 5.

The Limits of Deontology

A Kantian conception of morality is this: rational, autonomous agents, through the use of pure, practical reason can arrive at a moral code, a categorical imperative, independent of God, which is universally applicable to all persons. The sum total of morality is the duty to obey universal commands that are apparently evident to all rational, thinking persons. There are a number of theological assessments to make of Kant's claims. To identify just a few, Kant's deontology is a moral scheme wherein God is unnecessary, because humans have the ability through reason to ascertain truth (i.e., what rules or moral axioms to follow) and to act accordingly. The rules we are to follow make sense according to reason, even if they are believed to have been revealed at some point, which is secondary to their reasonableness if it factors in at all. For example, the Ten Commandments appear to make sense. For those who view them as a transcultural, transtemporal natural basis of moral laws for such things as judicial codes, their display in various settings serves to remind us that there is a moral order in the world. The commandments are believed to be understandable and ought to be doable by any reasonable creature concerned with a universal moral code, regardless if one actually *believes* or *participates* in the faith that gave rise to them and the moral vision of their narrative context. One can reasonably follow such "rules" as the Ten Commandments without a faith commitment. In a deontological perspective, faith is beside the point, because the highest claim on our lives is the imperative of duty *for the sake of duty*.

Kant's anthropology assumes that the essence of humanity is rationality and autonomy, not relationality and interdependence.[3] According to

---

2. Alasdair MacIntyre, *After Virtue*, 2nd ed. (Notre Dame, IN: University of Notre Dame Press, 1984), 215.

3. See Colin Gunton, *A Brief Theology of Revelation* (Edinburgh: T and T Clark, 1995), chapter 2. Gunton attributes the (over)attention to the doctrine of revelation in modern Christian

this perspective, our humanity is not discovered in relationships with the Triune God or in community with others. The moral life is discovered separate from these relationships, which are considered heteronomous inhibitors of the use of pure practical reason. The kind of rationality that Kant has in mind is objective, unattached from any presuppositions and particularities, such as belief in God and particular faith claims and commitments. The discovery of morality by the free, unfettered reason of the human mind is an overly optimistic view of humanity, especially in light of what history has revealed throughout the centuries about our actual capabilities, reasons, and interests in doing what is right. This Kantian commitment to free rationality not only is an illusion but also undermines the role of Christian faith in ethics. This move bifurcates faith from reason, belief from action, and salvation from morality, creating dualisms that are detrimental to the theological grounding of Christian morality and ethics. Christian faith and gratitude for grace as motivators for ethical action are conceived as extrinsic and suspicious incentives inhibiting our autonomy and ultimately having nothing to do with how we actually live in the world. In *Living the Christian Story,* John Colwell writes of this Kantian failure that

> every attempt to locate a universally accessible foundation for moral right-
> ness in independent rationality is doomed to failure. It fails because no
> human rationality is truly independent and, consequently, no human ratio-
> nality can be universally acceptable . . . the assumed possibility of detached
> objectivity is delusory. My notion of moral rightness is consequent upon
> my own history and the history and traditions of the community in which
> I participate.[4]

theology to Kant's influence and to foundationalism. Gunton sees this obsession with "knowing" as a "consequent gnosticising tendency" of revelation that ignores relating (page 18). This is in contrast to the essence of revelation, which is the revealing of persons, God to us, ourselves to God, and ourselves to each other.

4. John Colwell, *Living the Christian Story: The Distinctiveness of Christian Ethics* (Edinburgh: T and T Clark, 2001), 10. Not only is this rationalistic foundation doomed to failure, it also rests on an *"entirely hypothetical"* understanding of reason assumed by Kant, *"not susceptible to any form of proof"* that there is such a thing as a common morality, according to Mark Johnson in *Moral Imagination: Implications of Cognitive Sciences for Ethics* (Chicago: University of Chicago Press, 1993), 23–24. While I disagree with Johnson's caricature of Judeo-Christian morality as "moral law folk theory," I appreciate his critique of reason as it morphed from obedience *to* divine reason to obedience *based on* human reason. He writes: "Morality of this sort is basically a matter of 'doing what you are told' by a superior moral authority (typically, God). But as soon as morality comes to be understood as based on commands that are essentially rational (i.e., expressions of divine *reason*), morality becomes rational, since all the relevant moral laws can be grasped by human reason" (p. 21).

If moral rightness in a Kantian framework is to be derived *apart from* the "history and traditions of the community in which I participate," the way in which one approaches the Bible in ethics might be obvious. Submitted to a deontological commitment to universal rules and prescriptions, unattached from the God and the faith tradition from which it comes, the Bible can be believed and used by any reasonable person, an ironic concept given that the same principles of reason, when applied to the higher critical studies of the Bible and used by "enlightened" persons, served to erode its believability.[5] In this view, the Bible does not need a history or community of interpretation and practice to become the "living narrative" through which the living God beckons us forward. The Bible does not even need to be *believed*, but simply obeyed.

Are there deleterious effects if the Bible is subjected only to a deontological perspective that sees scripture as a set of categorical imperatives that any and all rational creatures ought to obey? Can the essence of Christian morality as shaped by and reflected in scripture be summed up as "trust and obey?" What might be the impact of this kind of deontology on our use of scripture, its uniqueness as revelation, and its role in shaping our moral orientation and character? My concern with this deontological approach is twofold. One is that it actually undermines scripture *as revelation,* since it limits scripture to little more than a book of revealed rules. Two, this view limits scripture's effectiveness in shaping our moral lives if the primary question posed is "What ought I to do?"

First, I see limitations in a simple deontological view and treatment of the Bible as a revealed rule book, one that, in practice, minimizes the use of scripture as a moral source. For all of the emphasis that evangelicals place on the authority of the Bible, a deontological perspective may reduce and diminish the Bible's importance as a source for moral guidance because it restricts ethics to *just* following principles, rules, and commands, and the Bible to a *mere* instrument in helping me understand what ought I to do. Moral formation requires more than just the ability to follow principles and rules. We need the requisite discernment, practical wisdom,

5. In *A Brief Theology of Revelation,* Gunton explores the ways in which the Enlightenment belief in the accessible and universal foundations of morality steers human reason in the wrong direction. He writes: "What then, is wrong with foundationalism? It is not that it seeks a common basis for rationality, but that it seeks the wrong one and in the wrong way. It seeks the wrong basis, because it seeks one that is merely secular: something inherent within human reason and experience. It thus expects human reason to ground itself. It seeks it in the wrong way, because it believes that it can find what it wants apart from revelation. Another way of putting the matter would be to say that it is intellectually Pelagian, believing that something eternally and universally true can be founded on human rational and scientific effort alone" (p. 50).

and virtues to know *how* these principles are to be lived out in a variety of diverse contexts. We need a moral character disposed to act in certain ways, and we need a moral vision around which to orient our lives. The scriptures shape and direct our moral sensibilities, vision, and capacities in many ways. Therefore, there is no one way in which the Bible provides moral guidance.

The scriptures do not bring us into a static relationship with "timeless rules or timeless principles."[6] The scriptures facilitate dynamic communion with God and provide the means for engaging in common understandings and commitments with other believers for the purpose of living faithfully with God and with others. According to Stephen Fowl, "Christians should best understand claims about scripture's authority as establishing and governing certain networks of relationships."[7] These relationships are with the texts of scripture themselves, with others, with history, with the world, with traditions, with ourselves, and most importantly, with God.[8] It is in these networks of interdependent relationships that our moral sensitivities and commitments are shaped. The scriptures provide the way for us to understand who God is, God's claims on our lives, and God's continual activity in the world. It is through scripture that human relationships are fostered as we come together to understand how unforgiving we are in light of God's forgiveness, how divided we are in spite of the reconciling power of the gospel, and how unloving we are in the face of violence toward others. We need the scriptures as revelation and for relationship with God and others, but dare I say that the scriptures need us to imagine and enact them in the world?

The second limitation to a deontological approach to the Bible is that, in practice, it restricts our engagement with the scriptures if the only moral question posed is "What ought I to do?" I do not believe that this question is irrelevant or one that ought not to be asked. If the scriptures are actually a source for the moral life, which I believe they are, this question is a critical one, yet the answers may come in various shapes,

6. See Stanley Grenz, *The Moral Quest: Foundations of Christian Ethics* (Leicester, England: Apollos, 1997), 245. Grenz writes: "Viewing the Bible primarily as the repository of timeless rules or timeless principles for human conduct risks overlooking the actual goal of revelation. The ultimate purpose of God's self-disclosure is to bring us not into a relationship with either a body of timeless laws or universal moral axioms, but into relationship with the self-revealing God, and as a consequence with one another and with all creation. The precepts and moral principles found within the pages of Scripture serve the Bible's central purpose, to facilitate fellowship or community."

7. Stephen Fowl, *Engaging Scripture* (Malden, MA: Blackwell, 1998), 3.

8. Ibid., 6–8.

through various genres, and in surprising ways, given scripture's often unrecognized power and radically subversive message. I am not disputing that the Bible contains deontological material. That this can be the sole basis for Christian morality is what I find restricting and troubling and an inadequate use of scripture in ethics.[9]

A deontological method in using scripture may result in its "domestication,"[10] further reducing its impact as a source for our moral formation, since we are robbed of the discernment and practice needed for understanding how these rules might apply to a context very different from the ones in which they were originally delivered. John Colwell critiques reading and interpretative strategies that relegate the Bible to a rule book as a misappropriation of *sola scriptura*.[11] This misappropriation marginalizes the ways in which faith, grace, the story of Jesus, the presence of the Holy Spirit, and the Christian community foster faithful reading strategies that take us deeper into the moral vision of scripture. Viewing the Bible as a book of rules, abstracted from its real purpose and meaning, is, according to Colwell, one reason for the loss of ethical confidence in Protestantism as we find ourselves fleeing to other sources of accepted moral wisdom that might be more suitable in a pluralistic society.[12] In other words, using the Bible as a rule book has diminished its importance and impact. This, along with our obvious selectivity and inconsistency in determining which rules apply to whom, and where and when, further diminishes our contribution to moral meaning beyond launching platitudes from pulpits and podiums. What is needed, according to Stephen Fowl, is a more sustained engagement with the scriptures for our moral lives. A mere foray into scripture to discover what I ought to do in any given circumstance weakens the need for a disciplined and sustained engagement with the Bible in conversation with others. Fowl writes:

9. See Allen Verhey, *Remembering Jesus: Christian Community, Scripture, and the Moral Life* (Grand Rapids: Eerdmans, 2002), 74. Verhey writes: "I do not deny the presence of prescriptions in Scripture, nor do I propose that they be torn from the canon, from that collection of writings (in all their 'great variety') which (as a whole) can and should rule the churches' [sic] life and speech. I do not deny that scriptural prescriptions can be appropriated in the deliberative process of giving reasons for specific moral judgments and rules. What I deny is this: that the fact that one can cite a scriptural prescription or prohibition is *sufficient* for the justification of a contemporary judgment or rule. One cannot simply and definitively answer the question, 'What ought I (or we) to do?' by citing a scriptural prescription or prohibition."

10. William Placher, *The Domestication of Transcendence: How Modern Thinking about God Went Wrong* (Louisville: Westminster John Knox Press, 1994), cited by Colwell in *Living the Christian Story*, 59.

11. Colwell, *Living the Christian Story*, 59.

12. Ibid., 61.

Christians' relationship with scripture is not only multi-faceted in that they are called to engage scripture in a variety of ways and contexts; it is also ongoing. This is so in two interrelated respects. First, the purposes and aims of the Christian life cannot be realized through brief encounters with scripture. Because the Christian life is an *ongoing* process of formation and transformation, a journey into ever deeper communion with God and with others, Christians can expect to engage scripture in more or less proficient ways throughout their lives. In addition, the formations and transformations that constitute the lives of Christians entail that they will need to bring an ever-changing set of interests and concerns to bear on scripture.[13]

A deontological approach to the Bible reduces the moral life to one that is concerned with simply following rules.[14] Ethics is restricted to decision making and taking positions on given issues, with little regard to other crucial dimensions, such as character formation and conscience. In this approach, I really do not need to engage in moral reflection with the scriptures or with the long-standing traditions of the Christian faith in their engagement with biblical texts or to experience fundamental conversion in my character or worldview. I simply need to "trust and obey."

This view of scripture also ignores the contexts and narratives behind scriptural prescriptions and commands. This hermeneutical violation has important ethical considerations when it comes to how we actually use scripture. Our history is replete with the ways scripture has been used to justify morally problematic practices, especially when it comes to deriving normative rules. Perhaps what we need are moral criteria guiding our use of scripture in ethics. One such criterion might be allowing the scriptures freedom to speak in their various voices and genres, working against the desire to control and domesticate them into any one way of speaking or attempting to squeeze them through our own ideological interests. This requires the hermeneutical skill and sensitivity to discern in what mode we should appeal to various texts of scripture, whether as rules, principles, paradigms, or descriptions.[15] It is to the task of hearing the commands in their own context that I now turn for consideration of the role of rules in Christian ethics.

13. Fowl, *Engaging Scripture,* 7 (emphasis mine).
14. I explore this concept of the danger of duty to morality in more detail in my article "Trust and Obey": The Danger of Obedience as Duty in Evangelical Ethics," in the *Journal of the Society of Christian Ethics* 25, no. 2 (Fall/Winter 2005), 59–77.
15. See Richard Hays, *The Moral Vision of the New Testament: Community, Cross, New Creation* (San Francisco: Harper, 1996), chapter 11.

Commands and Their Moral Vision

The reduction of the Bible to a book of rules ignores the requisite hermeneutical sensitivity and skill needed to handle scripture with integrity and care and ignores too its multiplicity of genres, with apodictic material as only one of many. To reiterate, I am not arguing that the Bible does not contain commands that are deontological in nature. Positively and negatively, we are commanded to perform certain acts and refrain from engaging in others. Duty as a moral criterion is a crucial one in ethics. However, for the purpose of moral instruction and formation, the point of a command is not obedience *for the sake of* obedience. It is therefore critical that we understand the contextual and contingent character of commands, while maintaining that they point in various ways to a more complex moral reality that extends beyond them, and which, by practicing and obeying the commands, the faith community can embody. The commands themselves direct us to a larger moral dimension of which the command is a servant and reflection of its meaning.

I turn to a brief discussion of the Ten Commandments recorded in Exodus 20:1–17 to illustrate the role of commands and the nature of obedience as it serves a larger moral purpose than just obedience *for the sake of obedience*. I use the Decalogue as illustrative because of our familiarity with it and for the common perception that it contains commands that are to be obeyed. This claim may be easily contested, but I make it nonetheless, especially since the display of the Ten Commandments in public places has drawn attention, from various groups wanting them displayed to those working strongly to advocate their removal. For these reasons alone many are at least aware that such a thing as the Ten Commandments exists, even if their content is unknown. In my exploration of the Ten Commandments I will look at the intention and narrative context of their delivery and what it meant, and still means, to obey these commands.

Divine Commands or Divine Invitation?

Is it appropriate or adequate to interpret the Ten Commandments through the lens of a divine command theory of ethics, given to tell us what to do? Divine command theory locates the authority of commands in the will of the authority giving them, typically understood as God. Obedience is expected because commands come from this authority. While the Ten Commandments may be interpreted this way, in that their origins are with God, it is perhaps of primary importance that the commands found in the Decalogue be understood first from the context that gave them their shape and purpose. One of the most crucial aspects for understanding these divine commands, according to Patrick Miller, is that they presuppose a set of mutual, consensual obligations that are attached to relationships prior to their intention to legislate and direct the corporate life of their hearers. These relationships are with Yahweh as the Lord God and with others in the faith community.[16] George Mendenhall argues that what one may understand as "commandments" are in fact not prescriptions for behavior, but instead are commitments, descriptions of ethical obligations that "must be voluntarily embraced and undertaken freely and gladly in grateful response for benefits and blessings already received."[17] The heart of the commandments therefore is covenantal, relational, and social, not judicial or legislative. Even though they were foundational for the stipulations that did form the structure of Israel's legal, religious, and moral codes known as the Law, they were first and foremost terms that established the nature of their relationships with Yahweh (Exod. 20:1–7) depicted in what is referred to as the first table. The commandments also provided the ethical orientation that was to govern Israel's relationships with others (Exod. 20:8–17), spelled out in what is often referred to as the second table. Without these relationships, the commandments are rent from the context that gives them meaning. Miller notes:

> The presence of directives or regulations parallel to the *second* table in *other societies* has been noted. But the covenantal context of the obligations found in the Decalogue assumes a relationship that begins with the "I-you" of the deity and the people and so includes stipulations that have to do directly with that relationship. The presence of the first table along with the second causes problems in contemporary life when the presence and power of the commandments is at issue in the larger civic community. For many individuals what is to be kept before the community is only the second table of the Decalogue, a move that takes the Ten Commandments out of the covenantal context and turns the stipulations into some kind of natural law. They may have that character; indeed the rationality of the divine commands, their rootage in a more universal sense of value and obligation, is readily apparent. But the Decalogue's obligatory character

16. Patrick Miller, "Divine Command and Beyond: The Ethics of Commandments," in *The Ten Commandments: The Reciprocity of Faithfulness,* edited by William P. Brown (Louisville: Westminster John Knox Press, 2004), 17.

17. George E. Mendenhall, *Ancient Israel's Faith and History: An Introduction to the Bible in Context,* edited by Gary A. Herion (Louisville: Westminster John Knox Press, 2001), 61.

arises out of the covenantal relationship and assumes the first table as a
required starting point.[18]

The commandments are part of a history, a story, a living narrative
that beckons its hearers to a faithful response characterized by obedience.
According to Miller, the giving of the commandments was the continuation of the story of Israel's exodus out of slavery, God's provision for its
deliverance, and the forming of a community that was to continue telling
this story of deliverance and freedom. Even though delivered in the form of
commandments, they still contain and reflect a narrative, one that shapes
moral character and virtue as they are followed as part of living out the
reality to which they point. It is the Lord God who saves and delivers a
people who, in turn, are "set apart" to reflect this *particular* reality by
being a covenant people in right relationships with Yahweh and others.
Miller goes on to observe,

> As the prologue illustrates, the commandments grow out of a shaping nar-
> rative, the story of the people's deliverance. The commandments are placed
> at a climactic point in a narrative that is understood to be definitive for the
> community's life, the context in which the commands make sense and are
> to be understood and appropriated. They serve to shape the moral life of
> later members of the community in an ongoing narrative of the community's
> life and individuals' lives, a story still ongoing.[19]

These commandments therefore are not arbitrary "from on high" prescriptions that were expected to be obeyed by anyone and everyone. Even
though they represented good social practices, ones that would ensure some
semblance of a cohesive and respectful social order, the commandments
were a faith proclamation, and the response to them in obedience is part
of faithfulness to the God who formed a community of people who were
to witness: first by affirmation that there is no other God like this one,
and second by living a social reality according to these commitments that
was in sharp contrast to the nations around them. While they may reflect

18. Miller, "Divine Command and Beyond: The Ethics of Commandments," 17. See also the
helpful essay by Nancy J. Duff "Should the Ten Commandments Be Posted in the Public Realm?"
in *The Ten Commandments:The Reciprocity of Faithfulness,* chapter 13.

19. Miller, "Divine Command and Beyond: The Ethics of Commandments," 23. I realize the
ways in which Israel's story has been taken up by visions of America as the New Israel and a
Christian nation, giving justification for the legitimacy of the Ten Commandments as a judicial
code for a democracy with Christian roots. This is an important and very large topic that is
relevant and related to my concerns, but one that I can just acknowledge, given the scope of
this project.

good social practices and have some degree of universal appeal, "there is no assumption that it is sufficient for the commandments to be posted,"[20] since they were to be taught and lived within and by the faith community, with obedience as the mark of consent to God's authority manifested in the commandments to shape the lives and moral ethos of the believing community. They are intricately linked with a story of faith, starting with Israel and taking shape in the church, as an acknowledgment of the relationships that exist between God and the people of God and faithful demonstrations of responsiveness by following the commands.

What does it mean, then, to obey the commands? If they are not to be obeyed for *the sake of obedience*, what are the purpose and morally formative dimensions of claiming allegiance to the God who delivered them and following the commands as an acknowledgment of God's authority and our faithfulness? I suggest that obedience is a practice by which we learn the "rules" of Christian faith and the means for developing virtuous habits that are reflected in the moral concerns of the commandments. Commands are not the sum total of Christian morality. Instead, they are a starting point for giving us an orientation, "a framework, for further moral reflection, discourse, and action."[21] Obedience to commandments results in an embodiment of the moral vision that gives them shape and meaning.

Narrative Context of Obedience

Obedience to commandments is not an end in itself. We have not exhausted our moral responsibilities when we simply do what we are told to do. Obedience, as a Christian practice, is a means for learning how to live in the world *as Christians* by orienting us to the moral narratives and vision that ought to give shape to the totality of our lives. The end is the purpose that obedience serves: the means of realizing God's will for the world, albeit imperfectly, and the means of forming us into people who live the will of God.[22] Obedience enables those participating in a tradition to learn the practices that constitute that tradition and to become more engrafted within that tradition. This is what James McClendon refers to as "The Community of the Ten Commandments."[23] When one obeys the

20. Ibid., 27.
21. Ibid., 16.
22. I realize that the "will of God" is a broad and diffuse expression. I will take it to mean here the two great commands of scripture: learning to love God with heart, mind, and soul, and loving others.
23. James W. McClendon, Jr. *Ethics: Systematic Theology,* vol. 1, 2nd ed. (Nashville: Abingdon Press, 2002), 182.

Ten Commandments, one is not simply obeying the command of God. To miss the connection between practices and commandments is to miss the morally forming dimensions of moral laws, such as the Decalogue. According to McClendon, "each Commandment (except perhaps the first and the last) has its connection with a *powerful practice* in the community that receives this law. As a guide to morality each reminds its hearers of a particular existing practice or set of practices, and provides a line of direction for life in that sphere."[24] These practices make sense within the context of a moral community that understands the intentions of these duties, which go beyond mere obedience to divine commands to the evocation of virtues and goods that create and sustain our moral lives.[25]

At this point, it may be helpful to provide examples from two of the commandments in the Decalogue to illustrate the relationships between commandments and obedience as a Christian practice. I will refer to the prohibitions against misusing God's name (Exod. 20:7) and adultery (Exod. 20:14). What is typically referred to as the third commandment, "You shall not misuse the name of the LORD your God, for the LORD will not hold anyone guiltless who misuses his name" (NIV), flows from the prologue of the commandments: "I am the LORD your God, who brought you out of Egypt, out of the land of slavery" (Exod. 20:2, NIV). Because these commands are from the Lord God who delivered them out of slavery, Israel was to have no other gods, they were not to fashion and worship idols, and they were to refrain from wrongfully using the name of God. Walter Brueggemann argues that the third commandment, taken in its context, is not exclusively related to the use of obscene language. Instead,

> . . . what must be understood is that the "name" of Yahweh bespeaks of God's powerful presence and purpose. The utterance of the name is the mobilization of the presence and power of God. . . . To make "wrongful use of the name," or as Walter Harrelson suggests, the use of the name "for mischief," means to invoke through utterance the power and purpose of Yahweh in the service of some purpose that is extraneous to Yahweh's own person. That is, the violation is to make Yahweh (who is an ultimate end) into a means for some other end.[26]

The act of restraint from misusing the name of God is one part of the command that is to be observed. It is offensive when with regularity we

24. Ibid., 185.
25. Ibid.
26. Walter Brueggemann, "The Book of Exodus," in *The New Interpreter's Bible*, vol. 1 (Nashville: Abingdon Press, 1994), 842.

hear expletives using the name of Jesus, in all of its various derivations, and the invocation of God's name in situations that are far from holy. However, this commandment as directed to the believing and hearing community is concerned with *their* and *our* misuse of God's name, invoking it in inappropriate, manipulative, ideological, and self-serving ways. This commandment not only involves a restraint on language, but is also grounded in the moral dimensions of the use of language, especially religious language with all of its power and appeal. The people of God reverence God not just by refraining from "swear words," but by conscientious attention to the ways in which "God-talk" is used to legitimate practices that are morally problematic by making claims that God is (perhaps always) on "our" side. Jan Milié Lochman comments that "to misuse the name of God means that instead of placing ourselves at God's disposal, we place him at ours, domesticating his holy name for our unholy or pseudo-holy purposes. The God of liberation is turned into a domestic deity, a household god."[27]

I am drawn to reflect on the implications of this command in its covenantal context for evangelical ethical practices related to the use of God's name. Evangelicalism is "word"-centered and "word"-driven. We see scripture as God's word as central to faith and practice, as well as the use of words as important for communicating the good news of Christ. However, we are also tempted to use God's name to justify political programs and social ideologies that may have nothing to do with the gospel and, in fact, may be inimical to it.[28] When we do, we run into the danger of violating this command by using *and* misusing God's name for our own personal and political purposes. We can refrain from swearing and obscenity and still disobey this commandment. When we invoke the name of God, a powerful use of religious language, to baptize actions and ideas that may have serious moral consequences and bind God to particular social and political ideologies, we have disobeyed the third commandment by a careless, "pixie dust" use of God's name, sprinkling it wherever and whenever we wish. Obedience to the third commandment requires an understanding

27. Jan Milié Lochman, *Signposts to Freedom: The Ten Commandments and Christian Ethics* (Minneapolis: Augsburg, 1982), 54.

28. I live in the "swing state" of Ohio. The religious conservative vote is courted with great regularity by Republican candidates seeking to shore up this base. Ohio is also the home of the Ohio Restoration Project and the "Patriot Pastors" (see www.ohiorestorationproject.com). These examples I have in mind about the use of God's name in ways that legitimate programs and ideas by giving them a divine sanction. See Peter Berger, *The Sacred Canopy: Elements of a Sociological Theory of Religion* (Garden City, NY: Doubleday, 1967).

of our own motivations and inclinations that may tend to put God at *our* disposal, using God's name to justify what *we* fancy to do at the moment. The third commandment requires and teaches humility, a virtue that helps us name our presumptions and arrogance when using God's name for a variety of causes and programs. The right use of language requires habits and disciplines that require thoughtfulness and discernment for the ways the power of language either helps or inhibits the purposes of God and serves or harms other people. Practicing the commandment may help heighten our ethical sensitivities to these issues and enable us to embody the purpose and vision to which it points.

The second illustration pertains to the seventh commandment, the prohibition against adultery (Exod. 20:14). The stipulation of this command flows from the larger narrative of God's design for marriage, which is the wholesome sexual union between a man and a woman in the covenant of marriage as an expression of union and covenant in the most profound and intimate of ways. Adultery is defined as "sexual intercourse between a married or betrothed woman and any man other than her husband."[29] The prohibition against adultery also applied to sexual relationships between married men and the wives of fellow Israelites. The substance of this commandment does not necessarily mean at the very *basic* level the prohibition against having a sexual relationship with someone else's spouse is the ultimate expression of faithfulness. In other words, the sum total of marriage fidelity is not completely encapsulated by the prohibition against adultery, as important as this prohibition is for establishing the most fundamental of parameters around the covenant of marriage. In the context of marriage, this was a given assumption, a starting point if you will, of both the physical and symbolic nature of this covenant. The moral orientation behind this prohibition is the fundamental narrative of Yahweh's covenantal, faithful, and practiced love for us and our response in kind. Just as the image of adultery, harlotry, and whoredom is used to characterize the deteriorating quality of Israel's relationship with Yahweh, so too does infidelity in marriage take many forms, with sexual infidelity as just one of them, as signs of eroding trust, relationship, faithfulness, and intimacy.

I can refrain from adultery as a sexual act and still be unfaithful in marriage. The commandment *may* keep me from having sex with my neighbor's husband, but it is limited in ensuring the character and quality of my own marriage because it cannot make me faithful *to* my spouse.

29. *The Anchor Bible Dictionary,* vol. 1 (New York: Doubleday, 1992), 82.

This I learn by commitment, by practice, by rehearsing how our lives came together, and by thanking God for this particular reflection of divine love and self-giving. The prohibition against adultery is a fundamental aspect of fidelity in marriage but does not a faithful marriage make without the practices of mutuality, service, honor, and dedication to another person's good and well-being. Refraining from extramarital sex is only the start for realizing the moral vision of Christian marriage. In speaking about the narrative context of rules and the prohibition of adultery, Nancey Murphy's insights on the New Testament witness are just as applicable to the Old Testament in reference to the role of rules as servants of God's moral vision. She writes:

> For a New Testament example, consider the following: "no adultery" is a rule constitutive of the practice of marriage—any marriage practice. However, marriage for Christians is significantly different from what it is for non-Christians. New Testament teaching links it with witness to the faithfulness of God. Marriage is thus a subpractice within the broader constitutive Christian practice of witness. So the rule "no adultery" takes on a deeper significance for Christians. Infidelity within marriage essentially destroys the value of the practice in testifying to the fidelity of God—it prevents participants from attaining what Scripture teaches is a primary internal good toward which the practice itself aims.[30]

At this point it may be necessary for me to repeat again that I am not against duty and obedience, neither am I prepared to jettison these important criteria from our moral discourse. I do believe that the commandments and their narrative contexts and moral vision still matter and are obligatory for us as Christians. Jesus affirmed the moral content of the law in the Sermon on the Mount. After delivering the core of his ethical teachings in the Beatitudes, Jesus reminded his hearers that he did not "come to abolish the Law or the Prophets . . . but to fulfill them" (Matt. 5:17). His sermon goes on to illustrate the more rigorous moral sensitivity required by his kingdom teaching to the ethical dimensions and requirements of his new law parallel to the requirements of the Ten Commandments. I return to this idea in the next chapter, where I give attention to the moral orientation and ethos of the kingdom of God as moral vision and as a normative criterion for Christian moral formation and ethics.

---

30. Nancey Murphy, "Using MacIntyre's Method in Christian Ethics," in *Virtues and Practices in the Christian Tradition: Christian Ethics after MacIntyre*, edited by Nancey Murphy, Brad Kallenberg, and Mark Thiessen Nation (Notre Dame, IN: University of Notre Dame Press; reprint, 2003), 39.

Obedience as Christian Practice

My point is that we must take duties and obligations to scripture *more* seriously when it comes to the forming of our moral lives and orientation, so that our obedience actually serves the purposes for which the commands of scripture are given. For this purpose we must clarify the role of obedience in Christian morality. If the sum total of morality is not just obedience, what does it mean to obey commands, such as the prohibitions against adultery and misusing God's name? Instead of viewing obedience as allegiance to rules *for the sake of obedience*, perhaps obedience can be viewed as a practice that teaches us essential aspects of Christian life. Obedience as a practice assists us in developing virtues and fulfilling obligations consonant with the moral vision of scripture around which our lives are oriented, which is to "be imitators of God, therefore as dearly loved children" and "to live a life of love, just as Christ loved us" (Eph. 5:1–2). Obedience, when practiced in light of the Christian story, beckons us to develop the requisite habits so that living out the demands of and allegiance to our faith in God become part of us. Christian morality is then expanded to encompass concern with who we are and who we are becoming over the long haul as opposed to what we are told to do at any moment or in any given decision.

Obedience may be a practice, but is it a virtue? That is, is obedience a good, a virtue, for its own sake? In their book *Christians among the Virtues: Theological Conversations with Ancient and Modern Ethics*, Stanley Hauerwas and Charles Pinches provide provocative insights and helpful answers to the question "Is obedience a virtue?"[31] They answer the question with "well, it depends" on what one means by obedience and virtue. First, it depends on how one understands obedience. Hauerwas and Pinches make a distinction between obedience and compliance. The difference is that "we can comply with a rule or a command without obeying it; so too we can 'pretend to obey,' which would mean something like that we feign consent to some ruler's commands while merely complying with them."[32] As noted in the previous discussions on the narrative context of the Decalogue, I may comply with the commands outside their relational and narrative context, such as the prohibition against adultery, yet still disobey them by ignoring the requisite moral dimensions of fidelity in

31. Stanley Hauerwas and Charles Pinches, *Christians among the Virtues: Theological Conversations with Ancient and Modern Ethics* (Notre Dame, IN: University of Notre Dame Press, 1997). See chapter 8.
32. Ibid., 134.

marriage. What enables obedience as a practice to *nurture* virtue is not feigned consent, but the willingness to be transformed by the habits that obedience generates. There is no guarantee that obedience qua obedience will shape my character and moral orientation, because much depends on the kinds of virtues that are being developed through the practice of obedience. Obedience itself is not a virtue if by this I mean that obedience *as* obedience is inherently good.

Perhaps the question to be asked, and one that Hauerwas and Pinches answer, is this: *when* does the practice of obedience teach virtue? As noted previously, one's consent is an important consideration when assessing the role obedience plays in training a person in a tradition. Hauerwas and Pinches, however, are careful not to ground this understanding of consent in the classic liberal framework of the consent of the governed in a democratic polity based on ideologies of individual freedom and rights. The basis for obedience as a means for learning virtue is covenantal and relational, not principled or ideological. It assumes the legitimate authority of the one asking for obedience, and the willful consent of the one who freely obeys given the acknowledgment of a relationship that exists between them, while also recognizing that these two wills may be in conflict.[33] For the Christian, obedience as a practice is related to our relationship with God and with the Christian community as we continue to practice a living faith. It is in this context that obedience enables us to learn the ways and reasons for acting *as* Christians. Obedience is what enables us to be trained in the practices and goods of our Christian tradition.

Alasdair MacIntyre goes to great length to explore the relationships among practices, virtues, and a community's moral tradition.[34] According to MacIntyre,

> A practice involves standards of excellence and obedience to rules as the achievement of goods. To enter into a practice is to accept the authority of those standards and the inadequacy of my own performance as judged by them. It is to subject my own attitudes, choices, preferences and tastes to the standards which currently and partially define the practice.[35]

MacIntyre's account of a practice relies on the assumption that all life is an embodied story or narrative that we learn to live. Our lives are intertwined, constrained, shaped, and part of the larger narratives of others.

33. Ibid., 135.
34. MacIntyre, *After Virtue,* 186–87.
35. Ibid., 190.

What gives meaning, form, and coherence to human life are narratives and the practices they contain that save us from randomness. MacIntyre refers to the process of learning a narrative through practice as "embedding."[36] He writes:

> A living tradition then is an historically extended, socially embodied argument, and an argument precisely in part about the goods which constitute that tradition. . . . Once again the narrative phenomenon of embedding is crucial: the history of a practice in our time is generally characteristically embedded in and made intelligible in terms of the larger and longer history of the tradition through which the practice in its present form was conveyed to us; the history of each of our own lives is generally and characteristically embedded in and made intelligible in terms of the larger and longer histories of a number of traditions.[37]

What keeps traditions living, like the Christian tradition, according to MacIntyre, are the virtues that sustain these traditions, virtues that are realized as individuals practice the rules and realize the ultimate good of these traditions in their own lives and communities.[38] Obedience as a practice is a means by which we become embedded in the narrative of the God who gives us life and in our response to scripture that beckons us to participate in the life and love of God and others. The practice assumes a relationship with God and an acknowledgment of God's right to rule our lives, and a desire to live our lives consonant with the purposes or narrative of God. It sees commitment not as a static, one-time decision for Christ, but one that is acted on over and over again through various practices of obedience. It is our way of acknowledging our ultimate allegiances, the permission given to be shaped by rules of *this* particular story, and to become embedded in its meaning, which gives order, coherence, meaning, and purpose to our moral lives. As summarized by Hauerwas and Pinches,

> When Christians obey God, they obey the *Christian* God. As they tell the story, God is a person, whom one might attempt to deceive . . . by pretending to obey as Ananias and Sapphira, or to whom one might offer one's obedience precisely because he had learned in God's history to count God trustworthy, as did Abraham. Obeying this God has the context of a historical and personal relation. Within it, God issues commands which Christians must obey. But the relation is not constituted entirely by the commands

36. Ibid., 212.
37. Ibid., 222.
38. Ibid., 223.

and the obedience. Christians, for example, come to trust God, or hope in God's promises as they learn of God in the stories of God's faithfulness in preserving Israel or sacrifice in offering up his son Jesus. Learning these things, they can speak of "trusting" or "hoping" as part of their obedience, now understood in an expanded sense.[39]

To speak of obedience as a practice of learning the rules and virtues that constitute Christian faith may seem to indicate that there is just one practice or one virtue in the Christian life, that of obedience. However, as I have attempted to clarify, obedience is not the end of our moral obligations. Obedience is the means by which we learn and practice our moral obligations consistent with the "rules" of the Christian faith. Following prescriptions and proscriptions in the forms of commands and rules may require obedience without an understanding of the reasons or the larger dimension of the practice, even though this larger dimension is important. Sometimes we must "do what we are told" even if our wills and affections are not inclined to do so and even if we don't understand the reasons. Since the practice contains the good to which it is directed, according to MacIntyre, we are still participating in the achievement of the good through obedience even as we are still learning "why we do what we do" and are being shaped by the good practice in spite of ourselves.

Obeying the Scriptures

I hope it is clear that I believe we do need to obey the scriptures as *scripture*. If scripture is the primary source to which we look for moral guidance and wisdom, how do we engage with this book in our search for direction and orientation? What does it *really* mean to trust and obey the Bible? I offer a few suggestions here for consideration.

First is that we must learn to actually read the Bible.[40] Much in evangelical discourse and practice focuses on articulating one's view of the Bible, whether it is inerrant or infallible or any word derivation thereof. What one thinks about the Bible's authority is important but not the end of the matter. How one actually reads and responds to scripture is quite another.

39. Hauerwas and Pinches, *Christians among the Virtues,* 141–42.

40. I am indebted to my colleague and friend Dr. Dan Hawk for sharing this insight. Dan is an Old Testament scholar with deep pastoral sensitivities and commitment to the church. He commented at one point in our many conversations that, as evangelicals, we talk a lot about what we think of the Bible and its authority. According to Dan, however, one of the greatest needs we have as evangelicals is learning how to actually read the scriptures.

Stephen Fowl posits that "one of the chief tasks facing Christian communities concerns the formation of their members into being wise readers of scripture."[41] Learning to read scripture takes time, diligence, commitment, and a community of readers who are also committed to this task. It also assumes a level of discomfort in our commitment to realize that scripture is complex and discordant at times, not to be breezed over lightly with the hope of finding the one meaning or the one principle with which we can walk away. That is where I find our rhetoric at odds with our practices as evangelicals. For all of the emphasis placed on the authority of the Bible, the actual use and reading of scripture is quite minimal. Small groups, while formed as Bible studies, tend to be more focused on the therapeutic or social needs of their members. Bibles are condensed into one-minute, one-day, and one-year volumes to aid in accumulating as many "baby Bible facts" in the shortest time and most convenient way possible.[42] Sermons, while listing scriptural texts, move quickly to ad hominem talks or stories that will connect more easily with audiences seeking entertainment on Sunday mornings. We may purport to believe in scripture's authority, but our reading strategies and actual use may say otherwise.

Second, we learn to obey the scriptures by allowing them to interpret us as a faith community that has already affirmed our commitment to hear these words as authoritative for our lives. While hermeneutical methods are useful for learning to "rightly handle the Word," the move toward application at the end of the process is perhaps premature without some sense of wondering how these texts might interpret our lives and the churches of which we are a part. This question enables the scriptures to master us as opposed to us mastering our interpretation of various texts. The scriptures expose presuppositions, false ideologies, dysfunctional Christian communities, distorted views of God, distorted views of self, and a myriad of other realities that inhibit our capacities and willingness to embody the narratives and moral vision of scripture. Scripture is revelatory not just about God, but about humanity, communities, the nature of power, social evil, and us. This exposure by scripture is a gift, because it then provides opportunities and ways to envision how our lives might be different if we actually obeyed and followed the numerous ways in which scripture reorders our perspectives, our understandings, and our actual ways of living before God and with others. Allen Verhey provides helpful insights into how scripture functions

41. Fowl, *Engaging Scripture,* 179.
42. This phrase was used by Professor Robert Hubbard, my Old Testament professor at Denver Seminary, who was often bemused by what these eager evangelical seminary students chose to fixate on in scripture.

to form our moral lives.[43] He provides three pairs of virtues necessary for the practice of reading scripture that enable us to remember Jesus. These are holiness and sanctification, fidelity and creativity, and discipline and discernment.[44] About sanctification Verhey writes:

> Sanctification is the standard of excellence in reading Scripture that is ready to set this canon alongside our lives and our common life as their rule and guide. It is the readiness to set the remembered story alongside all the stories of our lives—stories of sexual desire, stories of sickness and healing, stories of wealth and poverty, stories of politics—until our conduct and character and communities are judged and made new by the power of God, are formed in remembrance of hope, and themselves render the story rendered by Scripture. Sanctification invites and welcomes attention to the saints as the best interpreters.[45]

Learning to obey the scriptures requires actually reading them and engaging with them with others in our faith community. Learning to obey the scriptures assumes that we will allow these rich texts to interpret, sanctify, and reorient our lives. Obeying the scriptures also assumes that we will in fact follow them. This is what Nicholas Lash refers to as "performing the Scriptures."[46] For Lash, the reading and careful interpretation of scripture matters, but it is the "performance" of scripture that brings our reading and interpretation full circle in that now we live these texts as an authoritative source for our lives. We obey scripture by enacting its story in our own lives. This "performance of scripture" is a full-time task for the Christian community because,

> For even the most dedicated musician or actor, the interpretation of Beethoven or Shakespeare is a part-time activity. Off-stage, the performers relax, go shopping, dig the garden. But there are some texts the fundamental form of the interpretation of which is a full-time affair because it consists in their enactment as the social existence of an entire human community. The scriptures, I suggest, are such texts. This is what is meant by saying that the fundamental form of the Christian interpretation of scripture is the life, activity, and organization of the believing community. The performance of scripture *is* the life of the church. It is no more possible for an isolated individual to perform *these* texts than it is for him to perform a Beethoven quartet or a Shakespeare tragedy.[47]

43. Verhey, *Remembering Jesus,* chapter 3.
44. Ibid., 68.
45. Ibid.
46. Nicholas Lash, *Theology on the Way to Emmaus* (London: SCM Press, 1985), 38–46.
47. Ibid., 43. I will return to this concept of "performance" in the next chapter as it applies to the kingdom of God and Christian discipleship as the means and ends of Christian ethics.

Many evangelicals belong to churches with doctrinal statements. Typically the first statement is related to the authority of the scripture and reads something like this: "We believe the Bible to be the inspired, the only infallible, authoritative Word of God."[48] Yet I suspect that if we embodied this commitment in actual practices and performances, many of our churches and Christian organizations would be unrecognizable as Christian bodies. Imagine the implications for leadership styles, church polity, decision making, attitudes toward and coziness with ruling political parties, economics, oppression, war and violence, and immigration if we really took scripture seriously by obedience as performance, along with serious, sustained, and engaged reading, and with a "readiness to be formed—and reformed—by it."[49]

Conclusion

So, do I still sing "Trust and Obey" when it is listed on the service? By all means and with far more appreciation and enthusiasm than I ever did before. I sing it with gusto because of the reality to which it points when one trusts and obeys all of the scripture in the various ways in which it shapes our lives and Christian communities. I am called upon to obey scripture as I follow the moral vision contained in it and seek to allow scripture to "come alongside" and interpret my life. As we read, we are beckoned to follow and perform the stories of the Bible for the conversion and realigning of our lives with God. The Bible's impact and authority go far beyond whether it offers prescriptions in telling us what to do. Scripture's authority is taken seriously as it calls us to be certain kinds of persons, in certain kinds of communities, living out the vision of God's good intentions for creation made known in Christ. It is the entirety of scripture, along with its rules for the Christian life, that we are called to follow. We do come to these texts expecting guidance and seeking wisdom. But we need to learn to converse with these texts, *and with one another over these texts,* questioning and probing their meaning and application then and today as a sign and practice that we actually *do* take scripture seriously by engaging with its meaning, claims, and possibilities for our lives enacted through performance as trusting and obeying.

48. National Association of Evangelicals, http://www.nae.net/index.cfm?FUSEACTION=nae.statement_of_faith.
49. Verhey, *Remembering Jesus*, 56.

3

We've a Story to Tell

Which One and Why?

I remember the scenes well. The evening worship service had been revamped from its more traditional format of extended hymn singing, evening prayer, and a more informal yet intense time of biblical teaching. It no longer appeared that this particular configuration was meeting needs, as determined by dwindling attendance. There were a number of factors feeding into the desire to have a different kind of worship service on Sunday evenings. There were concerns expressed about effectiveness and the time and energy it took to maintain a service for so few people. A desire to reach more people with the gospel message through a service that was more seeker-sensitive also factored into the decision to recreate the evening worship experience. As a result a contemporary service started, and its success was immediately apparent since there were times when it was standing room only. The auditorium was full of new faces, mainly individuals who attended other churches in the morning but were looking for something more contemporary to supplement their normal morning experience in worship. The design of the evening service was different each week, ever changing to catch the audience by surprise. The ambiance preferred by the directors of the evening service was to be as unchurchy as possible, with the hope of attracting individuals who would normally be repelled by any sniff of formalized religion. To accomplish this end, the auditorium, which used to be the sanctuary, was transformed into different venues, such as bar scenes, nightclubs, sports arenas, gyms, and dorm rooms. The participants gathered upon the stage and fulfilled their various roles as announcers and emcees, stand-up comics, singers, and actors in skits and dramas, usually culminating in the solo performance of the gifted speaker giving the message that evening. This was intended to "set the stage" by creating a familiar environment in which it might be easier to hear and connect with the presentation of the gospel, so that more people might get saved. It was a form of evangelism that valued "meeting people where they're at" by using whatever means were necessary to accomplish this end.

I remember these scenes well because they were so different from what I had conceived and expected of "church." I remember the scenes because of how familiar they were and how much I actually disassociated them with anything related to good news for myself or for others. I realize that the edge in my voice now may cast me as some kind of old fogy who may be inherently opposed to any kind of change and experimentation with forms of worship, or as one who sees "church" as an experience limited to a particular mode of worship or structure in the confines of a building restricted to people who want to gather in safe and familiar surroundings simply for this purpose. I hope I don't view such a dynamic organism as the church in this way. I hope that my concerns are in fact fueled by a deep love and respect for the church as a witness to the radical kingdom of Jesus Christ that *is different* from what is normally expected of a church experience. I did yearn for an experience of walking into a church and recognizing it *as* a church, a place of worship, a sanctuary, precisely because it *is different* from the scenes played out all through this culture and others that allege to promise human happiness and fulfillment by any means possible.

My experience on the staff of a large evangelical church in the early nineties leads me to ponder a number of theological and ethical issues. I will pose just a few questions I see pertinent for evangelical ethics and relevant for the concerns of this book. I place these concerns in dialogue with utilitarianism, wondering if the greatest good of the Christian faith really is the greatest number "getting saved" by whatever means possible. *Is* this the greatest good of Christian faith? What might be the implications for Christian discipleship as a narrow way when the means used purports to make it easy, simple, and acceptable for the greatest number?

John Colwell describes the gnawing I experience when confronted with these questions. He writes:

> Wherever the Church begins to put its confidence in advertizing strategies, management techniques, or feeling-centered counselling therapies, it ceases to be faithful. Wherever social programmes displace sacramental indwelling, the focus of true holiness is jeopardized. Wherever the gospel is offered as a commodity instead of proclaimed as command, truth is abandoned. And in each instance the specific promise of the Spirit's presence and activity is forfeited. Indeed, it may well be that where the Church may appear (at least from a secular perspective) to be most effective and flourishing it is, in reality, least faithful. Before trumpeting apparent growth we should pause to consider what actually it is that is growing. To seek growth at the expense of faithfulness is, in reality, to diminish. If the gospel is proclaimed as the supposed remedy for every "felt" need, it may gain popularity but there can be little expectation for transformation.[1]

In an attempt to untangle some of my ethical concerns with the kinds of practices I described in the opening paragraph, I take up again a conversation with one of the moral theories, John Stuart Mill's utililtarianism, presented in chapter 1. My return to Mill is short, since my chief aim in this chapter is to open up possibilities for a richer appreciation of Christian discipleship as moral formation and a vision of the church, not measured by its effectiveness in utilitarian terms but by the quality of its life and faithfulness as the ethical community of Christ. I briefly highlight some of the implications of this proposal for the ministry and practices of the church, while returning to them for a fuller exploration in chapter 5.

The Limits of Utilitarianism

John Stuart Mill's principle of utility is this: what is observable about human behavior is that we desire happiness. Therefore, the principle of utility is that we ought to pursue what will achieve the greatest happiness for the greatest number of people. It is the principle of utility that gives us a measuring stick for morality, since actions are deemed good and just when they produce the desired effect for the majority of people. "What is" as observable in human behavior, such as the desire for happiness however individuals choose to define it, is what "ought to be." Morality in a utilitarian perspective builds on this assumption and provides little

1. John Colwell, *Living the Christian Story: The Distinctiveness of Christian Ethics* (Edinburgh: T and T Clark, 2001), 164.

guidance as to the moral content of actions, or the moral dimensions of the ends of human life from any perspective except that which individuals desire as their own happiness. Even though Mill attempted to emphasize that the means for achieving a desired end had moral considerations, the principle of his moral claims was still utilitarian in that the ends could and would justify the means used to attain them.

In chapter 1, I offered the suggestion that utilitarianism has appeal because it measures moral worth by effectiveness and results. It works well in a context where ethics is seen as mediating and ameliorating various competing ethical claims by its principle of the greatest good for the greatest number as the best we can do in obtaining moral consensus. The open-ended and self-defining nature of happiness is easily appropriated in a context where individuals have the freedom to determine their own happiness and well-being as long as it does not impinge on others. These utilitarian ideals reflect in many ways the sociopolitical and cultural climate in which American evangelicalism has been birthed and "democratized."[2] Utilitarianism is a good complement to the values of a liberal democracy, with its emphasis on an individual's freedom to pursue his or her own self-defined goods or conceptions of happiness. I mentioned previously the equating of the American story with a particular Christian interpretation of our history. Utilitarianism provides a point where this tendency comes together in our rhetoric and practices. The values of freedom and individualism in an American democracy are baptized as Christian values and a normative epistemological framework for assessing the moral life and for establishing ethical criteria. This may explain in part the patriotic fervor in many evangelical traditions that justifies fighting for *our* freedom and the securing of *our* rights as a Christian vocation by any means available.

What are my concerns with utilitarianism from the perspective of Christian morality? There are four initial concerns. First, the influence of utilitarian individualism has resulted in a less-than-developed understanding and appreciation of the church and the communal nature of the Christian life. From a utilitarian standpoint, the church exists to meet the needs of individual religious consumers seeking happiness and self-fulfillment. A utilitarian perspective may foster an understanding of the church as functional, not for the purposes of helping us in our utility and calling to live out a Christian narrative, but for the purposes of meeting individual needs in the pursuit of our own happiness. The call to discipleship and the

2. See Nathan Hatch, *The Democratization of American Christianity* (New Haven: Yale University Press, 1989).

communal shaping of the moral life by a community of Christ followers is irrelevant or secondary at best.

Second, this ill-defined conception of happiness and freedom lacks theological and moral content related to the richness of salvation as more than just a decision for Christ. This lack of definition is convenient for ignoring and dulling the rigors of Christian morality that are at the heart of the Christian life. Because utilitarianism doesn't assume moral consensus, and perhaps even relies on the hope that there might not be moral consensus, we are free to pick and choose which aspects of Christian faith bring us the most happiness or reflect our already held moral convictions. The narrative of our lives, wishes, and desires is free to interpret the Christian narrative in ways we see fit, as opposed to the other way around. Salvation may be for our souls but influences little else.

Third, this emphasis on the greatest good for the greatest number and what serves their needs is in contrast to the scriptural obligations to care for the least of these, for the minority and for those on margins of social and political power. This is especially problematic if one has even a cursory view of human history, and even church history, and the tyranny of the greatest good defined by the majority and their tyranny over the minority. We know that the majority can be wrong and often have the resources to muster the ideological power and political support to enforce the view that might makes right and the majority always wins.

My fourth concern is the ways in which utilitarianism easily becomes a rationalization of the ends justifying the means. I see a number of difficulties in this regard, to which I alluded in the opening paragraph. Goodness is measured by results, and means are chosen that may produce the desired outcomes, regardless of the quality and content of the means chosen or the ends desired. This may be especially true if the greatest good is seen as the greatest number getting saved by whatever means possible. If this is the moral vision informing evangelical perspectives on the purposes and ends of the Christian life, what are the implications for the quality and demands of Christian discipleship as morally formative and for the church as the ethical community of Christ? How might this view determine the ministry practices of the church and undermine their impact to actually be morally forming practices? The question I pose to students in Christian ethics is not how many persons attend your church but what kind of moral characters and disciples are formed *as a result* of learning and living *with* the people called your church? These are my concerns that I concentrate on in this chapter as I look at the relationships between

Christian discipleship, moral formation, and the narrative context of the church as kingdom community.

The Kingdom Way

The premise under which I am operating is that discipleship and morality are not options or insignificant to the claims of Christian faith. While I recognize the call to follow Jesus Christ is a necessary part of evangelism, the totality of the Christian life cannot be summed up or understood as simply "getting saved." I understand morality to flow from essential relationships—one's relationship with the Triune God and relationships with others. These relationships are essential for the ways in which they shape and transform our lives, and the concept of "getting saved" is but one entry point into these life-changing relationships. Just as discipleship is not optional to Christian faith, so Christian morality is not an option, an "add-on" informed by other sources and commitments. The claim I make is that Christian morality has its source in our relationship with Christ and flows from that relationship as an embodied, dynamic, and living aspect of our lives *as Christians.* It is not personal, or "just between God and me." The moral dimensions of Christian faith are deeply and inherently social and lived out in the context of Christian community and the world. Christian faith is not just a one-time decision but a way of life.

The Christian faith as a way of life reflects Jesus's own pronouncement in John 14:6: "I am the way and the truth and the life. No one comes to the Father except through me" (NIV). This text is located in the Upper Room discourse starting with John 13. Jesus is giving his final words to his disciples before his crucifixion and death, so there is a sense of urgency to these last-minute instructions. Jesus is not only speaking but actively demonstrating his love through humble service, such as washing the feet of the disciples (John 13:1–17). He is showing them the "way" to the Father by his own life and actions. Jesus's life was the embodiment of the wisdom and righteousness of God and is now offered for the disciples and the rest of humanity as the means by which relationship with the Father is restored. In the context of John 14:6, it is assumed the disciples were also expected to follow the ways of Jesus, a terrifying thought in light of the road to the cross that Jesus was about to follow and the humble act of service he had just performed. "The way" would likely have been understood by the disciples as the common metaphor for the way of wisdom and righteousness, a distinct style and manner of living that is observable.[3] This concept of the way is found in the scriptural descriptions of people who followed Christ (Acts 9:1–2, 19:8–9), since they were known and identified by their distinctive way of living faithfully to Christ as their Lord. John's Gospel and the image of the way invite us not simply to the means of salvation, but to the ways of Christ as truth. The way is an important metaphor for understanding the nature of the Christian life patterned after the life of Christ and embodied in the narrative of the kingdom of God, making Christian morality an incarnation of "kingdom ethics."[4]

That the kingdom of God was Jesus's primary message and the central theme of the New Testament is little disputed among biblical scholars and theologians. What it may have meant, what it means today, when it was to be fulfilled, and its relationship to Israel and the various societies in which Christianity has taken root have not generated the same level of agreement or consensus.[5] My concern is not with these disputed dimensions of the kingdom of God, but instead with its role as the means of Christian moral formation and the ways it fosters imaginative vision and moral possibilities in helping us realize, however sketchily, the purposes and ends of God.

What is the kingdom of God? According to Bruce Chilton and J. I. H. McDonald, *kingdom* may be understood as reign, rule, and sovereign domain, yet these words alone fail to capture what is essential for grasping the theological and ethical importance of the kingdom. Its essence, according to Chilton and McDonald, is God's intervention.[6] God initiates deliverance for humankind. Yet relegating the kingdom to just God's actions for the sake of humanity is to miss the relationship between God's actions and the human response to this grace and mercy. According to Chilton, the kingdom is essentially performative, a synergism of initiative, response, and action. It is God's performance, or actions, on our behalf and the responsiveness this elicits from us, which is our performance in kind. The kingdom of God is like a magnet, bringing together the two

3. See Craig S. Keener. *The Gospel of John: A Commentary*, vol. 2 (Peabody, MA: Hendrickson, 2003), 940, and "Way," in *The Eerdmans Bible Dictionary* (Grand Rapids: Eerdmans, 1987), 1048.

4. See the excellent work by Glen Stassen and David Gushee, *Kingdom Ethics: Following Jesus in Contemporary Context* (Downers Grove, IL: InterVarsity Press, 2003). I will return to their work later in this chapter.

5. See Howard Snyder, *Models of the Kingdom*, 2nd ed. (Eugene, OR: Wipf and Stock, 2001), for an overview of various typologies of the kingdom.

6. Bruce D. Chilton and J.I.H. McDonald, *Jesus and the Ethics of the Kingdom* (London: SPCK, 1987).

poles of God's incursion into human life and human receptiveness to this incursive invitation. After reflecting on the parable of the sower (Mark 4:1–20), Chilton and McDonald write:

> Instead of imagining two distinct forces, eschatological and moral, with a field of critical tension between them, we might rather think of the Kingdom as a single magnet with two poles. At one end is the divine performance of the Kingdom, an inceptive reality which attracts hope. At the other end is human performance, an enacted response which itself elicits action. . . . Indeed the creative interface between the two is of the essence of the Kingdom which is presented.[7]

It is the human response to *and* "performance" of the message of the kingdom that brings the eschatological and moral dimensions together, according to Chilton and McDonald. By *eschatological* they mean God's intervention both now and in the future. The manifestation of God's desired future, God's *telos,* is the reality of the kingdom now that has transformed the course of history and human lives. This radical intervention of God elicits, if not demands, a human response, since "the ethical performance of the Kingdom is not only an appropriate response, it is a necessary one, if the perception of the Kingdom is to be achieved . . . because the Kingdom is of a God whose claims are absolute, it necessarily addresses itself to people as a cognitive and an ethical challenge at one and the same time."[8] The ultimate "performer" of the kingdom is Jesus.[9] Yet since humans are assumed to have agency as "performers" and are addressed as such in the teachings of Christ, the continual embodiment of the kingdom depends on those who take its claims seriously, demonstrated by responsiveness and realignment of our lives according to the moral vision of the kingdom of God. Jesus inaugurated the kingdom of God through his birth, life, death, and resurrection. This was truly and deeply eschatological and continues to be so. Christians incarnate the importance and implications of kingdom living *because* we profess loyalty to Jesus the King. This is truly and deeply moral.

The kingdom of God for Chilton and McDonald is ultimately performative and praxis-oriented. While the biblical and theological dimensions are crucial for understanding the kingdom, the intention was and is ultimately transformative, ethical, and practical. The kingdom is a way

7. Ibid., 24.
8. Ibid., 31.
9. Ibid., 61.

that is to be lived.[10] This is not meant to reduce Jesus to a moral teacher whose teachings were good but little else. The power and authority of Jesus's life, ministry, and teaching are manifested and actualized in that they *produce performances* on the part of his hearers. Jesus's authority as the bearer of the kingdom of God is acknowledged by the responses of his hearers and "it is realized *par excellence* not in the dream world of apocalyptic nor in temple cults, legalistic casuistry, ascetic discipline nor power politics, but in personal and community life that is responsive to the call of God."[11]

Chilton's work is used and expanded on by Glen Stassen and David Gushee in their rich and notable book *Kingdom Ethics: Following Jesus in Contemporary Context*. Stassen and Gushee describe the ethics and practices of the kingdom of God in a sustained engagement with the Sermon on the Mount recorded in the Gospel of Matthew. They bring together the character of God's actions, the meaning of the kingdom of God, its imperatives, its virtues, its practices, and its end, and in so doing, provide the reader with a thorough picture of Christian ethics.[12] Stassen and Gushee focus their moral reflection on this record of Jesus's teaching "because the way of discipleship and the commands of Jesus are most explicitly taught in the Sermon on the Mount."[13] If Jesus is normative for Christian ethics, as they argue, then we must take seriously the actual life and teachings of Jesus in moral reflection and ethical behavior.

According to Stassen and Gushee, the Sermon on the Mount presents multiple dimensions of the moral life, such as moral vision, moral virtues, and moral obligations oriented around the overarching narrative of the kingdom of God. The result is a comprehensive proposal for Christian ethics that finds the sources for its moral norms in the prophetic ministry and teachings of Jesus in the Sermon on the Mount. Their proposal is holistic and compelling for a number of reasons. First, it connects Christian faith with ethical commitments and practices. To be a disciple of Christ is to follow Christ in very particular ways. Our ethic starts with our basic convictions about who God is and the normativity of Jesus for Christian ethics.[14] Second, character is shaped by the development and exercise of virtues that are rooted in Jesus's teaching in the Beatitudes. What makes the virtues of humility, righteousness, mercy, goodness, purity of heart,

10. Ibid., see chapter 4.
11. Ibid., 79.
12. Stassen and Gushee, *Kingdom Ethics,* see section 1.
13. Ibid., 30.
14. Ibid., 59–68.

and justice *Christian* virtues is their source in the very character of God known explicitly through Christ. They are the virtues that Jesus himself exhibited. Third, these virtues inform our moral reflections and perceptions, and guide our decisions, when used in conjunction with scripture, reason, and wisdom from others. Fourth, "kingdom ethics" as articulated by Stassen and Gushee is essentially the way of discipleship. We take our "cues" about what matters, how to "see," how to act, what to do, and who to be based on our loyalty to Christ and participation in and performance of kingdom values and commitments.

These links between discipleship and morality are important for understanding the means and ends that come together in Christian ethics. The end we serve is God's kingdom, and the means by which we serve is following Christ as his disciples. We do this through performance, according to Chilton and McDonald. For Stassen and Gushee, we do this through the life of discipleship shaped by the moral vision and practices of kingdom ethics. For the late William Spohn, the Christian moral life is summed up by "go and do likewise."

The Kingdom of God and Moral Imagination

In *Go and Do Likewise: Jesus and Ethics,* Spohn uses the "tripod" of the life of Christ known in the Gospels, virtues ethics, and practices of spirituality as the lenses through which to understand and live out the norms and claims of Christian ethics.[15] This triadic way of conceiving the Christian moral life is essentially paradigmatic in that it provides the patterns or ways in which we understand who we are (Christian identity), what kind of people we are becoming (virtue), and what kind of life we ought to live as our lives are shaped by the story of Jesus (spiritual and ethical practices). In his analysis of the parable of the good Samaritan (Luke 10:25–37) and the giving of the new commandment by Jesus (John 13:31–38), Spohn writes:

> In both John and Luke, the standard for action-inspired-by-love is a narrative pattern. The conjunctions "just as" and "likewise" refer moral reflection back to the prime analogate for guidance. Since the prime analogate displays a moral pattern, it functions in a morally normative way: you ought to act likewise. This type of guidance differs from the usual case of moral normativity, namely a general principle shaping action in concrete situations. The biblical scenarios guide action in a more concrete manner.

15. William Spohn, *Go and Do Likewise: Jesus and Ethics* (New York: Continuum, 2006), 12.

They call for action that is appropriate or "fitting" to a pattern of relations embedded in an image or story. Moral inquiry thereby becomes analogical because it asks what the paradigm suggests.[16]

The prime analogate is the person and concrete actions of Jesus, who is the prototype, the ultimate paradigm of Christian morality. The analogical pattern by which we orient our lives and action is the paradigm of the kingdom of God. It is the kingdom of God that is the "framing metaphor" for the Christian moral life. As an analogy, the Christian life ought to correspond to the pattern and paradigm of Jesus and the kingdom of God.

How does the kingdom of God present the pattern for morality and function as our basic metaphorical and imaginative framework for Christian ethics? For Spohn it starts with a conversion of our perception. Perception is our capacity to see *and* to interpret. The moral dimension of our seeing is the capacity to see rightly. It matters not just *that* we see, but what and how we see and interpret the meaning of our lives, since "perception is a function of character; it is not a morally neutral faculty but one that sees only that which the person already values."[17] John McIntyre in *Faith, Theology and Imagination* also conveys the significance of imagination in Christian ethics. "Imagination asks us to suspend our loyalties to see a new way of looking at a situation" by reorienting our perspectives.[18] Imagination, according to McIntyre, is not the same thing as wishful thinking but instead is looking *into* reality and seeing it with a different perspective, informed by the gospel, in order to perceive and strategize how life could be different.[19] Imagination shakes us out of our familiarity with the gospel story, comfortable with how it goes, what seems to matter, and how it ends; freeing us from what we think is so ordinary, to envision new possibilities.[20]

Conversion to the kingdom of Christ, the transference from darkness to light (1 Peter 2:9–10) is a total relocation from which we see the world. True conversion is the radical reorientation of our lives according to our membership, our new citizenship in the kingdom of God. Conversion is not just or only "getting saved" as the end of the Christian life. Conversion is both an entry point and the continual process by which we actualize the

16. Ibid., 61.

17. Ibid., 86.

18. John McIntyre, *Faith, Theology and Imagination* (Edinburgh: Handel Press, 1987), 34–35.

19. Ibid., see chapter 1.

20. Ibid., 54.

story of Jesus, develop virtues, and engage in ethical practices. Conversion "inevitably involves a change in our basic metaphorical frameworks."[21] For Spohn, this is the meaning of conversion and salvation. It is radical transformation that corrects our perception and transforms it (read: converts it) to an orientation that is *continually* being transformed by Christ through practices essential to discipleship, practices such as reading scripture, service, spiritual disciplines like meditation and prayer, and community, all of which sharpen our moral perception.[22]

If moral perception is developed through a fundamental reorientation and conversion of how we see the world according to the kingdom of God, then analogical imagination is how we put into practice the virtues and practices of the kingdom that are shaped by moral perception or "rightly envisioning the world." Analogical imagination is the link between the gospel narratives and our envisioning of the possibilities of how these narratives shape our moral perceptions and practices. Spohn describes the analogical imagination as that which "bridges the moral reflection of Christians and the words and deeds of Jesus. It provides the cognitive content for obeying the command 'Go and do likewise.'"[23] In his hermeneutical method for appropriating the ethics of the New Testament, Richard Hays calls for an "integrative act of the imagination."[24] After engaging in the descriptive and synthetic tasks of interpreting scripture, whereby we read texts carefully and in the context of the entire canon, we are pressed to then relate the variety of texts and the modes in which they speak to our particular situations. This hermeneutical task requires imagination and willingness to see things differently, so that "whenever we appeal to the authority of the New Testament, we are necessarily engaged in metaphor-making, placing our community's life imaginatively within the world articulated by the texts."[25] Hays goes on to say that,

> the central point is this: the use of the New Testament in normative ethics requires *an integrative act of the imagination,* a discernment about how our lives, despite their historical dissimilarity to the lives narrated in the New Testament, might fitly answer to that narration and participate in the truth that it tells. . . . Here we speak, however, not merely of human artistic wit: in such acts of imaginative integration, the church has historically

21. Spohn, *Go and Do Likewise,* 67.
22. Ibid., 112–19.
23. Ibid., 50.
24. Richard B. Hays, *The Moral Vision of the New Testament: Community, Cross, New Creation* (San Francisco: Harper, 1996), 6.
25. Ibid.

recognized the work of the Holy Spirit. Where faithful interpreters listen patiently to the Word of God in Scripture and discern fresh imaginative links between the biblical story and our time, we confess—always with reverent caution—that the Spirit is inspiring such readings.[26]

Moral imagination is required as a bridge between the kingdom of God brought to us by Jesus Christ and the moral vision and ethical possibilities that the kingdom presents as normative for Christian ethics. It requires "imaginative analogies,"[27] heightened sensitivities to new corresponding possibilities in order to envision how our lives and communities might be transformed to live and perform the kingdom of God. Moral imagination is envisioning and enacting possibilities for transformation that our lives and our communities could actually *be* different and transformed by the reality of the kingdom. As Stassen and Gushee remind us, kingdom ethics provides us not only with virtues by which we live, but also with moral vision and transforming initiatives as "regular practices that are commanded by Jesus" so that the imperatives and visions of the kingdom might be enacted, performed, and realized.[28] Moral imagination is not wishful thinking or a flight of fancy. It involves active engagement with scripture, with others, and with the realities of our world. Moral imagination means that we take seriously the sources of our moral perceptions that we bring to bear on moral judgments.[29] Moral perception and imagination make it possible to keep us from accepting "what is" as "what ought to be." Instead it helps us to realize and embody "what should be" as we envision moral possibilities in light of the kingdom of God. Moral imagination is reliant on a serious engagement with the claims of the kingdom of God as the source of our moral vision and norms. The kingdom is to be performed. It is performed by people who see another way, other possibilities, and who work hard to discern how to live out these kingdom claims and vision in a utilitarian world.

The Utilitarian Limits to Imagination

It is fitting at this point in the discussion to reflect on and apply these insights to a concrete example, given this chapter is focused on a critique

26. Ibid., 298–99.
27. Ibid., 298.
28. See chapter 6 in Stassen and Gushee, *Kingdom Ethics.*
29. See chapter 8, "Moral Imagination," in *Moral Imagination: Implications of Cognitive Science for Ethics,* by Mark Johnson (Chicago: University of Chicago Press, 1993), for interesting insights into various dimensions of moral imagination.

of utilitarianism in evangelical ethics. I will use the example of war, because moral deliberation on the topic of war has been and is currently quite contentious. This seems to be more so in an evangelical context for a number of reasons and highlights the ways in which moral reflection on such topics take place outside the imaginative metaphorical framework of the kingdom of God.[30] Presenting options in Christian tradition on war, such as just war and pacifism, in the abstract is one thing. Morally reflecting on the actual experience of war, particularly since the U.S. involvement with the war on terror and the invasion of Iraq, is quite another matter.

I have observed a number of dynamics pertinent to the ways evangelical Christians tend to talk about war and violence, nationhood, the kingdom of God, and the source of their moral commitments and practices. My primary location for observation has been in seminary classes in Christian ethics, as well as at churches and with friends. My first observation is how difficult it is to have this conversation. While students express an interest in using tools of moral reflection on this topic, few discussions raise their level of discomfort and anger more than the topic of war. Many come from military backgrounds or have themselves been involved in various branches of military service or preparation. Some are training for military chaplaincy. It may be a difficult discussion because it hits close to home in deeply personal ways. The second tendency I have observed is how little Christian faith informs opinions on war. This may be the result of the lack of encouragement and experience in actual moral deliberation and discourse in evangelical contexts.[31] In the introduction I offered the possibility that evangelical ethics tends to be quite apologetic. There is a defensive stance on ethical issues that is more akin to apologetics than moral reflection; the right thing to do is to take a stand on an issue. There are two difficulties with this approach. One is that it does not lend itself well to conversion of perception or analogical imagination. For many of us, our minds are often already made up on a variety of ethical issues, thereby minimizing the need for a more robust analysis of the multiple layers of moral problems. Evangelicals are not alone in this. However, evangelicals seem to have a propensity to minimize social analysis required for social ethics, such as war, and limit the topics for moral ire to a few select concerns. This is the second difficulty with this apologetic approach to ethics. The issues receiving moral attention are quite limited. For example,

30. I am indebted to my colleague and friend Dr. Luke Keefer, for his precise and prophetic insights on the kingdom of God as the operating paradigm for ethics, especially as it applies to a Christian commitment to peacemaking.
31. See Verhey, *Remembering Jesus,* especially part 1.

abortion and sexuality draw quite a bit of interest and heat, while issues pertaining to economic justice and war and peace receive far too little.

The third tendency, and where it becomes more problematic and disturbing, is the hodgepodge use of scripture as a source for moral reflection on war, to see the presence of war in the scriptures as justification for war. While I recognize the hermeneutical difficulties with the myriad texts that portray holy war as what God commands and as justification for annihilating enemies, the jump from the complexity of scriptural portrayals of war to conflict, violence, and war among sovereign nations in a modern context is one that requires far more attention, care, and sophistication than is typically available in many evangelical churches, or in churches in general.[32] The typical focus on "just" spiritual issues in teaching and preaching in evangelical churches, and the desire to avoid controversial issues like war, along with the nationalistic impulses of many evangelical churches, may partly explain this tendency. The "trust and obey" method of using the Bible as a source for moral deliberation may be another reason for this predilection. The desire to take the Old Testament seriously as part of the canon may add to the befuddlement and lack of hermeneutical sensitivity of how to relate the two testaments on topics such as war and violence. It also ignores the fact that war is not the only story the Old Testament tells about conflict and relationships with enemies.[33]

Adding to the complexity of our deliberations on war is the fact that the scriptures and Christian tradition are not univocal on this topic. As mentioned previously, the presence of war in the Bible and God's involvement in it does present some challenges for the exercise of analogical imagination in moving from scripture to the actual justification and practice of war. In conversation with scripture, Christian tradition has typically presented us with three options for thinking about war. They are crusade or holy war, justified war, and nonviolent pacifism. The more recent proposal of just peacemaking championed by Glen Stassen seeks to combine the concerns of just war and pacifism, whereby the need for justice is taken seriously yet obtained by nonviolent means appropriate for securing peace consonant

32. See the helpful book by Peter C. Craigie, *The Problem of War in the Old Testament* (Grand Rapids: Eerdmans, 1983, c1978).

33. See the selection of essays in *A Peace Reader,* edited by E. Morris Sider and Luke Keefer, Jr. (Nappanee, IN: Evangelical Publishing House, 2002). Of particular note are "Peace in the Old and New Testaments," by John R. Yeats, and "War in the Old Testament: A Journey toward Nonparticipation," by Terry L. Brensinger.

with the gospel of peace.[34] What, however, has become more disturbing to me, and what is pertinent to the overall concern of this chapter, are the reasons why moral reflection on war is so difficult and why war as a good, especially when waged by one's own country, is so easily accepted. My concern is this: the metaphorical framework for reflecting on war is not in actuality the kingdom of God but instead is the kingdom of America, revealing both the nationalistic and the utilitarian nature of our moral commitments as evangelicals.[35]

Even after careful reflection on the use of scripture and the options in Christian tradition, their merits and shortcomings, the preference typically resides with a crusade mentality or with just war. However, the reasons given are typically not theological or ethical. The reasons for supporting war are characteristically pragmatic and functional. In essence they are based on a principle of utility. In practice the moral perspectives on which evangelical Christians tend to rely for reflecting on the topic of war are strongly utilitarian. The means are justified by the desired ends. Reasons given to justify the decision to go to Iraq to fight the war on terror go like this: "We had to do something," "We have the capabilities," "We have a right to protect our borders," "Keeping Saddam in power would be worse than the damage inflicted by war," "More people were harmed by Saddam's tyranny," "We must liberate oppressed people," "We cannot have another 9/11," "If we don't stop them, they will bring the fight to our streets." The moral vision informing these reasons is more nationalistic than theological, because the "we" are Americans, and whatever means by which happiness and security are acquired for the greatest numbers of "we's" is justified. When asked for the ways these reasons are informed by Christian faith, and how a different conception of "we" may lead one to a different conclusion, the answer typically given mimics Martin Luther's doctrine of the two kingdoms: There is the kingdom of God and the kingdom of the world. The kingdom of God is about spiritual matters, and the kingdom of the world is about sin, punishment, and securing justice

---

34. See Glen Stassen, *Just Peacemaking: Transforming Initiatives for Justice and Peace* (Louisville: Westminster John Knox Press, 1992), and *Just Peacemaking: Ten Practices for Abolishing War* (Cleveland: Pilgrim Press, 1998).

35. While writing this book at Tyndale House in Cambridge, England, my husband and I took a weekend trip to York. At York Minster is a memorial to the women who died in World War I. Edith Cavell was a British nurse who was executed in 1915 in a German prisoner of war camp. Her name is listed on the war memorial at York Minster on a panel with these words: "Standing as I do in view of God and eternity, I realize that patriotism is not enough. I must have no hatred or bitterness toward anyone. Edith Cavell, Brussels, October 15, 1915." See www.edithcavell.org.uk.

by means of the sword. According to Stassen and Gushee, this kind of response reflects our tradition of "evasion and dualism" when it comes to the topic of war and Christian peacemaking.[36]

Kingdom thinking therefore does provide a metaphorical moral framework for thinking about such things as war, but which kingdom? How might the kingdom of God as modeled and taught by Jesus give us a metaphorical moral framework for reflecting on war? If we accept the kingdom of God as the means by which our moral perception is changed and the metaphor that fuels our ethical imagination, the implications for our reflections on war may be obvious. It calls on us to take seriously deliberations about war on *Christian* terms with a perspective that is shaped by our membership in the kingdom of God. My point here is not to fully elaborate the merits of either just war theory or pacifism. This is a debate that ought to be taken seriously in moral reflection, one whose complexities I have grown more to appreciate given that an actual war is going on as I reflect on this topic.[37] My purpose is to illustrate how discussions on war are filtered through a pragmatic and utilitarian lens in moral deliberation, which reflects the sources to which we really turn when making moral assessments. My experience in teaching Christian ethics and involvement at evangelical churches is that even after a careful, well-thought-out presentation on Christian pacifism as a viable kingdom response to war based on the teachings of Jesus (Matt. 5:38–42)—which is my position, to be fair to the reader—the reasons given by these audiences for rejecting pacifism as a moral option are functionally utilitarian.[38] Even with some concession that this may be the ethic of Jesus, peacemaking and pacifism arc typically dismissed as viable options because they are seen as too utopian, too impractical, too unrealistic, too time-consuming, and too ineffective, in spite of the agreement that love for enemies actually might be the way and ethic of Jesus. What is valued is what will work and bring about success.

36. Stassen and Gushee, *Kingdom Ethics,* 128–32.

37. For a good overview for various positions on war from a Christian perspective, see chapters 7 and 8 in Stassen and Gushee, *Kingdom Ethics.* See also Edward LeRoy Long, *Facing Terrorism: Responding as Christians* (Louisville: Westminster John Knox Press, 2004).

38. Even though I am arguing that utilitarianism informs moral deliberation in an evangelical context, I also suspect that the Reformed inheritance from Augustine through Luther and Calvin, coupled with the patriotic fervor of many evangelical groups, contributes to the justification of war, and even holy war. It was Augustine who wrote to defend war and to legitimate a Christian's participation when war was waged for just reasons. This Augustinian legacy contributed to the two spheres of thinking of later Reformers, particularly Luther, which carved out a distinct role for the government as the servant of God. The church now has its sphere of ethical concerns and the state has its own.

Imagining Kingdom Communities

I used the scenario described in the introduction of this chapter and my reflections on discussions of war to illustrate the presence and limits of utilitarianism in Christian morality, particularly in an evangelical context. Utilitarianism essentially confines our moral perception and imagination. The situation I seek to address is summed up in the introduction to *In Good Company: The Church as Polis*, by Stanley Hauerwas. Quoting the Rev. Joe Dinoia, Hauerwas writes:

> Christian soteriological doctrines must be set into the whole pattern of the Christian life. Accordingly, any description of salvation must suggest how "the dispositions to attain and enjoy the true aim of life develop over the course of a lifetime of divinely engendered and sustained 'cultivation.' Christian salvation means finally becoming a certain kind of person, one who can enjoy the end of life that the Christian community commends."[39]

To combat the pragmatic and results-oriented culture that has so influenced a utilitarian understanding of what is good and to be valued, we need to foster moral perception and imagination in evangelical church life and ministry practices, so that we develop and cultivate the "dispositions" to enjoy the "end of life that the Christian community commends." The desired end is the worship of God through a community of Christian disciples committed to the means and ends of kingdom living. The realization of this end is contingent upon certain types of Christian communities that embody the desired end in the means of their commitments and practices. I end this chapter by lifting up the possibility and need for Christian communities that embody and live the practices of the kingdom and equip others to imagine and develop the requisite dispositions consonant with *living* the saved life.

The place to start might be with a more robust understanding of "church" and its relationship to the kingdom of God in evangelical thought and practice.[40] I will refrain from a lengthy excursus on the intricacies of the relationship between kingdom and church. I trust it will be sufficient to state my conviction that I see the church as the creation, servant, and

39. J. A. Dinoia, *The Diversity of Religion: A Christian Perspective* (Washington, DC: Catholic University Press, 1992), 61, as quoted by Stanley Hauerwas, *In Good Company: The Church as Polis* (Notre Dame, IN: University of Notre Dame Press, 1995), 8.

40. See the informative collection of essays in *The Community of the Word: Toward an Evangelical Ecclesiology,* edited by Mark Husbands and Daniel Treier (Downers Grove, IL: InterVarsity Press, 2005).

manifestation of the kingdom that has come to us through Jesus and continues to live in his people who gather as the community of Christ based on Matthew 16:13–20, and assumed in the various New Testament epistles written to the churches. The church as the *ekklesia* has its origins in Christ's declarative response to the confession of Peter, "You are the Christ, the Son of the living God" (Matt. 16:16). In reply Jesus declared that the church, or *ekklesia,* would be built on the confession of Peter, and he granted to Peter the "keys to the kingdom of heaven" (Matt. 16:19). *Ekklesia* was borrowed from the political realm and denoted a gathering of citizens meeting regularly. Hans Küng writes of the *ekklesia* that it is the repeated assembling of those "called out" for political purposes to conduct the business around which they gather.[41] It is a continuation of the *kahal* in the Hebrew scriptures, or the gathering of the people of God.[42] This new community, "the church," was called, created, and named by Jesus as his own. The church was given the "keys to the kingdom" based on the confession of Jesus as the Anointed One. The church is called out as a dynamic, communal, and continual gathering to carry out the business and "politics" of Jesus the King.[43]

Howard Snyder refers to the church as the agent of the kingdom.[44] The implication that Snyder draws is that the church is active in its demonstration that the kingdom has come, parallel to Chilton's concept of "performance." The church demonstrates its kingdom consciousness through its commitments and actions, such as the ethics of the kingdom embodied in Christian morality and discipleship.[45] The church is the called-out body of believers who enact kingdom ways and commitments before a watching and waiting world. This is the mission of the church: to proclaim that the King has come not just through word, but by deed and the demonstration of the radical values of the "upside-down Kingdom."[46]

The kingdom of God creates the church. It calls out a people, an *ekklesia,* who go about the King's business in public, whose lives, decisions, ways of relating to others, and loyalties to the King are the source of their moral perceptions and imaginations. It is why Stanley Hauerwas affirms

41. Hans Küng, *The Church* (London: Search Press, 1973), 82–87.
42. Ibid., 82.
43. See John Howard Yoder, *The Politics of Jesus,* 2nd ed. (Grand Rapids: Eerdmans, 1984).
44. Howard A. Snyder, *The Community of the King,* 2nd rev. ed. (Downers Grove, IL: InterVarsity Press, 2004), 14.
45. Ibid., 28–32.
46. See Donald Kraybill, *The Upside-Down Kingdom* (Scottsdale, PA: Herald Press, 1990).

that the church does not need a social ethic, but the church is a social ethic in that it embodies the story of Jesus.[47] The kingdom of God is not a program or a social or political ideology. The kingdom of God creates a *community* of "peculiar people" called "the church," whose lives and practices embody their ethic.[48] The church as an agent of the kingdom of God serves the greatest needs of humanity. By living out kingdom ethics, the church can contribute to the need for justice, peace, mercy, hope, righteousness, and reconciliation in a broken world. In so doing, the church will be relevant in meeting humanity's essential needs.

Why do I think this is an important recovery for evangelical ethical practices, particularly related to my critique of the utilitarian nature of evangelistic practices in an evangelical context? It is because of the inclination to see the church as secondary, irrelevant, or unnecessary for the moral formation of its characters and for the actual substance that feeds our Christian lives, such as practices of worship, scripture, prayer, community, and service. This could be attributed to various influences in evangelicalism, such as a skewed form of pietism that characterizes one's decisions and positions as "between me and God," the revivalist spirit that emphasizes personal conversion, or the various democratizing influences that are a part of evangelical traditions in the United States.[49] I suspect, however, that our views of the church as evangelicals are shaped just as much, if not more, by our uncritical acceptance of the ideologies of individualism, pragmatism, and consumerism, which makes the church unnecessary for anything other than meeting one's personal needs. I am concerned with practices that communicate our views of the church as functionally utilitarian and instrumental. The danger is that the church becomes the means by which religious consumers meet their personal needs and fulfill their happiness.

If the church as a kingdom community is necessary for the actual embodiment of the gospel whereby the church is the means for realizing the ends of God's kingdom, then we also may be a step closer to confronting the utilitarian nature of church practices by realizing that

47. See Stanley Hauerwas, *The Peaceable Kingdom: A Primer in Christian Ethics* (Notre Dame, IN: University of Notre Dame Press, 1983), 99–102.

48. See Rodney Clapp, *A Peculiar People: The Church as Culture in a Post-Christian Society* (Downers Grove, IL: InterVarsity Press, 1996).

49. See Hatch, *Democratization of American Christianity*. See also the essays in part 1 of Husbands and Treier (eds.), *The Community of the Word:Toward an Evangelical Ecclesiology:* D.G. Hart, "The Church in Evangelical Theologies, Past and Future"; Dennis Okholm, "Fundamental Dispensation of Evangelical Ecclesiology"; and Jonathan Wilson, "Practicing Church: Evangelical Ecclesiologies at the End of Modernity."

the purpose is not the "greatest number getting saved." This leads to a second possibility for envisioning the church as a kingdom community: that salvation and ethics are intricately bound together. In other words, the "saved" life is a moral one.[50] In *The Kingdom of God*, John Bright observes of the relationship of the "social gospel to the gospel of individual salvation" that

> the two are not to be set apart as has so often been done, for they are two aspects of the same thing. Indeed, they are as intimate to each other as the opposite sides of the same coin. We can no longer, as "liberals" have done, preach the ethics of Jesus and leave aside his person and work as if it were a cumbrous and superfluous theological baggage. At least if we do so, we must know that we do not preach the Jesus of the New Testament faith. Nor can we, as "conservatives" have tended to do so, sneer at the "liberal" for not preaching a full gospel and then, because we urge men to salvation through faith, feel no need to confront ourselves and our people with the demands of the righteousness of the Kingdom. This, too, is not to preach the Christ of the New Testament, but an incomplete Christ.[51]

To preach the Christ of the New Testament is to preach the entirety of Jesus's life and its implications for the Christian life. It is his whole life that is salvific, not just our understanding of what happened to our souls at the moment of Jesus's death on the cross. One of the chief legacies of the Protestant Reformation is the belief that salvation is offered to us by grace and accepted through faith. However, according to John Colwell, much of North American and British evangelicalism has misappropriated and misunderstood Luther's *sola fide* (by faith alone) and *sola gratia* (by grace alone) by failing to appreciate the moral dimensions of salvation for the formation of character and ethics. He writes:

50. The following is an illustration of the lack of relationship that many evangelicals see between salvation and ethics. In a forum cosponsored by Christians for Biblical Equality and Ashland Seminary, various perspectives on family and marriage, gender, and ministry were presented for their implications in pastoral ministry. As expected, discussion ensued around the meaning of Galatians 3:28, "There is neither Jew nor Greek, slave nor free, male nor female, for you are all one in Christ Jesus." A number of students lent their hermeneutical expertise to clarify that Paul was talking only about salvation here, meaning men and women are equal before God but not before each other. I find that the "typical" evangelical student is inclined to attribute this passage to "just" salvation, not to a radical reorientation of our relationships with others *because of* our salvation. There appears to be a tendency in evangelical ethics to separate salvation from ethics. This propensity tends to both spiritualize and overpersonalize the gospel as pertinent for "just" salvation as opposed to a way of life that is radically transformative.

51. John Bright, *The Kingdom of God: The Biblical Concept and Its Meaning for the Church* (New York: Abingdon Press, 1953), 223–24.

Evangelistic programmes informing "converts" that they have "become Christians" by virtue of having come to the front of a meeting in response to an appeal, repeated "the sinner's prayer," or signed a "decision card," are merely more blatant instances of the assumption that becoming a Christian is merely a cerebral process, a matter of intellectual assent to a series of propositions. By contrast, more recent evangelistic programmes that focus on a defining experience, feeling or generated atmosphere, not only tend to lack significant intellectual content, they also tend to detach Christian "experiences" from the rigors of daily discipleship. . . . Here then is one possible basis for a loss of ethical confidence within some elements of contemporary Protestantism: confidence to speak and live in a manner that is ethically distinctive is absent simply because the ethical essence of faith is denied.[52]

I find Colwell's insights applicable to much of North American evangelicalism that places itself in the historical and theological trajectory of the Protestant Reformation, vis-à-vis Luther and Calvin, with an emphasis on a forensic perspective of justification by grace through faith that declares us legally righteous. To be saved is to be *declared* in "right standing" with God as a part of the *ordo salutis* separate from sanctification, or continual growth into Christlikeness.[53] However, as biblical scholars writing on "the new perspective on Paul" have proposed, this concept of a legal declaration of righteousness does not necessarily reflect a biblical portrait of what it means to be "righteous."[54] Righteousness or justification is not just "being made right with God"; it connotes living right with God, fulfilling moral obligations consonant with a new orientation and perspective. To think of being declared "righteous" without an accompanying commitment to actually *act* righteously is not what the biblical writers had in mind in their instructions on the Christian life. Salvation is not simply God's declaration of righteousness. To be declared righteous is also to do what is right. Justification and sanctification, therefore, go hand in hand and ought not to be seen as separate events in the total economy of salvation. If (and when) separated, the very "basis of the moral life" erodes, since salvation, alleged as the most important event of our lives, has little or

52. Colwell, *Living the Christian Story*, 49.
53. I recognize again how diffuse and contested the history of evangelicalism is in this regard. Evangelicalism out of Wesleyan and Anabaptist streams has a more unified understanding of the relationship between justification and sanctification, in that while they are separate theological concepts, ethically they go together.
54. See Stephen Westerholm, "The Righteousness of the Law and the Righteousness of Faith in Romans," *Interpretation* 58, no. 3 (July 2004): 253–64; Stephen Westerholm, *Perspectives Old and New on Paul: The "Lutheran" Paul and His Critics* (Grand Rapids: Eerdmans, 2004); and James Dunn, *The Theology of Paul the Apostle* (Grand Rapids: Eerdmans, 1998).

nothing to do with how we actually live.[55] The righteous are known to
be a people who live rightly before God and the world patterned after
the way of Christ. To be saved is to live the saved life. This tendency to
bifurcate justification by grace from sanctification sees "getting saved from
sin" as one end, if not the primary end, and living a life consonant with
and growing into the claims of Christian faith as secondary.

Our salvation from utilitarianism requires a richer view of the church
as an agent of the kingdom of God, to use Howard Snyder's term, and a
more holistic appreciation and appropriation of salvation. The way to bring
these two commitments together is the forging of stronger connections
between the imperative of moral formation of Christian disciples and the
context of the kingdom community as the environment that shapes the
moral perceptions and imaginations of Christ followers. How might this
happen? Perhaps the answer is obvious: It happens through what story
we tell—by what we say and by what we practice.

I return to these proposals in chapter 5 and the conclusion, but for now
it suffices to comment on what I mean. First, the kind of conversations
and discourses taking place in our churches matters. Allow me to return
to the example of the way discussions on war take place in evangelical
contexts. Prior to the threat to invade Iraq, there was not one prayer
offered in the church with which I was involved. On this subject, the
silence was deafening. The prayers offered continued to be focused on
the material and psycho-spiritual needs of middle-class Americans, with
little reference to a world beyond ourselves. To date, when prayers refer
to the war, they are limited to American soldiers and their families and for
their protection. What story does our verbal prayer life tell in this regard?
It communicates our provincial and personal aspirations and disregard
for "others" who are not a part of our "we." I use this as an example of
the strong messages we send about what *we* value in this most formative
and important dimension of Christian life. Our values appear in what we
actually pray for.[56]

To become a community where moral formation occurs, we must commit to becoming what Allen Verhey refers to as a community of moral
discourse, deliberation, and discernment.[57] It matters not just that we
talk, but also what we talk about and how we go about that discussion.
In evangelicalism "talk" is rampant, given the verbal nature of our tradi-

55. Stanley J. Grenz, *The Moral Quest: Foundations of Christian Ethics* (Leicester: Apollos,
1997), 118.
56. See chapter 22, "Prayer," in Stassen and Gushee, *Kingdom Ethics*.
57. Verhey, *Remembering Jesus*, chapter 2.

tion reflected in our "word"-driven practices, such as scripture as Word of God, preaching, teaching, witnessing, etc. *Discourse,* however, implies thoughtful dialogue, conversation, exploration of possibilities, and careful attention to the power of language to shape moral perceptions and imaginations. Often in the desire to avoid controversial issues "for the sake of unity," we opt for silence on important issues or positions that may seem more agreeable given the class locations and commitments of congregants, reifying what we already believe to be true. However, to become a community where we *can* talk about issues of moral significance and be shaped by these very conversations, these issues must make it to the forefront of carefully framed and conducted conversations that are more than just repetitions of sound bytes and easy-to-digest moralisms. Providing opportunities for moral discourse, deliberation, and discernment in the context of the church in a kingdom perspective will enable us to grow in our abilities and capacities to morally reflect on issues *in light* of our faith claims and Christian commitments.

What we talk about and how we go about this are important. Yet moral formation is a continuous process and commitment that occurs through actual practices and "exercises" of our faith as a way of living out the Christian narrative. In the rich collection of essays edited by Miroslav Volf and Dorothy Bass, *Practicing Theology: Beliefs and Practices in Christian Tradition,* Craig Dykstra and Dorothy Bass define Christian practices as "things Christian people do over time to address fundamental human needs in response to and in light of God's active presence for the life of the world."[58] Examples of such practices include truth telling, hospitality, generosity, reconciliation, and spiritual disciplines.[59] Practices both flow from belief and continue to act on us by molding our lives around what we believe. Practices shape us in that they require continual reflection on what we do and the reasons why we engage in certain practices or refrain from others. They are the ways we enact the narratives and traditions that have formed our lives. By practicing the elements of our traditions, not only do we keep them alive, but they become part of us. Without a commitment to practicing our morality, we are left with moralisms, or simply a belief *in* morality. "Discipleship—and therefore the Christian faith—is about

58. Craig Dykstra and Dorothy C. Bass, "A Theological Understanding of Christian Practices," in *Practicing Theology: Beliefs and Practices in Christian Life,* edited by Miroslav Volf and Dorothy C. Bass (Grand Rapids: Eerdmans, 2002), 18.

59. See the essays in Volf and Bass (eds.), *Practicing Theology.* See also Christine D. Pohl, *Making Room: Recovering Hospitality as a Christian Tradition* (Grand Rapids: Eerdmans, 1999).

doing the words of Jesus."[60] I would add that discipleship as the means of Christian moral formation and ethics is about learning how to practice the ways of Jesus in order to enact the *telos* of the kingdom of God.

Conclusion

What might I say now about the scene I depicted at the beginning of this chapter? Outreach and evangelism are *good* practices to pursue and do require creativity, openness, thought, and imagination. Practices themselves, however, require moral reflection, since practices contain the "good internal to the activity."[61] We need to ask, "What are the goods that these practices communicate, and to what goods do they direct us?" I leave the answer to this question up to the imagination of the reader. Suffice it to say that I wonder what kinds of ends are projected and what kinds of Christians are formed through practices such as these. The evangelical church in the United States does not need more religious consumers in the "spiritual marketplace."[62] The evangelical church does not need another war over the Bible or worship styles. We need people who are captivated by the moral vision of the kingdom of God. The answer to this question will depend on how we conceive of the church as an agent of the kingdom of God—or even *if* we do—and the substance of the moral life as kingdom people who practice the ways of Jesus as his disciples. The ends we have in mind and the ends that our practices serve require the time and commitment for moral reflection. Without this, our practices will continue to be shaped by our very pragmatic and results-oriented perspective that squelches moral imagination and perception by accepting what works for what is good, a perspective that justifies means and practices by the ends we actually desire in spite of our claims otherwise.

60. Stassen and Gushee, *Kingdom Ethics*, 485.
61. See Alasdair MacIntyre's definition of a practice in *After Virtue*, 187.
62. See Wade Clark Roof, *The Spiritual Marketplace: Baby Boomers and the Remaking of American Religion* (Princeton, NJ: Princeton University Press, 1999).

4

Sweet Hour of Prayer

Save Me from the World's Cares

I remember with gratitude the Christian fellowship with which I was involved during my junior year of college. I learned through these friends many practices necessary for sustaining faith and a growing commitment to Christ. This was a group that regularly read scripture, prayed, attended church, talked about matters important to Christian faith and practice, lent support in times of need, and reached out to others. We were all university students living with what were perceived to be inordinate amounts of pressure and consistent feelings of being "burned out," especially during exam time and before holidays. As in all communities, there were interesting persons with interesting views on various issues. There was one student involved in our fellowship who had a vibrant prayer life that was an encouragement and help to many of us. During her first term, she failed to study and did not show up for exams. She indicated that she had not received direction from God as to how and what to study and that prayer was perhaps the most important means of preparation. She was hoping for spiritual inspiration to infuse her study time so that God could use it for God's glory. As a result, she failed her qualifying exams and flunked out of school. As our group rallied around her to provide support, we were a bit perplexed by the reasons she gave for her decision to pray in lieu of preparation and study. Even after the painful repercussions of her decisions and practices, she was confident that what mattered most was that she was right with God in what she did.

It was difficult to dispute this point. We human beings are a complex bunch, and our relationships with the divine are as multifaceted and unique as we are as individuals. I cannot help but reflect on this experience for the ways it highlights aspects of evangelical piety and practice with our emphasis on "being right with God" for understanding what it means to be virtuous and for doing the right thing. In this chapter I explore this kind of rhetoric and practice, and its impact on the moral life, through the prism of virtue ethics. To put this another way, is "being right with God" the end, guarantee, and indicator of a virtuous life? Is "being right with God" enough for our moral lives?

The Limits of Personal Virtue Ethics

Aristotle's theory of virtue ethics is this: The acquisition of specific virtues, or those qualities that make a person good, enables one to achieve a life of happiness, which is the end and substance of the moral life. Virtues are both internal goods and qualities that enable us to realize what makes for a life of well-being and happiness. Aristotle's theory was developed in the context of the ancient Greek city as the *polis*, which the virtuous citizen was to serve. This context is necessary for understanding salient features of Aristotle's theory, features that share some common affiliation with Christian morality yet also diverge in significant ways.

Aristotle's theory and Christian morality share a belief in the social nature of human beings. Human well-being and flourishing occur in various relationships where life is shared and common goods are realized. For Aristotle these relationships are friendships with people like us. He believed that it was with people "like us"—of the same social rank, class, educational background, and gender—that our virtues would be formed. For Christians the most fundamental relationships, where the moral life is formed, are with the Triune God and the kingdom community of the church. Our relationship with the Triune God is marked by its difference. A fundamental assertion of Christian faith is that the Triune God is not like us. What enables this divine relationship to be morally forming is the fact that we need a God who is not like us, whose virtue and moral goodness actually reveal our lack, and whose power makes possible our participation in the divine nature (2 Peter 1:3–11). It is in light of God's difference from us that we understand our shortcomings and moral failures. The same holds true for the community of the church. The last thing I need is another person "like me." It is in these differences—those between God and us, and in the diversity of God's people—that I am able to see my limitations and the ways they produce moral myopia. I can accept these differences as epistemological gifts that enable me to see what I cannot or will not see on my own.

There is also a dynamic aspect to the moral life shared by Christian ethics and Aristotle's virtue ethics. The moral life is not a given, but one that needs to be nurtured and practiced by developing habits in light of an informing vision. Christians may call this the process of sanctification inspired by the Holy Spirit working through spiritual disciplines to transform us more into a person like Jesus Christ, whereas Aristotle locates this in the will of a human being, in her or his aspirations and efforts to be good as part of living the good life. The moral life is lived in light of a *telos* that provides shape and orientation to our understanding of what is good and why we ought to live in light of this informing vision. Aristotle's *telos* was the good of the Greek city and its need for virtuous citizens. For Christians our informing narrative is the kingdom of God and the necessity of faithful members helping us to live according to this "way."

I suggested in chapter 1 that Aristotle's ethic might be attractive in a context where personal integrity is respected as an important aspect of moral character and where personal piety is valued. Virtue ethics can account for these as ingredients of a moral life. Evangelicals place a strong emphasis on personal integrity. Pastors and leaders rise and fall on issues of integrity, albeit in limited areas such as money and sex. But as important as personal integrity is, it is just one dimension of morality. Integrity has a communal dimension in that it is formed by narrative and developed through habits and actually lived out in various social contexts where it is ultimately put to the test. I also surmised that virtue ethics may appeal to evangelicals, since virtue language is familiar in the scriptures. The Bible portrays virtuous persons as models that are pleasing to God. The Sermon on the Mount contains a list of virtues appropriate to living in the kingdom of God. The grand virtues of faith, hope, and love permeate much of the Pauline corpus, along with other virtues like goodness, kindness, gentleness, patience, and self-control as fruit of the Spirit. There is a resonance with virtue ethics that resembles what is treasured in evangelical piety as the product of righteousness and evidence of spiritual growth.

There are two areas of significant divergence between virtue ethics and Christian morality that need further consideration, lest Aristotle's ethic be appropriated in ways that ultimately damage the distinct aspects and sources of Christian morality. The first is the differences between Aristotle's *polis* and the *ekklesia* of Jesus Christ. The second is the disparities between the virtues needed to serve Aristotle's city and the kind of virtues needed to live out the kingdom of God, where Jesus is the norm for the Christian moral life. The *kind* of community in which virtues are formed and developed matters for the *kinds* of virtues that are needed to live out a community's moral purpose and ultimate end. Virtues are formed in light of narrative, so it matters that the Christian narrative be the primary one for the formation of *Christian* virtue.

What was the social milieu of Aristotle's philosophy and the context out of which his ideas were formed? According to John Bryant in *Moral Codes and Social Structure in Ancient Greece*, Aristotle's life and work were always associated with the elite and rulers of society. Bryant observes that "the philosopher's involvement in the major historical currents of his era was both direct and significant."[1] This involvement would no doubt affect the ways in which Aristotle viewed the purpose and nature of ethics, and his role as philosopher, especially if his own location was among the elite of Greek society. The Greek city or *polis* was characterized by its heavy social stratification and rigid class and racial boundaries. It was an exclusive society where membership and privilege were restricted to Greeks. Barbarians, slaves, and "others" were viewed as less capable of being and becoming good citizens. Their roles were to serve the elite, since according to nature some were destined to rule and others were destined to be ruled.[2] Alasdair MacIntyre reminds us that in ancient societies, morality was tied to one's place in the social structure. Doing one's duty according to one's status and role was to fulfill one's moral obligation.[3] Therefore, trying to change one's assigned social location and role was a wrong thing to do. Aristotle's ethic relied on these assumptions about social stratification and the inherent fitness of the elite to rule.

In spite of the belief reflected in *Nicomachean Ethics* that goodness was attainable by all persons, Aristotle's ethic was restricted to the elite

---

1. John Bryant, *Moral Codes and Social Structure in Ancient Greece: A Sociology of Greek Ethics from Homer to the Epicureans and Stoics* (Albany: State University of New York Press, 1996), 336.

2. Ibid., 349.

3. Alasdair MacIntyre, *After Virtue* (Notre Dame, IN: University of Notre Dame Press, 1983), 122–30.

since he believed that the mass of humanity, or the common folk, were actually incapable of moral goodness because of their natural state. It may be tempting to see another similarity with Christian ethics on this point. Sin prevents us from achieving moral goodness. Yet for Aristotle, it was not sin understood in a Christian context that thwarted the attainment of moral goodness. It was one's social location and status according to an assumed inherent inferior nature that made one incapable of realizing and practicing moral goodness, which had nothing to do with a conception of sin. It is here that Bryant locates a central tension in Aristotle's moral theory. According to Bryant, Aristotelian virtues, such as generosity and good humor or wit, were restricted to those able to enjoy the comforts and privileges of leisure necessary for obtaining a life of happiness, since the privileged in their pursuit and practice of aristocratic virtues were served by those regarded as unfit, such as slaves and women, for a virtuous life. He writes:

> Aristotle in effect restricts complete *eudaimonia* to those of high social status and material affluence, a decidedly aristocratic perspective that rules out the possibility that laboring and commercial strata—whether free or servile—can ever participate freely in the life of moral excellence. Aristotle's status-based normative orientation is particularly visible in his account of the major ethical virtues, several of which pertain almost exclusively to an aristocratic life-style.[4]

The celebration of Greek nobility and military courage would likely have no place for such virtues as humility and peace as vital qualities of the *ekklesia* of Jesus Christ. It is here we find a second area of variance between Aristotelian and kingdom virtues. The *kinds* of virtues needed to serve the Greek *polis* may be radically different than the kinds of virtues that serve the kingdom of God. MacIntyre writes:

> At once it is impossible to delay the remark that the most striking contrast with Aristotle's catalogue is to be found neither in Homer's nor in our own, but in the New Testament's. For the New Testament not only praises virtue of which Aristotle knows nothing—faith, hope and love—and says nothing about virtues such as *phronêsis* which are crucial for Aristotle, but it praises at least one quality as a virtue which Aristotle seems to count as one of the vices relative to magnanimity, namely humility. Moreover since the New Testament quite clearly sees the rich as destined for the pains of

4. Bryant, *Moral Codes and Social Structures in Ancient Greece*, 360–61.

Hell, it is clear that the key virtues cannot be available to them; yet they *are* available to slaves.[5]

The contrast between an Aristotelian ideal of community and the community composed of "people of the kingdom way" might be obvious. The early church was composed of the "others," those on the margins of society, the poor in spirit for whom the gospel really was good news. The gospel continues to invert various conceptions of an Aristotelian *polis* by regarding the last as first and the first as last. Jesus's community of believers is known, or ought to be known, by our unity in our various diversities. It is not cultural, class, or ethnic sameness that brings us together. It is the one Lord, one faith, and one baptism in which we find our unity and community and the strength and grace to live with our diversities as gifts. The power of the gospel makes it possible to live with our differences in ways that we actually learn from one another and are transformed in the process. It is in our differences that our virtues are learned and put to the test as we seek to live a common life under the lordship of Christ, where in humility we "consider others better than ourselves" according to the example of Jesus (Phil. 2:1–11). Christian virtues therefore have strong social dimensions. The ways in which we learn and practice the virtues are in relationships with others. They are the means by which we learn how to live in community with others not like "us." It is not enough to be "right with God" and make claims to moral superiority. One cannot be right with God and not be right with others. Learning how to live right with others requires the development and practice of Christian virtues lived out in our varied social contexts with all of their moral complexities.

Christian Virtues

Virtue ethics has points of congruence with and an important place in Christian morality. The kind of people we are matters to God. Who we are informs the decisions we make and how we act in the world. This also matters to God. However, what makes virtue ethics "Christian?" I must first explain what I mean by *virtue* and on what basis virtues might be called "Christian."

I will start with Alasdair MacIntyre's definition of virtue, given the influence of his work in *After Virtue* on Christian virtue ethicists. MacIntyre defines virtue as "an acquired human quality, the possession and exercise

5. MacIntyre, *After Virtue*, 182.

of which tends to enable us to achieve those goods which are internal to practices and the lack of which effectively prevents us from achieving any such goods."[6] Virtues are human qualities and characteristics that can be labeled "good" and to which humans aspire *because* these qualities are good and crucial for living a good life. What does MacIntyre mean by this? Placed in the context of his overall argument in *After Virtue*, this is an appeal for a recovery of narrative as necessary for virtue formation after the "failure of the enlightenment project."[7] The failure of the enlightenment project is that it offered the illusion that our lives are "unstoried" and not bound to any tradition. The irony according to MacIntyre is that the story of liberal individualism has provided the account we have accepted as normative, since "for liberal individualism a community is simply an arena in which individuals each pursue their own self-chosen conception of the good life, and political institutions exist to provide that degree of order which makes such self-determined activity possible."[8] Virtues in *this* narrative of liberal individualism are related to the achievement of the goods ingrained in this narrative. It is the good of each freely choosing individual determining and designing the narrative of his choosing. The irony therefore of liberal individualism is that it does have a narrative, a conception of "the good," and it does have virtues that are realized in practices, virtues that have no cohering story for self-defining and self-ruling individuals. Virtues such as autonomy and freedom are routinely practiced to realize the good that each individual is now free to construct as one's own *personal* story. I return to the influence of individualism and its impact on evangelical understandings of personal piety and morality later in this chapter. It is sufficient to say at this point that MacIntyre identifies the usurpation of moral narratives by liberal individualism, which fragments communities and shatters our sense of moral integrity since our ethic is now devoid of a narrative or co-opted by the false impression that we do not have or even need one. He writes:

> I have suggested so far that unless there is a *telos* which transcends the limited goods of practices by constituting the good of a whole human life, the good of a human life conceived as a unity, it will *both* be the case that a certain subversive arbitrariness will invade the moral life *and* that we shall be unable to specify the context of certain virtues adequately. These two considerations are reinforced by a third: that there is at least one virtue recognized by

6. Ibid., 191.
7. Ibid., chapters 5 and 6.
8. Ibid., 195.

the tradition which cannot be specified at all except with references to the wholeness of a human life—the virtue of integrity or constancy.[9]

The case MacIntyre makes is that if our lives are essentially the living out of stories or narratives, then the stories around which we orient our lives are crucial for the kinds of practices and virtues needed for achieving such goods contained within the moral *telos* of our narratives. Virtues therefore require a narrative context in which to be developed and practiced, let alone to be called "good." Without narrative, a morally orienting *telos*, our sense of what is virtuous is arbitrary and random and therefore impracticable. In other words, virtues are indefinable and indescribable and therefore cannot actually be practiced because there is no reason or means for actually calling them good and worthy of pursuit. They are whatever we make them to be. Virtues have no meaning and make no sense unless there is a frame of reference by which we measure the quality of virtues, the good they contain, and the ends which they serve.

What might be the implications of MacIntyre's conception of virtue for Christian morality as "an acquired human quality, the possession and exercise of which tends to enable us to achieve those goods which are internal to practices and the lack of which effectively prevents us from achieving any such goods?" Stassen and Gushee appropriately note that in spite of the renaissance of virtue ethics, "virtue ethicists are often strangely ambivalent or indefinite about which virtues Christians should nurture."[10] Joseph Kotva in *The Christian Case for Virtue Ethics* attempts to delineate the specific Christian claims and biblical and theological sources for virtue ethics to make the case that virtue theory coheres well with Christian ethics.[11] For Kotva, what makes virtue ethics Christian are the relationship between God's grace and our response, the normativity of Jesus Christ, and the communal nature of human beings.[12] Even though Kotva does not specifically address Stassen and Gushee's concern by answering *which* virtues Christians should nurture, he provides hints and his work is a helpful beginning for the concerns I am addressing in this chapter. Following Kotva's lead while taking some detours, I suggest three necessary indicators for understanding what kind of virtuous life might be

9. Ibid., 203.

10. Glen Stassen and David Gushee, *Kingdom Ethics: Following Jesus in Contemporary Context* (Downers Grove, IL: InterVarsity Press, 2003), 33.

11. Joseph J. Kotva, Jr., *The Christian Case for Virtue Ethics* (Washington, DC: Georgetown University Press, 1996).

12. Ibid., chapter 4.

called "Christian" and how we ought to go about pursuing the virtuous life in an attempt to move beyond personal piety. These are the virtues that Jesus practiced and demonstrated, the moral dimensions of spiritual formation into the image of Christ, and the working out of the virtuous life in its narrative and social dimensions.

Jesus Christ and Christian Virtues

First, Christian virtues have something to do with Jesus Christ. MacIntyre's definition is a preliminary point for explicating the quality, shape, and *telos* of virtues in a general sense. Jesus Christ is our frame of reference for explicating the quality, shape, and *telos* of virtues we should nurture in order to call them *Christian*. Virtues were not just taught by Christ in his parables and sermons as ideals or principles. Jesus himself is the exemplar of the virtuous life. It might be easy to attribute the virtuous life to Jesus based on his divinity. Yet the virtues that Jesus taught were *demonstrated* in the life he lived through his humanity and in his social and personal interactions. It is Jesus's humanity that gives us the window through which to view the quality and shape of a life that pleases God. Jesus did not just teach about the virtue of mercy. Jesus was merciful. Humility was not an abstract idea in Jesus's teaching. Jesus himself was the model of humility. Jesus did not present theories of justice. Jesus was reconciling, securing justice and righteousness as marks of shalom. It is not enough to simply ask, "What would Jesus do?" The more appropriate question is "What did Jesus actually do?"[13] and how did his divinely *incarnated* life model the ideal life that has its source in the goodness and virtues of God? The life Jesus actually lived presents us with the framework for comprehending the nature of Christian virtues. They are the qualities Jesus exemplified in his own humanity as he pointed us to God. After his exploration of various christological views, Kotva summarizes the implications of the life of Christ for Christian ethics and virtues as follows.

> Christian faith is a matter of becoming a certain sort of person. It is a matter of becoming like Jesus. Rules and principles can help us toward that goal, but the goal involves more than following rules. It is a goal that involves a way

13. I am thankful to Waverly Earley for this insight, which she raised in a Christian ethics course at Ashland Theological Seminary. See F. Scott Spencer, *What Did Jesus Do? Gospel Profiles of Jesus' Personal Conduct* (Harrisburg, PA: Trinity, 2003).

of being in the world. It is a goal seen in the totality of Jesus' life and way. It is a goal that requires the transformation of the self into his likeness.[14]

Spiritual Formation as Moral Formation

The first indicator, therefore, for qualifying virtues as Christian is the life of Jesus as the norm for the Christian moral life. If Jesus himself is the pattern for the virtuous life and if we take our cues from him, then our relationships with Christ have significant moral implications if we are serious about the transformation of our selves into his likeness. The second gauge for articulating the distinct nature of Christian virtues concerns the relationship between spiritual and moral formation. I understand spiritual formation in both its most basic and most difficult sense as the process by which we are transformed into the image of Christ by the work of the Holy Spirit through practices that position us for *this* kind of transformation (2 Cor. 3:12–18, 1 Peter 1:13–16). I share Kotva's assumption that this process is initiated by God's grace, empowered by the Holy Spirit, and reliant on our openness and willing participation in practices that situate us for life-changing experiences that serve this transformation into being like Christ.

However, I would like to press further the point by making a more explicit link between spiritual and moral formation in presenting this claim. Spiritual formation *is* moral formation. In other words, one cannot be transformed into the image of Christ, the norm for Christian ethics, without an accompanying commitment to the moral and ethical concerns of Jesus. Why do I desire to press and defend this assertion? I do so because of the renewed interest in spiritual formation in evangelicalism. While I embrace this interest and some of the practices, I do so critically. I am concerned about the ways in which spiritual formation is subverted by individualism, the therapeutic, and personal piety, then amplified and exacerbated in a consumer culture, so that spiritual formation in actual practice is equated with the search for personal self-fulfillment and healing, instead of the image of Christ or the kingdom of God as the *telos* of the Christian life.

Spiritual formation has been at the heart of Christian faith and practice for centuries. To cover the history of Christian spirituality here would be a disservice to its richness, given the scope and limitations of this particular

---

14. Kotva, *Christian Case for Virtue Ethics*, 89. Kotva interacts with and integrates the Christologies of C. Norman Kraus, Hendrikus Berkhof, and Edward Schillebeeckx to ground his case for Christian virtue ethics.

project.[15] I trust it is sufficient to affirm that the language and concerns of spiritual transformation and maturity, and their connections with the moral dimensions of Christian faith, are not new but instead have always been an integral part of it. It therefore often strikes me as ironic, and somewhat amusing, that the language of spiritual formation has appeared as a recent discovery in American evangelicalism, in light of the history of Christian spirituality in our various theological and ecclesial traditions long before this new finding. What is novel perhaps are the unique ways in which spiritual formation has been appropriated and practiced in American evangelicalism given the influences of individualism and our therapeutic milieu which has robbed spiritual formation of its moral dimensions.

Sociologist Richard Bellah and his colleagues in *Habits of the Heart* were among the first to alert us to the influences of individualism and the therapeutic on religious expression and practices.[16] According to these sociologists of religion, religious expression has morphed through four strands of American culture.[17] The first is the biblical strand, best depicted by John Winthrop, the Puritans, and the vision of the new colony as a "city on a hill" with a special mission given to it by God. Bellah and his colleagues characterize the second strand as republican, with its genesis in the creation of our democratic systems that attempted to bring power and participation to the lowest level of society. This lowest level was composed of landowning white men. The fulfillment and creation of better selves were realized through principles of justice and equality that alleged to give equal opportunity for all in "life, liberty and the pursuit of happiness." The third strand of American culture is utilitarian individualism, expressed in the emerging middle class with growing economic power to participate in the American Dream, so that "the most important thing about America" is "the chance for the individual to get ahead on his own initiative."[18]

The fourth and contemporary strand, and the one of which Bellah and his colleagues give a sustained analysis, is the therapeutic one of expressive individualism. Expressive individualism is fueled by a vision

15. See the following sources for good overviews of the history of Christian spirituality: Richard Foster, *Streams of Living Water* (New York: HarperSanFrancisco, 1998); Bradley P. Holt, *Thirsty for God: A Brief History of Christian Spirituality* (Minneapolis: Fortress Press, 2005); and Cheslyn Jones, Geoffrey Wainwright, and Edward Yarnold (eds.), *The Study of Spirituality* (New York: Oxford University Press, 1986).

16. Robert N. Bellah, Richard Madsen, William Sullivan, Ann Swidler, and Steven Tipton, *Habits of the Heart: Individualism and Commitment in American Life* (Berkley: University of California Press, 1985).

17. Ibid., 28–35.

18. Ibid., 33.

that self-fulfillment, self-discovery, and self-expression are the aims of an individual's life. Religion therefore becomes just one means by which an individual finds self-fulfillment and meaning, and can easily be changed or discarded if it fails to do so, exemplified by the amalgamation of religious belief known as "Sheilaism."[19] Whereas religion may once have provided the glue and coherence for moral commitments and a sense of community, religion is now that which is self-chosen for the benefits it provides to an individual seeking his or her own sense of well-being and wholeness, thereby fragmenting and disintegrating the moral frameworks that religious faith provides for adherents.

The authors of *Habits of the Heart* focus their study primarily on broad expressions of Protestantism lived out by white middle-class Americans. Their insights, however, are applicable to evangelicalism, given that evangelicals do tend to fit these descriptions and do receive a degree of attention from Bellah and his colleagues. While evangelical congregations and adherents may work against forms of expressive individualism, individualism and the therapeutic concern with personal happiness and self-fulfillment have found their own unique expression in American evangelicalism. They note similarities between a mainline Presbyterian church and an independent, conservative evangelical church in this regard. Bellah notes these similarities in the following way.

> Both Larry Beckett's conservative church and Art Townsend's liberal one stress stable, loving relationships, in which the intention to care outweighs the flux of momentary feelings, as the ideal pattern in marriage, family and work relationships. Thus both attempt to counter the more exploitative tendencies of utilitarian individualism. But in both cases their sense of religious community has trouble moving beyond an individualistic morality. In Art Townsend's faith, a distinctively religious vision has been absorbed into the categories of contemporary psychology. No autonomous strand of good and evil survives outside the needs of individual psyches for growth. Community and attachment come not from the demands of a tradition, but from the empathetic sharing of feelings among therapeutically attuned selves.[20]

However, lest one is left with belief that a conservative evangelical church does not succumb to the same temptations as this mainline liberal church, Bellah notes from his observations that Larry Beckett's evangelical church has absorbed the ethos of expressive individualism in different ways and

19. Ibid., 221, 235.
20. Ibid., 231–32.

has perhaps adjusted its theological commitments to serve the needs of seekers desiring fulfillment. Again Bellah writes:

> Larry Beckett's evangelical church, in contrast, maintains a vision of the concrete moral commitments that bind church members. But the bonds of loyalty, help, and responsibility remain oriented to the exclusive sect of those who are "real" Christians. Direct reliance on the Bible provides a second language with which to resist the temptations of the "world," but the almost exclusionary concentration on the Bible, especially the New Testament, with no larger memory of how Christians have coped with the world historically, diminishes the capacity of their second language to deal adequately with current social reality. There is even a tendency visible in many evangelical churches to thin the biblical language of sin and redemption to an idea of Jesus as the friend who helps us find happiness and self-fulfillment.[21]

The sociological study of religion in *Habits of the Heart* conducted by Bellah, Madsen, Sullivan, Swidler, and Tipton demonstrates the ways in which religious faith expressed in American culture has been reshaped in a market society that capitalizes on individual choice, preferences, and desire. When this is coupled with the therapeutic strand of our contemporary middle-class location, the implications for the expression of faith, and hence Christian morality, may be obvious. Religious commitments themselves become both utilitarian and expressive. They are valued for what end they produce for an individual seeking his or her own fulfillment, and they are esteemed as a means of self-expression. They are purely private and predictably personal. Moral commitments in this context are unstable, unpredictable, individualistic, and secondary to the needs that religious faith meets in one's personal life.

Evangelicals, in spite of our commitments to the authority of scripture and the norming theological commitments of historic Christian faith, are not immune to these trends as we too participate in the search for meaning and personal fulfillment in the spiritual marketplace, as provocatively noted by Wade Clark Roof.[22] According to Roof, the contemporary terrain of religious expression in the United States can be characterized by the plethora of options for spiritual seekers in our quest for an authentic,

---

21. Ibid., 232. I was first introduced to *Habits of the Heart* in a church history class taught by Dr. Bruce Shelley while I was a student at Denver Seminary. I remember the insights that Dr. Shelley provided in class by his observation that if one listens closely to sermons and teachings in many evangelical churches, it appears that people no longer need salvation, they just need healing.

22. Wade Clark Roof, *The Spiritual Marketplace: Baby Boomers and the Remaking of American Religion* (Princeton, NJ: Princeton University Press, 1999).

self-affirming religious experience. In general, the spiritual marketplace is characterized by three prevailing trends.[23] The first is the breadth of interest in spiritual matters, whether it is among those who are seeking a deeper meaning in their current religious practices or persons attempting to find new avenues of spiritual expression. The second trend that Roof notes is the shift from religious certainty to a mood of "quest" or "seeking," which is more self-reflexive and concerned with self-understanding and improvement than an affirmation or solidification of particular theological beliefs. The final trend is somewhat paradoxical, given the second. Roof presents this third trend as a "spiritual yearning" that seeks to move beyond the self-centered, therapeutic culture in which baby boomers grew up.[24] However, he still acknowledges the self-focus that this final trend represents. He writes, "Popular spirituality may appear shallow, indeed flaky; yet its creative currents, under the right conditions, can activate our deepest energies and commitments. Even in its most self-absorbed forms, today's spiritual ferment reflects a deep hunger for a self-transformation that is both genuine and personally satisfying."[25]

For some, their spiritual quest may involve a return to their childhood churches or a return to older historic and theological traditions.[26] For others, like the individuals in *Habits of the Heart*, some options are an eclectic mixture of various beliefs and practices strung together to meet their personal needs. For many it is the discovery of religious meaning outside institutional structures, through nature, Eastern religions, or various forms of religious self-help organizations and small groups. For evangelicals in particular Roof notes that the spiritual quest has prompted the rise of seeker-sensitive churches and the use of other avenues, such as media and technology, to reach our quest culture. Much of this is the result of the continual need for all religious groups to adapt to cultural trends for survival.[27] For evangelicals, these adjustments may be part of the missional impetus inherent within our tradition to address the needs of any given culture with a gospel message by being relevant. This is often the reason given for accommodating our language and evangelistic emphases to the larger concerns of culture by "meeting people where they're at."

However, it is likely that this quest mentality for personal fulfillment via religious experience is also significantly shaping the actual beliefs and

23. Ibid., 9.
24. Ibid.
25. Ibid.
26. Ibid., chapter 1.
27. Ibid., 79.

ethical commitments of evangelicals. These are not benign adjustments that have no implications for the connections we make between faith and morality. Roof refers to this reshaping as the "redrawing of boundaries" that all religious groups experience.[28] In particular he notes the impact this has on evangelicalism as it has absorbed and adjusted itself to the larger spiritually seeking culture.

> "Born-again" spirituality thus has an affinity with an introverted self as articulated in recent decades in the broader American culture. As the followers themselves see it, it is a self in relation to God as described in the never-changing New Testament plan of salvation. Closer scrutiny, however, reveals an expansive self very much influenced by the wider culture. Books, music, witnessing, testimony, and ritual performance within the subculture all employ a rhetoric emphasizing that the individual who has directly experienced God may then discover the "real self." That this discovery occurs in a shared faith community is common but, by and large, the setting itself is secondary to the highly subjective narrative of an individual pretty much on his or her own, in a process of spiritual transformation. "Journey" and "recovery" languages keep the focus on growth and self-development, thereby reinforcing a personal, psychological account of the meaning of salvation. This narration of self is elaborated by recourse to psychocultural themes such as spontaneity, control, intimacy, and self-affirmation embedded within the culture, which define and make vivid rich dimensions of personal experience.[29]

What are we to make of these trends noted by the writers of *Habits of the Heart* and Roof in *Spiritual Marketplace*? In what ways might these trends have an effect on the ways we understand the relationship between faith and morality, and Christian virtue and the kingdom narrative for Christian ethics? The first impact of this individualistic, therapeutic perspective on Christian spirituality is the privileging of oneself prior to all other selves. What matters is the health and well-being of one's personal soul as more important than the well-being and flourishing of other persons. There appears to be an excessive amount of attention directed to the need for one to be "healthy," able to "love one's own self" before attention can be given to the interests and concerns of others. In other words, how can I love others if I cannot love myself? While I do not mean to discount or ignore the place that soul care has in one's overall spiritual and moral development, this inordinate amount of attention to *one's own* spiritual well-being borders on spiritual narcissism, a spiritual

28. Ibid, chapter 6.
29. Ibid., 183–84.

self-absorption that is more akin to a therapeutic commitment to one's own happiness than to Jesus's teaching that "whoever finds his life will lose it, and whoever loses his life for my sake will find it" (Matt. 10:39; see also Luke 9:23–27).[30] The attention that we place on ourselves in evangelical spirituality and the often disproportionate concentration on the state of our own souls overlooks the connections and interdependence of our own spiritual health, moral maturity, and *responsibility* and *ability* to tend to the needs and concerns of others as crucial to spiritual maturity, discipleship, and kingdom ethics. Perhaps the healthiest thing we can do for ourselves is to stop thinking about ourselves and tend to the needs, concerns, and situations of others, lending us an empathetic and wider perspective so crucial for morality.

In his survey of popular literature on contemporary spirituality, L. Gregory Jones notes the ways in which "much contemporary spirituality is shaped by consumer impulses" and is "captive to a therapeutic culture" to the detriment of Christian ethical concerns at the heart of Christian spirituality.[31] The result is a spiritual journey that lacks a *telos* that has anything to do with Christ and is essentially a "ceaseless motion of self-discovery or, more likely self-invention."[32] Not only is Jones concerned with the diffusion of Christian spirituality into a nondistinct, even non-Christian one, he is also alarmed at the ways this trend undermines the connections between authentic spirituality and our moral sensibilities.

---

30. I want to be careful in making this claim, given the ways in which women, especially in evangelicalism, have been relegated to the roles of caring for others and self-denial, often at the expense of our own spiritual and moral development. For this reason, I am not a fan of an ethic of care suggested by Carol Gilligan in *In a Different Voice: Psychological Theory and Women's Development* (Cambridge: Harvard University Press, 1993), and Nel Noddings in *Caring: A Feminine Approach to Ethics and Moral Education* (Berkeley: University of California Press, 1984). I read their projects as advocating an ethic of care based on an essentialist understanding of gender that sees women, *because we are women,* more inclined to care and attend to the needs of others. While I appreciate the attention given to care and responsibility in the nexus of relationships as an important moral criterion, contributions Gilligan and Nodding have made, I do think their theories tend to exacerbate this kind of self-sacrifice for women because of the ways we have been socialized to find meaning in caring for others *because* we are women. For an important feminist analysis on this concern, see Judith Plaskow, *Sex, Sin, and Grace: Women's Experience and the Theologies of Reinhold Niebuhr and Paul Tillich* (Washington, DC: University Press of America, 1980).

31. L. Gregory Jones, "A Thirst for God or Consumer Spirituality? Cultivating Disciplined Practices of Being Engaged by God," in *Modern Theology* 13, no.1 (January 1997): 3–28. Jones uses the works of Bernard of Clairvaux and the contemporary work of Thomas Moore in *Care of the Soul* to illustrate the distinctions between authentic and inauthentic Christian spirituality and the dangerous ways that Moore uses language to promote either a sub- or non-Christian form of spirituality.

32. Ibid., 4.

He attributes this erosion to what he calls the "bifurcation of spirituality and politics" as

> . . . one of the reasons that contemporary spirituality can be consumed as a luxury consumer good, primarily designed for middle- and upper-class folks. One will not be confronted with the massive suffering around the world, or even around the corner from where one lives. Nor will the reader be confronted with Amos's stinging prophetic indictments and Jesus's call to costly discipleship. Rather, the reader is invited to an increasingly inward journey that leaves the world largely as it already is.[33]

A practiced, disciplined, and focused attention on the concerns and situations of others may actually be a pathway to our own spiritual and moral wholeness. It may also enable us to keep our own particular problems and concerns in a more balanced and realistic perspective. This might be an important corrective to a second concern arising from the individualistic and therapeutic milieu of current evangelical spiritual practices and their effect on ethics. My concern is that the unbalanced attention given to one's own sense of healing and wholeness, as shaped by our therapeutic context, may subvert the attention needed for the concrete material needs of other people. Akin to Maslow's hierarchy of needs, if our basic material and survival needs are met, which they are in the middle-class location that most white evangelicals inhabit, then we have the ability and leisure to focus on more psycho-spiritual needs of personal health and wholeness, however we choose to define them. Our problems as we define them may tend to be "problems of privilege," which could actually minimize the problems and suffering in a global context fraught with poverty, violence, oppression, and other tragedies that threaten the lives of millions of human beings.

Christian Virtues as Social

If the first indicator of Christian virtue comes with reflecting on the actual life of Christ as the norm of moral goodness and if transformation into the image of Christ is the *telos* of spiritual formation, with an implication that our selves will also "be clothed" in the moral concerns of Jesus, then the third indicator of a virtuous life that can be called "Christian" is the social dimension and application of Christian virtue in contested moral spaces as an ethical necessity. In other words, Christian virtues are not an individual's personal possession of piety. Being right with God is

33. Ibid., 21.

no guarantee that one will live a life characterized by righteousness and justice. Christian virtues are lived out, exercised, and applied in social contexts just as Jesus did. This third indicator may be a correction to the consumption of spirituality for one's own therapeutic self-enhancement and the bifurcation of "spirituality and politics" that robs Christian spiritual practices of their moral dimensions. To ground this part of my argument, I turn to a discussion on justice as a cardinal virtue of Christian moral reflection and ethical action.

One of the difficulties in advocating for a "spirituality of justice,"[34] as a necessary rectification for a reductionistic understanding of virtue and personal piety, lies in the assumptions about justice and its surrounding rhetoric in an evangelical context. For many our conceptions about justice are hinged to ideological assumptions inherent in our legal and political systems. Justice is about rewarding good and punishing wrongdoing. Or justice may be seen as the more equitable distribution of goods in spite of structural arrangements that may have created inequitable access to goods and services in the first place. Concepts such as freedom, rights, fairness, and equal opportunity are also bundled into conversations about justice as if these terms are synonymous and as if the securing of such rights and conditions ensures that justice has been done. While these are important aspects of justice, to collapse justice into these concepts is to miss what is unique and far more demanding in a *Christian* understanding of and commitment to justice. Without an account of a biblical and theological framework for justice, we are left with, to borrow again Jones's phrase, a bifurcation of "spirituality and politics" and dualism between one's personal sense of piety and self-righteousness and actual practices of justice.[35] C. Norman Krause attributes these dualisms to Neoplatonic and Gnostic influences on Christian faith. He writes:

> The dualistic traditions strongly influenced by Neoplatonism and gnostic Christianity make personal piety the requisite expression of spirituality and, correspondingly, devalue the spiritual character of social ministry. According to this conception of the Christian life, the fruit of the Spirit in a person's life *may* provide motivation for social action, but spirituality *is not* immediately identified with compassionate social action. Instead, spirituality is associated with ascetical, monastic community (in contrast to secular-

34. Ibid., 24.
35. By *politics,* I do not mean, nor does Jones, the party politics of Republicans and Democrats. *Politics* means public life and is an important antidote to both the privatization and the politicalization of religious faith.

temporal society), mystical contemplation, devotional piety, evangelistic witness, and charismatic worship.[36]

How do we begin to address the concerns that Jones and Krause raise about the split between one's sense of personal piety and just, compassionate social action? Where do we start with framing a picture of justice from a Christian perspective that gives us a way for understanding the social nature of virtue? First, it is important to examine the linkages between the biblical images of justice, righteousness, and peace. In Hebrew, *mishpât* (justice), *tsâdaq* (righteousness) and in Greek, *dikaiosunē* (righteousness or justification) describe the process, status, or conditions by which persons and circumstances are declared and made to be right, just, good, and virtuous. As Raymond Reimer notes these words are "roughly synonymous, having to do with restoration, wholeness, setting things right, healing that which was broken, making peace—peace between humans and God."[37] This kind of biblical justice is essentially relational, as opposed to ideological, in that it involves the making right of God's relationship with humanity and our relationships with others based on movement and initiative, God toward us and us toward others. The justice of God and the pursuit of justice by Christians go hand in hand. "Doing" justice is our response to the justice, mercy, and compassion of God toward us. The capacity and response of justice is a product of one's own spirituality. It is an indication that we have internalized and appropriated the implications of God's reconciling actions with humanity that moves us beyond a narrow focus on and satisfaction with our own righteousness before God and toward the living out of God's reconciling justice in the world as we live to make things right.

Behind a biblical concept of justice is the grand theme of shalom (*shâlêm*), the image of safety, harmony, peace, and completeness. Shalom is a situation brought about by justice and righteousness, a right ordering and maintaining of relationships that are harmonious and safe and offer well-being and hope to others. Shalom requires the presence of justice and righteousness to create and maintain harmony and wholeness. The "original position" of justice is not John Rawls's social contract theory,

36. C. Norman Krause, "Spirit and Spirituality: Reclaiming Biblical Transcendence," in *Vital Christianity: Spirituality, Justice, and Christian Practice*, edited by David L. Weaver-Zercher and William H. Willimon (New York: T and T Clark, 2005), 33, emphasis mine.

37. Raymond H. Reimer, "Living Out the Peace of God: The Apostle Paul's Theology and Practice of Peace," in *Vital Christianity: Spirituality, Justice, and Christian Practice,* edited by David L. Weaver-Zercher and William H. Willimon (New York: T and T Clark, 2005), 93.

which views society as a collection of individuals agreeing on basic rights "from behind a veil of ignorance."[38] The original position of just and right shalom is the knowledge of God's creation of a world and communities intended for harmony, wholeness, plenty, security, and peace brought about by means which themselves are just and righteous. Justice is the recreation of the conditions of shalom that God intended for creation in the first place. It is the working toward the reestablishing and maintenance of harmony, wholeness, and righteousness within the entirety of the created order. In the *Soul of Politics,* Jim Wallis writes:

> In the Hebrew Scriptures, one finds the more holistic concept of *shalom* as the best definition of justice. It is a deeper and wider notion than the security of individual human rights. The vision of shalom requires us to establish "right relationships." It is a call to justice in the whole community and for the entire habitat. Shalom is an inclusive notion of justice extending even to the rest of God's creatures and the whole of the creation. Restoring right relationships takes us further than respecting individual rights. It pushes us to see ourselves as part of a community, even as members of an extended but deeply interconnected global family, and ultimately as strands in the web of life that we all share and depend upon. The biblical vision of *shalom* could be a basis for a new politics of community and the social healing we need so much.[39]

A biblical vision of shalom stems from God's creative intentions for the world, which is *still* loved by God. God is still working at reconciling justice. Abraham Heschel refers to justice as "God's stake in the world."[40] For Heschel, justice is the reflection of God's *pathos.* The taking on of God's divine compassion for justice and righteousness was the impetus behind the prophet's role of foretelling the message of God's justice since it is an "*a priori* of biblical faith not an added attribute to His (God's) essence, but given with the very thought of God. It is inherent in His essence and identified with His ways."[41] God's justice and righteousness meant that God was like no other god in the ancient world. Other gods were capricious and demanding of mere mortals, treating us like pawns, with no concern for the plight and well-being

38. See John Rawls, *A Theory of Justice* (Cambridge: Harvard University Press, 1972). See also Karen Lebacqz, *Six Theories of Justice* (Minneapolis: Augsburg, 1986), for an important critique of Rawls and other theories of justice from a Christian perspective, and Nicholas Wolterstorff, *Until Justice and Peace Embrace* (Grand Rapids: Eerdmans, 1983).

39. Jim Wallis, *The Soul of Politics* (Maryknoll, NY: Orbis Books, 1994), 73.

40. Abraham Heschel, *The Prophets*, vol. 1 (New York: Harper and Row, 1962), 198.

41. Ibid., 200.

of humanity. However this God, our God, was different because of God's intricate and concerned involvement with our plight and with the death-creating conditions of injustice and oppression. As Heschel observes "God's concern for justice grows out of His compassion for man."[42] He goes on to affirm that,

> Justice is not important for its own sake; the validity of justice and the motivation for its exercise lie in the blessings it brings to man. For justice . . . is not an abstraction, a value. Justice exists in relation to a person, and is something done by a person. An act of injustice is condemned, not because the law is broken, but because a person has been hurt. What is the image of a person? A person is a being whose anguish may reach the heart of God. "You shall not afflict a widow or orphan. If you do afflict them, and they cry out to me, I will surely hear their cry . . . if he cries to Me, I will hear, for I am compassionate" (Exod. 22:22–23, 27).[43]

Even a cursory reading of the prophetic material in the scriptures gives one a big hint that all is not well in a world characterized by the obsession with "wisdom, wealth and might."[44] What is important to remember is that the ire of the prophets was primarily directed to the people of God. While they may have lived in a world of violence, injustice, and oppression among nations, it was their own violence, injustice, and acts of oppression that were most troubling to the prophets. Why? Because they, and we, should have known better as the recipients of God's mercy, compassion, grace, and justice. It strikes me that much of the prophets' critiques were directed at the personal pietistic practices of the people of God. There was no shortage of fasting, praying, temple going, and even tithing (Isaiah 58, Micah 6:1–7). It seems, however, that the people of God assumed this was either enough or all that was required of them. Heschel writes:

> Of course, the prophets did not condemn the practice of sacrifice in itself. . . . They did, however, claim that deeds of injustice vitiate both sacrifice and prayer. Men may not drown out the cries of the oppressed with the noises of hymns, nor buy off the Lord with increased offerings. The prophets disparaged the cult when it became a substitute for righteousness. It is precisely the implied recognition of the value of the cult that lends force to their insistence that there is something far more precious than sacrifice.[45]

42. Ibid., 216.
43. Ibid.
44. Ibid., 8.
45. Ibid., 196.

Might it be possible that these pietistic practices acted as a shield, numb-
ing their participants through mantra-like, religious routine practices so
that they would not have to confront the injustice and oppression around
them, conditions they were actually creating by their inattention and shallow understandings of what it meant to be "right with God"? Heschel
certainly implies that the "noises of hymns," "increased offerings," and
religious practices themselves substituted for righteousness and drowned
out the cries of the oppressed and the victims of injustice.

However, it may also be possible that the lack of concern for righteousness and justice was intentional. The people of God at the point of
the prophetic critiques of the Old Testament, between 700 and 600 BC,
were at the center of the political and economic machine of the ancient
world. Israel had transitioned from a people with no power, except that
of God's, to a strong–yet–conflicted nation. They were now privileged
with their economic resources, military might, and political leverage.
Their privilege was at the expense of others who built their cities and
their religious sites, and ensured their comfort and security. It is at this
point that the prophets' anger at the spiritual practices of the people of
God is most disturbing and indicting. They (read: we) had participated
in creating oppressive conditions and were now hiding behind their own
sense of spiritual rightness as the people of God as a justification for their
actions. They did not need to attend to a "spirituality of justice," since
they were likely convinced that they were already "right with God" and
that this was itself enough for God. To commit to making things right,
consonant with the justice of God, would have been costly, since they
benefited from current social arrangements. Therefore, their own conception of personal piety and religious rhetoric was an easy way to convince
them that the most important thing was "being right with God," enabling
them to capitalize on the conditions of injustice for their own benefits,
well-being, and pleasures (Amos 2–6). A "spirituality of justice" would
have challenged their own conceptions of what it meant to be "spiritual,"
and true spirituality would have indicted their inattention to justice and
righteousness. It was easier to maintain the status quo and accept it for
what it was than to transform social arrangements based on the vision
of shalom and the reconciling righteousness and justice of God. If one
person or a group benefits from the ways things are and can defend it
with religious rhetoric and a sense of one's own *self*-righteousness, then
the stakes for justifying one's benefits and privileges increase while the
stakes for working toward God's reconciling justice decrease.

A biblical conception of justice is linked with righteousness as "making things right" based on God's creative intention for shalom. This view also fueled the prophetic critique of the personal pietistic practices of the people of God and of the ways in which they ignored the call to "do justice" (Micah 6:8), even as they prided themselves for their own sense of righteousness before God. Being right with God is no guarantee for living righteously in the world and no excuse for ignoring injustice. A biblical commitment to justice must also account for Jesus, the norm for Christian moral reflection and practice. Why care about justice? Because Jesus did.[46]

So what *did* Jesus do? Jesus's first public pronouncement clearly indicated for whom the gospel would be good news (Luke 4:14–30), a proclamation that elevated the threat to the security of his hearers. This gospel of Christ was good news for the poor, the prisoners, the physical outcasts, and the oppressed. No wonder his hearers *in the religious gathering* responded with outrage and fury. Perhaps they had anticipated a sermon that was "for them," one that would ease their guilt and make them feel better about their own particular problems and perspectives. Jesus did not deliver for *them* but for *others*. Much of Jesus's Sermon on the Mount (Matthew 5–7) was targeted to the religiosity of religious people who were far more concerned with *being* right about matters of theological and legal intricacies than with living righteously. Jesus called for a righteousness that surpassed and exceeded that of the Pharisees and teachers of the law, who were charged with making sure people "got it right" at the expense of the higher and more demanding requirements of the new law of Christ (Matt. 5:17–20). The Sermon on the Mount is steeped in Jesus's concern about the demands of kingdom living for Christian disciples that *exceeds* and *surpasses* right religiosity and misdirected personal pietistic practices. The vision of the kingdom of God *exceeds* and *surpasses* our common and accepted understandings of what it means to be "spiritual" and "right with God." It is a life characterized by attention to the poor, acts of mercy and forgiveness, peacemaking, truth telling, love for enemies, and generosity. This *is* what Jesus did. The implications for us may be obvious. These are indispensable virtues for a Christian account of justice because they are virtues necessary for realizing, albeit incompletely, the desired shalom of God. These virtues are marks of the

---

46. See Daniel J. Harrington, S.J., and James F. Keenan, S.J., *Jesus and Virtue Ethics: Building Bridges between New Testament Studies and Moral Theology* (Lanham, MD: Rowman and Littlefield, 2002).

righteousness of God expressed in our lives consonant with our commitment to the ways of Christ.

The witness of Christ was not a benign social witness, concerned with "just" spiritual matters. Jesus's mission was not "just" saving individual souls. Jesus's mission and ministry were far greater in scope and purpose. He was the means for the re-creation of shalom that surpasses and exceeds the sole concern with the status of individual souls getting right with God. Belief in and loyalty to Christ had enormous political and social implications for his followers.[47] Tax collectors ought not to continue in the hegemonic and oppressive practice of collecting taxes (Luke 19:1–10). Jesus shattered the social isolation of people with diseases and pathologies that placed them dangerously outside the margins of protection of their communities by inviting them back in (Mark 1:40–42, Luke 8:26–39, 14:15–24). Jesus healed some who were physically sick and tormented, making it possible for them to live with the shortcomings and frailties of human bodies (Luke 4:38–44). Jesus was concerned with just economic practices and the distribution of resources according to needs and not wants. Jesus limited the totalitarian demands of political leaders for unquestioned allegiance and loyalty (Mark 12:13–17). Jesus elevated women to their rightful place as human beings, capable of hearing God and responding with faithfulness and conviction to the call of God (Luke 7:36–50, 10:38–41).

Jesus also participated in practices we might call spiritual disciplines. Jesus prayed, fasted, went to religious gatherings, tithed, sought silence, and studied his scripture. However, there is no indication in scripture that these practices were privileged by Jesus as "better" or deemed to be more important or prior to his own social witness of justice and righteousness. They were all part of the life of Christ, demonstrating to us the totality of his life as a life that pleases God and one who is busy doing God's will in the world. Moral reflection on the implications of the life of Jesus and our own transformation into his image as the process of spiritual formation bring together our relationships with Christ and our commitments to a "spirituality of justice." Since virtues are learned and practiced, by the grace of God and the work of the Holy Spirit, these virtues work on us as we exercise them, shaping and transforming us into the image of Christ. We acquire the virtues of the Christian life as we practice generosity, mercy, compassion, peace making, and various components of doing justice and

47. See John Howard Yoder, *The Politics of Jesus*, 2nd ed. (Grand Rapids: Eerdmans, 1994).

making things right. We practice these virtues because we desire to follow Christ and be transformed into his image to realize our best selves, selves that are pleased to do the will of God who has created and is recreating shalom. Spiritual formation is moral formation. We cannot be satisfied and smug in "being right with God" without a robust concern and commitment to shalom creating justice and righteousness. Transformation into the image of Christ assumes and demands the transformation of our moral sensibilities and ethical commitments into those of Christ's. Following Jesus means following Jesus in all areas of our lives.

Justice as Social Spirituality and Witness

What might be some of the implications and applications of these insights for evangelical ethical practices? We might be reminded of John Wesley's famous dictum that there is "no personal holiness without social holiness." A right relationship with God inspires and motivates service to others out of love, compassion, mercy, generosity, and justice. Justice is not an addendum to our Christian commitment. It should be part of our own *pathos* as recipients of the just and loving *pathos* of God, expressed in our commitment to "go and do likewise."

Justice is our witness to the goodness, grace, and righteousness of God. I often hear in seminary classes and evangelical church groups that ministries of service and social justice are just a *means* of evangelism. In other words, we do them with the hope of having an opportunity to share the gospel, which usually means giving a verbal account of a message of salvation. When pressed to explain how this differs from mental manipulation and ulterior and hidden motives, answers are often quickly given that the gospel is ultimately concerned with one's spiritual needs and the state of one's soul before God so that the ends will justify these kind of means. The inference is that one's material and physical life is secondary to God and therefore less important for our concerns. I clearly beg to differ based on the scriptural accounts of our holistic creation in God's image, the prophetic material, and the life of Christ. Justice *is* a crucial aspect of our social witness. To do justice is to do the gospel in the name and spirit of Jesus Christ.

Justice is essentially relational as opposed to ideological, and justice is ultimately concerned with others as opposed to getting what we see as our due based on our puny conceptions of our rights. As Joseph Kotva reminds us,

Biblical justice is preoccupied with the needs of those who are poor, weak, disadvantaged, or oppressed (e.g., Deut. 24:17; Ps. 10:17–18; Isa. 10:1–2; Jer. 5:28; Luke 4:18–19). Biblical justice is less concerned with individual merit or excellence than with individual powerlessness and need. It is focused on aiding those in distress, not calculating desert. It is more interested in protecting the powerless and enabling everyone to contribute than in identifying what some already contribute. In a biblical context, need and powerlessness are the most basic criteria for the distribution of benefits. It is only after this priority is met that ability and desert become criteria for justice.[48]

A biblical portrait of justice reminds us that justice is first and foremost about "God's stake in history" and focused on others, not ourselves. In my context, discussions on justice typically center on the rights of evangelical Christians, who often perceive themselves as a beleaguered minority group in the United States whose rights are being eroded and taken away by ubiquitous secular humanists. Concerns for justice in evangelical ethics tend to revolve around the exercise of faith in public arenas by focusing on such things as prayer in schools, the teaching of intelligent design, and the promotion of evangelical faith as the dominant religious expression in the public sphere. I find these assumptions odd and even dangerous when I read the Book of Acts and am reminded of the position of the early church on the margins of the Roman Empire, which should temper our enthusiasm to demand too much from "Rome." Perhaps we need to trust and obey our scriptures that alert us to the dangers of the collusion between political and religious power, which essentially undermines the need to trust God.

This skewed sense of justice may also take on forms such as the ready acceptance of capital punishment as just retribution for heinous wrongdoing, justifications for war, tax breaks that distribute more benefits to the privileged, and cuts in social services for those who are blamed for all sorts of social problems. Justice is seen as reward for those worthy of reward and punishment for those unworthy of such rewards. This seems to me a misplaced and ill-defined notion of justice from a Christian perspective. I hope it is clear that by justice I do not mean the fight for what is perceived to be the diminishing rights of evangelical Christians with our racial and class interests to be a dominant faith expression in the United States. What I mean by justice are relationships and actions characterized by the prophetic impulse of the people of God whose commitment to justice flows directly from the heart of God, in and through the heart of God's people

48. Kotva, *Christian Case for Virtue Ethics*, 148–49.

to others in a world racked by violence, injustice, and sin on a multitude of levels, in desperate need of creative and recreating shalom. Being right with God is not enough. It is justice, mercy, and righteousness that God expects from those who claim to know the God of shalom.

Conclusion

I hope that I have not caricatured evangelical pietistic practices as unimportant or irrelevant for Christian morality and ethics, or evangelicals as uninterested in issues of social justice. What I detect, however, as illustrated in the opening paragraph, is a tendency to separate one's sense of spirituality from one's concrete actions in the world. There is safety and security in assuming that "being right with God" is equivalent to all that God requires in terms of righteousness and justice, and is some sort of guarantee that we will act accordingly in the world. The tendency is to privilege the spiritual over the material and to separate spirituality from morality. I appreciate the importance and necessity of practices such as prayer, meditation, fasting, contemplation, and solitude. They are vital practices that shape our faith and are necessary for spiritual formation. If they are directed toward formation into the image of Christ, the moral implications of spiritual formation may seem apparent. We cannot be conformed into the image of Christ and ignore the moral and ethical concerns of Jesus. Spiritual practices take us beyond ourselves, to a vital, growing relationship with Christ. Yet might they also take us beyond ourselves to a greater awareness of our world and the necessity for a "politics of spirituality" that takes seriously the need for justice as a cardinal Christian virtue *and* spiritual act on behalf of others as an indication of a right relationship with God?

I was touched and impacted by the vibrant prayer life of the friend I described in the opening paragraph. She was an example to those of us consumed with performance and doing well in our studies and on exams who may have been tempted to see these practices as separate from our Christian commitments. She is a reminder to me of the necessity of prayer and other pietistic practices that keep our world before God and our concerns voiced in prayer. Yet ethics also implies the risk of acting with uncertainty as to outcomes and possibilities. The necessity and risk of acting is also a spiritual performance, since it ultimately requires faith and the need to trust in the righteousness and goodness of God whose stake in the world is still just and reconciling shalom.

5

Reviving Evangelical Ethics

Moral Conscience, Community, and Competency

Christian moral reflection is a demanding and important responsibility for the church. The stakes are high. It requires more from us than just duty, just results, and just personal piety. While I am not jettisoning such important concepts as duty, ends, and virtues from our moral discourse, I have attempted to raise questions about the ways these criteria as I have presented them converge and diverge with the claims and concerns of Christian ethics. My particular focus has been on the ways in which deontology, teleology, and virtue have been appropriated and how they function in evangelical ethical practices to the detriment of a more engaged, dynamic, and robust perspective on Christian morality, its sources and practices.

Deontology, or duty, is an important criterion for articulating the nature of our responsibilities and commitments to others. Discerning what we ought to do is a crucial task for bringing our moral claims to bear on complex issues for the hope of transformation. Using Kant's categorical imperative as a foil, I demonstrated the limitations of the duty to obey a categorical imperative in Christian moral reflection. To collapse an understanding of duty into obedience is to ignore the complexity of our obligations, their contexts and reasons why we carry them out. I argued that when the duty to obey functions as a sole moral norm in evangelical ethical reflection, particularly when applied to the use of scripture as a source in our deliberations, we run the danger of missing the rich and continual ways scripture feeds our moral imaginations and informs our ethical deliberations. My hope and aim are to present greater possibilities for our appreciation and use of the Bible in evangelical ethics that is, in practice, actually far more attentive to and serious about the ways scripture can be used as a source in moral formation and Christian ethics.

Teleology, which places the moral weight on the consequences and outcomes of decisions, is also an important consideration for moral reflection. We ought to be concerned about the impact our actions and decisions have on others, what goods they may produce, and what harms they may avert or minimize. I raised the concern, using John Stuart Mill's work in *Utilitarianism*, that a focus on the ends can both be imprecise, perhaps intentionally so, in its understanding of happiness, and can quickly succumb to our pragmatic proclivities to value what works and what produces the results we desire as an indication of moral rightness. When this happens, means can be divorced from ends, so that we might claim justification for what we do, no matter how troubling it may be, because of the desired ends that are achieved. I find this pragmatic utilitarianism disquieting in evangelical practices related to church growth and Christian discipleship; it robs Christian morality of its key foundations in the ways of Christ, the kingdom of God, the church, and a holistic understanding of salvation. My desire is to value the necessity and role of a community who sees and performs the ways of Jesus and the vision of the kingdom of God as key features of Christian ethics.

Virtue ethics concentrates on the relationship between one's character and the moral quality of one's behavior as a product of one's character. Aristotle has offered important concepts for understanding the development of virtue through habits, practices, friendships, and a larger purpose embedded in a community's history and narrative as the primary means for achieving a life of well-being. There is much in Christian ethics that resonates with virtue, indicated by Christian ethicists' renewed interest in virtue as an important component of morality. On the flip side, virtue ethics can be easily subverted by the ideologies and narratives of individualism and the therapeutic, which have influenced American evangelicalism in significant ways. The practices that cause me concern are the emphasis on personal piety and spiritual formation as a means of therapeutic self-fulfillment. The results are a privileging of the well-being of oneself at the expense of others and the separation of moral and spiritual formation to the detriment of a Christian commitment to the virtue of justice as a primary expression of the righteousness and goodness of God.

I promised in the introduction that this work would be critical yet reconstructive in my attempt to address the questions I have raised about what *really* shapes evangelical ethical practices. I ended each chapter by tipping my hat on where I might be going in some of my proposals. The endings of chapters 2, 3, and 4 were brief and a bit frayed, so it is now time to more fully elaborate on the dynamics of moral formation in an evangelical context related to scripture, Christian community, and the development and practice of Christian virtues. This is my main objective for this chapter. I explore three dimensions of morality I see as vital for a more vigorous appreciation of the ethical life in an evangelical context. These are the development of conscience, the role of Christian community, and the actual practicing of moral reflection and ethical deliberation as a means for becoming an ethically competent thinker and practitioner. I perceive these as neglected and deficient areas in evangelical ethical thought and practice. Using the insights from previous chapters, I also discuss at various points how scripture, the vision of the kingdom of God, and the development of Christian virtue nourish and work together with conscience, Christian community, and the exercise of virtue in our various social contexts.

Developing Conscience

Moral development requires the formation and use of conscience. In Protestantism the language and role of conscience is not unusual yet perhaps not as developed or as rich as it is in Catholic moral theology.[1] Impressions of conscience have been influenced by certain Protestant proclivities and further by some evangelical ones. Martin Luther gave Protestantism an early and well-remembered dictum when asked to recant his growing protesting convictions on the nature of salvation, grace, scripture, and church authority. We remember well Luther's retort, "Here I stand, I can

1. See Sydney Callahan, *In Good Conscience: Reason and Emotion in Moral Decision Making* (New York: HarperOne, 1991); Walter Conn, *Christian Conversion: A Developmental Interpretation of Autonomy and Surrender* (Mahwah, NJ: Paulist Press, 1986); Russell B. Connors and Patrick T. McCormick, *Character, Choices and Community: The Three Faces of Christian Ethics* (Mahwah, NJ: Paulist Press, 1998); *Conscience*, Readings in Moral Theology, no. 14, edited by Charles E. Curran (Mahwah, NJ: Paulist Press, 2004); Richard Gula, *Moral Discernment* (Mahwah, NJ: Paulist Press, 1997); and Anne E. Patrick, *Liberating Conscience: Feminist Explorations in Catholic Moral Theology* (New York: Continuum, 1996).

do no other." This is often interpreted as an act of conscience, a standing for what one thinks is right against popular opinion. Luther acted on what he believed was right, which put him at odds with church authority. Conscience therefore may be seen in this Protestant expression as standing against authority and standing for one's own personal convictions about matters of right and wrong as a lone voice crying in the wilderness.

Our Protestant legacy has also left us with a high view of sin. Total depravity in Calvinistic thought, and redacted in all sorts of interpretations and uses of Calvin, has left many Protestants with an understanding of total depravity as the normative condition of every human being. Total depravity is often interpreted as the utter moral bankruptcy of each person, and the complete inability of anyone to do what is right or to seek goodness. I read Calvin's original thought on total depravity as meaning the totality of the created order, and all facets of our personhood have been impacted by sin even though humans retain and express, albeit imperfectly and sporadically, the *imago Dei,* a moral conscience, and the "light of reason."[2] However, an appropriation of Calvinist thought by evangelicals continues to elevate sin, which means that much of ethical thought and action focuses on how to ameliorate sinful conditions by keeping things from getting worse or settling for the "best we can do this side of heaven." The implications for how one views the presence and possibility of a moral conscience may be obvious. Either there is not one, or it is bad and bankrupt due to sin and irrelevant for moral reflection, since the human conscience ultimately cannot be trusted.

This legacy of Luther and Calvin on our impressions of conscience results in what Charles Curran identifies as an emphasis on "consequent conscience" in Protestant interpretations of Pauline thought.[3] The consequent or judicial conscience is that which kicks in after the fact and judges our actions after we have performed them. It functions to assess and mete out consequences of bad behavior and decisions *after* they have been done or made. It is what reminds us we are guilty, sinful, and wrong in what we have done. Since there is little or no expectation of a moral conscience and good moral behavior from totally depraved sinners, "this negative consequent conscience fits the classical Protestant notion of salvation coming

2. See John Calvin, *The Institutes of the Christian Religion,* translated by Henry Beveridge (Grand Rapids: Eerdmans, 1989), book II, chapter I, sections 4–9, and book II, chapter II, sections 13–26.

3. Charles Curran, "Conscience in Light of the Catholic Moral Tradition," in *Conscience,* Readings in Moral Theology, no. 14, edited by Charles E. Curran (Mahwah, NJ: Paulist Press, 2004), 6.

to the sinner who is conscious of sin and in need of a saving God."[4] The consequent conscience serves to remind us how really bad we are.

I see three additional tendencies in evangelicalism in particular that make difficult a more positive assessment of conscience and its necessity in moral formation and ethical deliberation. They are the fear of subjectivity, the desire for simplicity, and the penchant to spiritualize ethical issues. Part of the evangelical response to theological liberalism in the modernist/fundamentalist controversy of the early twentieth century was the distrust of personal experience as an authenticator of truth, with its threat to erode objectivity. Since then, objectivity of truth and the inability of human subjectivity and knowledge to ascertain truth have been at odds, pitted in a battle one against the other. Human subjectivity cannot be trusted. It is tainted by sin, fraught with weakness, blind, and desirous of its own ways, spurring objective truth at every turn. Even though evangelicalism is packed with the appreciation and applauding of personal, subjective religious experience, notably in such things as testimonies, personal conversion stories, direct encounters with God, and worship experiences, the relationship between objectivity and subjectivity remains contested and confusing for many evangelicals who place them at polar extremes. This has an effect on our appreciation and use of conscience, which is a subjective aspect of our personhood with all of the risks and dangers this implies. Yet, as I will later consider, our consciences are not left alone to develop. They need the sources of scripture, Christian community, and the virtue of practical wisdom to shape and direct them.

Not only our discomfort with subjectivity is a barrier to a fuller appreciation of the place that conscience has in Christian ethics; so is our desire for simplicity in moral matters. We are often befuddled by the complexity of moral questions and yearn for the days when it appeared that right was right and wrong was wrong and everyone knew it. Christian ethics in an evangelical context gravitates toward simplicity in analysis of ethical issues, assigning much blame to personal problems that can be solved spiritually as opposed to engaging in social analysis to ascertain the various and layered root causes in need of attention. Many of us have been taught that the world's problems can be solved spiritually, by more people getting right with God, or theologically, by getting right information about God. In previous chapters I articulated the ways in which evangelical ethics appropriates the theories of deontology, teleology, and virtue

4. Ibid.

because they are an easy way to see morality as just duty, just results, or just personal piety. If people would just do these things, the world would be a better place.

In reality, moral reflection and ethical deliberation are far more complex and require thought and care in knowing how to bring our Christian commitments to bear in very complex moral spaces. This requires conscience and skills in ethical deliberation that enable us to assess the various dimensions of moral difficulties. Conscience requires more serious engagement with the richness and complexity of scripture, a stronger reliance on Christian community as a means for learning why and how to be moral, and the necessity of practical wisdom in becoming competent in the exercise of our Christian moral convictions. Moral reflection and ethical discernment require the development and use of a holistic conscience that, according to Curran, relies on reason, grace, emotions, and intuition, a conscience that is attentive to various moral demands, complexities, and possibilities. Curran writes:

> The holistic understanding of conscience proposed here recognizes the complexity and manifold aspects of decision making. As significant differences also exist with regard to the object of our decision making, the process of our decision making is somewhat different in different contexts. Judgments about a marriage partner, a vocation to be or do a certain thing, whether or not to move to another city or to take a difficult job, differ from judgments about whether the country should have an all-volunteer army or the feasibility of nuclear power plants. More personal decisions will obviously take into account the particularities of the person; decisions on social issues require a knowledge of all the data involved in community decisions and rely less on the particularity of the person. Thus, not all judgments of conscience proceed in the same way but are somewhat determined by the matter under consideration.[5]

What is a holistic conscience? How might evangelicals draw on conscience to expand our understanding of the rigor and demands of Christian morality that might work against the proclivities I suggested? I start with Sydney Callahan's definition of conscience in her book *In Good Conscience: Reason and Emotion in Moral Decision Making* and take some liberties to adjust this definition to address the particular contributions I seek to make to evangelical ethical practice.

Callahan defines conscience as "a personal, self-conscious activity, integrating reason, emotion, and will in self-committed decisions about right

5. Ibid., 18.

and wrong, good and evil."[6] Callahan goes on to characterize the personal dispositions and activities required for the formation of conscience. It is personal, holistic, and oriented to moral values and goodness and achieved by self-conscious, self-integrated, and self-committed action.[7] What is important to note about Callahan's insights is that conscience is not a static possession or an aspect of our humanity that is separate from the various forces that have influenced us. Conscience *is* formed, either for good or for ill. Conscience is that which is dynamic and able to be shaped, fashioned, and exercised. This is why Richard Gula identifies three dimensions of conscience, reflecting its malleable potentialities in being directed toward moral goodness. These dimensions are capacity as "our fundamental ability to discern good and evil," the process of discovery that commits us to investigate and evaluate sources of moral wisdom, and the necessary judgments we make in our choices as part of acting according to conscience.[8] In consideration of these three dimensions, Gula defines conscience as "the whole person's commitment to value and the judgment one makes in light of that commitment of who one ought to be and what one ought to do or not do."[9]

Conscience is the active integration and use of our abilities to assess moral issues with our passionate moral commitments that reflect the heart of God's justice with *practiced* determination to live and act according to our moral convictions. A conscience that is "personal, holistic and oriented to moral values and goodness" *can* be achieved, a point crucial to the very nature of conscience as an integral aspect of our moral agency as human beings. This begs the necessity for the formation of an "antecedent conscience," which Charles Curran describes as the capacities and sensitivities we need prior to an action to guide and direct our decisions *in order to* act according to the orientation that our moral values and sense of goodness give us.[10] In other words, conscience gives us a reservoir, a "built-up potential for a kind of act or activity,"[11] from which to draw to make judgments about what is right and good as we continually face ethical dilemmas. Conscience is a source that guides us before and during our decisions and behaviors and, in turn, continues to cultivate and

6. Sydney Callahan, *In Good Conscience*, 14.
7. Ibid., 14–17.
8. Richard M. Gula, "The Moral Conscience," in *Conscience*, Readings in Moral Theology, no. 14, edited by Charles E. Curran (Mahwah, NJ: Paulist Press, 2004), 52–53.
9. Ibid., 53.
10. Charles Curran, "Conscience in Light of the Catholic Moral Tradition," 6.
11. Callahan, *In Good Conscience*, 15.

shape our moral character, making us people of conscience. Conscience sometimes is judicial, creating in us a "gnawing feeling" that may come with decisions and actions, helping us to reflect on them, hoping to do better the next time. The point is that conscience is both necessary and shapeable, both antecedent and judicial.

Callahan's definition might appear to appeal to an understanding of conscience that is just personal and self-directed. At first glance this appears no different than a sense of conscience that demands that *I* stand alone for what is right and wrong according to what my *personal* conscience dictates. But this is not what Callahan has in mind. The corrective to this interpretation of conscience rests with the acknowledgment that, whether we acknowledge it or not, conscience is formed intentionally or unintentionally, since we are essentially social creatures. In reality, therefore, it is never my conscience acting alone. Gula reminds us that,

> The root meaning of the word "conscience" is "knowing together with." This meaning underscores that moral knowledge is social. Convictions of conscience are shaped, and moral obligations are learned, within the communities that influence us. While the judgment of conscience is always made *for* oneself (what I must do), it is never formed *by* oneself. No one can ever identify moral truth entirely on one's own. We are too limited by experience and knowledge, or almost blind from being accustomed to sin to recognize moral truth all by ourselves. So we must always take counsel before acting in conscience. That means that we ought to consult the established sources of wisdom.[12]

It is important for us to attend to the influences, "the established sources of wisdom," which can shape our consciences since moral knowledge, according to Gula, is inherently social. For Christian moral formation, it is essential to purposefully draw on sources that feed, shape, stretch, and inform our conscience in order for us to integrate reason, emotion, and will in self-committed decisions oriented toward moral goodness. Two of those sources to which I return for further exploration are scripture and Christian community.

How does scripture shape and form a holistic, integrated, and antecedent conscience? In chapter 2, I argued that we might be in danger of limiting scripture's role in moral formation if we collapse the Bible to a simple deontological perspective of obeying what appear to be straightforward commands. For a more constructive understanding and as a place simply to start, I suggest that scripture shapes our conscience by helping us to

12. Gula, "Moral Conscience," 54–55.

face reality, by orienting our moral vision, by providing us sources of moral wisdom, and by placing us in a community where the scriptures are learned and lived, where faith informs action, which I will explore later as a second vital source for Christian conscience.

First, scripture shapes our conscience by forcing us to face reality *if* the Bible is *actually* read.[13] The Bible is a raw book. It does not sanitize the human condition, the destructive tendencies of human communities, or the rampant evil of the world. The situations the scriptures describe are our situations. Ethical problems and moral issues are found on the pages of the Bible itself, as stories of rape, murder, sexual exploitation, abusive religious and political power, nationalistic war, racism, genocides, executions, tribal conflict, betrayals, and palace intrigue, to name just a few, are described in excruciating detail. These are our stories. We do not have to make this stuff up, because it is recounted for us, in our sacred history, in the pages of scripture. And we have seen these issues over and over again in human history. Scripture does not shield us from unpleasantness, neither does it give us permission to shirk our moral complicities in the intricacies and interdependencies of the human drama. In fact, it forces us to face the degrees of evil and moral bankruptcy by naming them, an important first step in the development of conscience as we see these are not "their" issues but ours. Scripture names and narrates what is evil and wrong and forces us to see it for what it is in our own lives and communities. In order for conscience to be formed and shaped, it first needs to be alerted, sensitized, and even outraged by the degrees of malevolence and immorality in our world. The scriptures describe our world, a world in desperate need of conscience-stricken and conscience-driven Christians who have the ethical sensitivities and sensibilities to evaluate and discern what is offensive to God, what is destructive to humanity, and what is *really* wrong.

Second, the scriptures form our moral consciences by shaping, inspiring, and orienting our moral vision. Thankfully, the scriptures do not portray the realities of our world as only wicked and hopeless, leaving us at this point of despair. We also have portrayals of the pockets

13. See James M. Gustafson, "Ways of Using Scripture," in *From Christ to the World: Introductory Readings in Christian Ethics,* edited by Wayne G. Boulton, Thomas D. Kennedy, and Allen Verhey (Grand Rapids: Eerdmans, 1994), 21–26. Gustafson's method for using scripture in ethics, particularly his understanding of scripture as "revealed reality" and "revealed morality," is more fully elaborated in "The Changing Use of the Bible in Christian Ethics," in *Readings in Moral Theology No. 4: The Use of Scripture in Moral Theology,* edited by Charles E. Curran and Richard A. McCormick (New York: Paulist Press, 1984).

and promises of redemption and hope. Christian ethics is not just about identifying what is wrong. It is more about moving toward what is good and right. Acknowledging what is wrong is only the first step in shaping moral conscience. We are able to name what is wrong because we have an understanding of what is right, or what should be, against which to make this kind of judgment. Scripture provides us with this kind of moral vision on a grand scale.

Richard Hays suggests we consider "three focal images" that synthesize the multivocal texts of scripture. These images or motifs enlarge our moral imaginations and point our consciences toward moral goodness. They are community, cross, and new creation.[14] The community God designed and desires is one that is an "alternative order that stands as a sign of God's redemptive purposes in the world."[15] This alternative community actually embodies the moral vision of "God's redemptive purposes" in our lives together. This focus on community is corrective for an understanding of conscience that is personal and private, circumscribed by my individual convictions of conscience, which may have nothing to do with God's redemptive purposes. The image of community helps us "when seeking God's will not by asking first, 'What should *I* do,' but 'What should *we* do?'"[16]

The second motif, according to Hays, is the cross. He writes, "The cross is the paradigm for faithfulness to God in this world."[17] He goes on to say that "our actions are therefore to be judged not by their calculable efficacy in producing results but by their correspondence to Jesus' example."[18] This vision of what is good according to the cross stands in sharp contrast to the vision of pragmatic utilitarianism that measures moral goodness based on outcomes. The cross of Christ returns us to the centrality of Jesus and the totality of his life for Christian ethics and the development of a Christian conscience as we are transformed by the Spirit into his image. Christian ethics is about faithfulness and following the ways of Christ and the ultimate expression of his love for others, including enemies.

Finally, Hays reminds us that we are moving toward the "new creation," an image that fosters hope, courage, and faithfulness in this "not-yet-redeemed world,"[19] virtues that are crucial for the self-conscious, inte-

14. Richard B. Hays, *The Moral Vision of the New Testament: A Contemporary Introduction to New Testament Ethics* (New York: HarperCollins, 1996), 196–98.
15. Ibid., 196.
16. Ibid., 197.
17. Ibid.
18. Ibid.
19. Ibid., 198.

grative nature of conscience that enables us to act accordingly. Scripture, with the motifs Hays suggests, therefore orients our moral vision so that we are not just smugly satisfied with identifying what is wrong, especially when focused on everyone else but us. Instead, scripture provides us with the knowledge of what should be in light of God's creative and recreating shalom.

Scripture is a source for inspiring moral vision and for shaping antecedent conscience, which can direct and guide our actions toward what is good, who *we* ought to be in light of this, and what *we* ought to do as a result. It does this by engaging reason, emotion, and will as we enter and engage with the varied and rich texts of scripture. Scripture's role in helping us to face reality and fostering moral vision therefore requires that we become "wise readers of Scripture,"[20] attuned to the various ways in which scripture reveals reality and vision to readers committed to *actually* reading the Bible. Skills in wise and attentive scripture reading beg the need for time, a commitment to keep coming back to it, and a growing comfort with its complexities and its discomforting language and pictures of reality. For evangelicals in particular, this may necessitate that we fight the tendency to find the "one size fits all" method of interpretation and application, may challenge our use of the Bible as just a personal book for private devotion, and may reveal the limitations and dangers of our overly simplistic use of the Bible in ethics. Hays cautions Bible readers about our tendencies to squeeze scripture—in particular, focus on the New Testament—into one mode of thinking and use by reminding us that "we should guard against falling into a habit of reading New Testament ethical texts in one mode only . . . we must be wary of attempts to use one mode of appeal to Scripture to override the witness of the New Testament in another mode."[21] I explored how deontology might be one mode of reading scripture that compresses its messages through the lens of "just obeying rules," ignoring the far richer ways in which scripture shapes our moral conscience. The scriptures do contain deontological material that is important for ethics. However, the scriptures also contain large chunks of narrative material and other genres that are important for the formation

20. Stephen E. Fowl and L. Gregory Jones, *Reading in Communion: Scripture and Ethics in Christian Life* (Grand Rapids: Eerdmans, 1991, reprinted by Wipf and Stock, 1998). See chapter 2, "Reading in the Communion of Disciples: Learning to Become Wise Readers of Scripture." See also L. Gregory Jones, "Formed and Transformed by Scripture: Character, Community, and Authority in Biblical Interpretation," in *Character and Scripture: Moral Formation, Community, and Biblical Interpretation,* edited by William P. Brown (Grand Rapids: Eerdmans, 2002).
21. Hays, *Moral Vision of the New Testament,* 204.

of conscience along with rules and prescriptions. We need to learn to *read* these various genres for what they are and for the ways they nurture our conscience by helping us face reality, by orienting our moral vision, and by providing sources of moral wisdom, the third way in which scripture shapes our conscience.

Third, scripture is a source of moral wisdom. In the introduction, I described various facets of evangelical identity and practice. Evangelicals have a high commitment to scripture. Much of evangelical identity is formed around an appreciation for the authority of scripture as a means for understanding the self-revealing God. I surmise, however, that much of evangelical Bible reading is geared toward the accumulation of knowledge about the Bible, taking in the data of scripture through such things as memorization, participation in inductive study methods, and expository sermons. These are essential practices. Yet we read scripture not just to amass more knowledge about "facts" but to nourish our moral capacities to act as our knowledge may direct us. Knowledge is the accumulation of information about certain things. Wisdom is the ability to apply and use our knowledge in morally compelling and transformative ways. This is one of the reasons why wisdom is often identified as a virtue, whereas knowledge is not. Wisdom requires skill, discipline, and discernment, qualities I will discuss later.

I see the narrative nature of scripture as a morally compelling way to bridge knowledge and wisdom and to move beyond a style of reading that is concerned with the accumulation of Bible facts to one that enters into the actual stories of scripture for the purpose of interacting with the multiplicities of plots, characters, twists and turns, and moral lessons. The narratives of scriptures engage our reason, emotions, and will. We are puzzled by many of the stories, and they cause us to ask hard questions. We identify with many of the characters and are introduced to new ones. We become angry at the tragedies and laugh at the absurdities of our human drama. As Sydney Callahan notes, there's nothing like a good story to pique the curiosity and concerns of our conscience. Narratives heighten moral sensitivities and make ethical claims by the situations they describe. The persons acting in these narratives, both God and humans, provide for us sources of wisdom as they act in the dramas of scripture. Callahan writes:

> Stories created by the imagination and actual historical events move and shape our moral lives. . . . There is a "power of enhancement" and empathetic emotional engagement in a parable and story. Mind and heart, reason

and emotion are simultaneously stimulated to respond to a narrative. The moral images in a narrative are more emotionally compelling, more real, more vivid, more concrete and contextual than a set of abstracted principles and rules. Stories don't simply impart information; they demonstrate and recreate experience through imagery and forms. . . . Great spiritual masters of the past understood the power of narrative and created parables and teaching stories. As the listeners to a story become engaged and transported into the story, they become emotionally and empathetically hooked, only to suddenly find that the story demands a moral response from those who have ears to hear.[22]

The narrative dimensions of scripture call us to engagement with texts that contain situations and characters in many ways consonant with our own. We "see" reality played out in narratives. We "see" the ways in which humans respond in noble, good, and just ways as well as exploitative ways. We "see" the hand of God at play, and often sense God's invisible involvement in narratives, wondering what this means for human agency and responsibility. Narratives call us to discern what is really going on as the story plays itself out, to wonder whether the outcome might have been different if the characters involved had made different decisions or acted in alternative ways. We also detect the ways noble persons averted catastrophes by their courageous decisions and actions. These stories give us concrete examples for moral guidance and wisdom, for who we should (or should not) be and what we should (or should not) do, and the heavy implications of moral agency. Narratives take us beyond just knowing the details of the story to interpreting what they mean and how they are to inform the way we live by giving us an invaluable source of wisdom for the moral life.

How might this work in actual practice when reading scripture? The power of narrative reading struck me while wrestling with the hermeneutical difficulties of war in scripture as I was preparing for a class. I was also working through the Book of Genesis during this time, reading again the stories that I thought were so familiar—at least until I hit Genesis 33. The story of Genesis 33 recounts the impending meeting between Jacob and Esau for the first time since Jacob cheated Esau out of his birthright. I had been taught that Jacob's behavior, while bad, was justifiable, since it was through Jacob, whose name became Israel, that God's purposes would be fulfilled, thereby justifying the means for securing the birthright. In the previous section (Gen. 32:22–32), Jacob had "wrestled with God" where he met God face to face, did not die as a result, had his name changed to Israel, and left

22. Callahan, *In Good Conscience,* 206–7.

limping. I learned that this text was about the private wrestlings with God that we would all experience at some point in life. However, in the narrative context this confrontation with God is followed by a confrontation with Esau, where Jacob's life was again spared by the one he had offended and wronged. Jacob prepares to meet Esau, expecting, I assume, some degree of retaliation evidenced by lining up his family in order of importance and by his readiness to offer gifts as recompense to Esau. Esau's response is startling, given the context, the wrong done, and the understandable desire to demand back what was lost. Esau is the one who runs to Jacob and offers the first embrace (33:4), refusing to accept the penitential offerings that Jacob had assumed would be due him, with the response, "I already have plenty, my brother. Keep what you have for yourself" (33:9). Jacob's response is equally startling. In Esau's embrace, the estranged brother and possible enemy, Jacob again sees the face of God and lives (33:10).

Some of us can relate to Jacob, most of us can understand Esau's position, and more than a few of us can relate to the various family members of the narrative who are also part of this story and who are ranked in order of their importance to someone else. But in this narrative all of us witness the surprising power of forgiveness when offered by the one offended. This narrative gives us an alternative different from what we had expected, and what we would have surely been able to justify. We suspect the story may have been different if Jacob had not wrestled with God and left limping, or if Esau had not been content with what he had, recognizing it as plenty. We know the story would have been different if Esau sought his rightful due and took revenge, killing others first to get to Jacob. Thankfully, this narrative surprises us and takes us beyond what we expect to what might be possible in our various circumstances that are similar to the one described for us in our sacred scriptures. It allows the possibility for us to act like Esau and Jacob, in the complexities of our situations, by offering forgiveness and seeking it. This narrative, along with many others in scripture, places us in the story where we are confronted with who we are, with our choices, with the quality and shape of our relationships with God and with others, and with alternative ways of seeing the world.

In *Formation of the Moral Self*, Johannes van der Ven identifies narrative as a crucial aspect for character formation, the last element following moral salience, moral passions, reasons and goods, and virtues.[23] It is possible to

23. Johannes A. van der Ven, *Formation of the Moral Self,* (Grand Rapids: Eerdmans, 1998), 379–86. Van der Ven's book is a rich exploration of the dynamics of moral formation, utilizing the insights of Paul Ricoeur's work in narrative.

surmise from Van der Ven's work that moral salience, passions, and virtues cannot be formed without a narrative context, since it is through narratives that these aspects of character are formed. Moral salience requires that we recognize the complexity and contingency of situations, because it is "important to be aware that the situation one is in requires action or refraining from action, and the nature of that action or nonaction must be decided by reading all relevant aspects of the situation."[24] The integration of passions, reason, and goods, integral to Callahan's definition of conscience, is identified by Van der Ven as also crucial. Moral formation involves formation of passions and reason directed toward the good since "this complementarity between passions and reasons should play a key role in character formation, because together they form an anthropologically sound infrastructure for the good life."[25] As for virtues, they must be modeled and practiced in order for us to learn them. And for this, we need examples and models of virtuous persons who can help us. Narrative, as the "final condition for character formation,"[26] helps us develop the wisdom needed to recognize the "complexity and contingencies" of situations. About the relationship between narrative and character Van der Ven writes:

> Storytelling is important because it offers the possibility of participating in the life, words and deeds of the great characters whom the story embodies. Storytelling functions as a kind of modeling, as described by cognitive-social learning theory, by offering an example with which the listeners or readers can identify. This modeling is not static but dynamic, in that it presents complex situations that characters move through. It carries the audience through the contingencies of time by inviting them into its side-shadowing of possible futures, showing them the responsibilities each of these futures entails for them, and confronting them with the choices to be made in the here and now. It makes them see how chance can be taken as challenge, probability understood as opportunity, and fate transformed into destiny.[27]

Narrative portrays the dangers of emotions and zeal unleashed from reason, and the sterility and control of human reason without passion. Narratives direct us toward a picture of the "good" and its possibilities when reason and emotions are directed to moral goodness and value. Narratives teach us virtue. They provide characters who also respond to the

24. Ibid., 380.
25. Ibid., 382.
26. Ibid., 384.
27. Ibid.

"complexities and contingencies" of various situations, characters who do good, characters who convert and repent when they do not, characters who surprise us, characters also engaged in the task of working toward, or thwarting, God's good purposes. Narratives teach us *how* to live and, in doing so, offer us a great source for moral wisdom indispensable for the formation of conscience. The narratives of scripture do not just give us information. They *show* us the various ways and possibilities of living the moral way through their own complexities that force us to return to them again and again, searching them to understand *who* we are to be and *how* we ought to live. The scriptures are an indispensable source of moral wisdom that fills the reservoir of our conscience by guiding and directing us through the "complexities and contingencies" of various situations described in narratives that are essentially our own.

The scriptures provide us with three starting points for shaping our moral conscience: the capacity to identify and discern what is wrong, moral vision that orients toward God as the source of moral goodness that drives our motivation and impetus to do what is right, and sources of moral wisdom through the rich genre of narrative. Conscience also requires a community of learning, since morality is inherently social. In other words, a scripture-shaped conscience requires a community where the scriptures are taught, lived, and practiced. Location in a Christian community is a second important source for shaping a Christian conscience as an integral part of moral formation.

Christian Community and Conscience

In chapter 3, I presented the dangers that pragmatic utilitarianism poses to Christian discipleship and ecclesiology. The church is the place where the narratives of scripture are taught, lived out, and practiced. If this is a necessary commitment crucial to the formation of conscious, then it matters which story or narrative informs and shapes the faith and practices of the church. This reexamination of narrative is what Stanley Hauerwas calls for in his book, *A Community of Character: Toward a Constructive Christian Social Ethic*.[28] In particular, his essay "The Church and Liberal Democracy: The Moral Limits of a Secular Polity" is critical of both liberal and conservative churches for the ways we have imbibed and accepted the values and ideologies of liberal democracy as the narrative

---

28. Stanley Hauerwas, *A Community of Character: Toward a Constructive Christian Social Ethic* (Notre Dame, IN: University of Notre Dame Press, 1981).

framework by which we interpret the value and purpose of Christian ethics.[29] He writes:

> Ironically, the most coercive aspect of the liberal account of the world is that we are free to make up our own story. The story that liberalism teaches us is that we have no story, and as a result we fail to notice how deeply that story determines our lives. Accordingly, we fail to recognize the coercive form of the liberal state, as it, like all states, finally claims our loyalty under the self-deceptive slogan that in a democracy the people rule themselves because they have "consented" to be so ruled. But a people who have learned the strenuous lesson of God's lordship through Jesus's cross should recognize that "the people" are no less tyrannical than kings or dictators.[30]

I have suggested that when evangelical Christians ignore or fail to recognize the centrality and ways of Christ and the vision of the kingdom of God as normative for Christian ethics, we default to the classic theories of deontology, teleology, and virtue, covering them with just enough of a veneer to make them look compatible with moral claims rooted in Christian faith and life in spite of the large divergences of these stories. The classic theories have much in common with the ideologies and values of liberal democracy that we have absorbed and accepted as ultimate goods. People are believed to be free to pursue their own definition of happiness because of the belief that our humanity is defined by autonomy, self-governance, and liberty from traditions and narratives not of our own choosing. The church and the traditions of the Christian faith become irrelevant to our moral bearings, and salvation is shrunk to one's personal decision to accept Christ and be saved from sin. Because duty to rules and laws becomes paradigmatic for the moral life, an inordinate amount of attention is focused on changing the laws of society, with little regard for the moral character and actual witness of the church in society when addressing issues of social justice. Our unwillingness to challenge the assumptions and ideologies of liberal democracy may erode the conception of the church as a community that embodies the story of Christ.

When evangelical Christians fail to take account of our primary loyalty to Jesus and his kingdom, the informing narrative, whether we realize it or not, becomes the patriotic story of the liberal democracy called the United

---

29. Hauerwas has Niebuhrian Christian Realism in mind in his critique. Even though the characterization of churches as either "liberal" or "conservative" is a bit broad and too general for my liking, I appreciate Hauerwas's critique, given that much of evangelicalism defines issues according to the broad categories of "liberal" and "conservative."

30. Hauerwas, *Community of Character,* 84.

States. This narrative is accepted and "taught" in a myriad of ways that I find limiting for our ability to fashion and form a conscience attuned to the realities and moral vision described in scripture, one that looks to scripture and Christian community for moral wisdom in assessing what is *really* at stake. For example, what does the presence of American flags in church sanctuaries communicate about our understandings of nation and church? The flag is a powerful symbol that evokes strong feelings and memories and opinions about nation, and it has its own narratives. Are these remembrances more important than our memory of how Christ's story has changed our story? I find it troubling that we pray—a practice that rehearses narrative—for God's protection of our military personnel, a practice not bad, but one that is questionable when we ignore the plight of innocent victims of violence and war who escape our petitions to God for protection, justice, and peace. I must confess that I sometimes get goosebumps when patriotic songs are sung as hymns of praise on various national holidays, celebrating the nation's narrative as blessed and set apart for God in spite of our actual history. Even as I participate in this practice, my conscience is troubled by the assumptions in the words being sung by Christians who claim ultimate loyalty to Christ and his kingdom as the counternarrative of our lives. This troubling causes me to rethink my actual participation in singing patriotic songs, especially in church.

How do these kinds of narratives affect conscience, and how can we reform our practices for the renewal and formation of conscience that is fed by scripture and the narratives of the church as a kingdom community? It matters not just that we preach but what we preach. It matters not just that we participate in communion, but whether or not our practices are actually communal reflections of the Triune God. It matters not just that we gather in small groups but that we actually assess the purposes of our life together in service to others, not ourselves. It matters not just that we worship but for what purpose and in what ways. It matters not just that we witness but what we witness about.

Not only do we look to scripture to help us face reality and to foster moral vision rooted in God and the ways of Christ, but we look to scripture and to others for sources of moral wisdom utilizing the narrative nature of scripture and the Christian community to stretch and shape our conscience. These help us to *learn,* to fill and replenish the fount of our moral conscience. The formation of conscience requires a place to deliberate, reflect, and practice our moral commitments. This is the third requirement for the formation of conscience, a place to learn practical wisdom as a necessary virtue or habit in Christian ethics.

Conscience and Practical Wisdom

Conscience is a vital feature of morality and ethics. While the aspiration to live according to conscience, to the values one professes and the virtues to which one aspires, may be simple, the application of our ethical commitments to complex and contested moral terrain requires skills. Not only do we need to know *what* we believe about the sources and requirements of our moral claims, but we also require assistance in knowing *how* to bring our moral claims into complex ethical situations for the purpose of transformation. We need practical wisdom in knowing how to live. Our consciences need to be exercised to develop the capacities and competencies in moral reflection and ethical deliberation necessary for practical wisdom.

What is practical wisdom? I return to Van der Ven's utilization of Paul Ricoeur in *Formation of the Moral Self*. Practical wisdom is the skill that enables moral deliberators to move from the abstract to concrete situations, or "wisdom-in-situation."[31] This "wisdom-in-situation," an expression Van der Ven borrows from Ricoeur, considers two dynamics present in moral deliberation. The first is "singularity," or "the uniqueness of the situation, and it means that general ideas or principles cannot be applied without qualification, because to do so would damage exactly those characteristics by which one situation would be distinguished from another."[32] In other words, ethical deliberation requires that we refrain from treating every and all situations as if they were the same and requires a method that duplicates itself in each situation. Not all situations are the same, and practical wisdom helps us to start the assessment by asking, "What is really going on *here*?"

The second dynamic under consideration is "contingency." Contingency is the recognition of the various actors and the open-ended nature of situations that allows for the possibility of change.[33] For Van der Ven, contingency is a "dialectical process" that brings "passivity and activity" together.[34] Situations are what they are both by human action and by chance. Ethics often means we find ourselves in situations not of our own choosing or creation. This does not mean, however, that we are left

---

31. Van der Ven, *Formation of the Moral Self*, 77. Van der Ven consistently uses *phronesis*, the Greek work translated as "practical wisdom." I refer to practical wisdom throughout this section for the purpose of simplicity and recognition.

32. Ibid., 77.

33. Ibid., 78.

34. Ibid.

without resources or will as actors in these situations. Contingency is the recognition that there are random elements in all ethical situations because we really do not know how things will turn out. This does not mean, though, that we are relieved of agency and responsibility in acting in certain ways. Contingency need not mean that we are paralyzed and left victim to unpredictable circumstances. Instead it begs the need for wisdom and discernment in knowing how to act in *this* situation consonant with the sources of our ethic and given the various possibilities and unknowns before us. Practical wisdom is the skill necessary to articulate and negotiate the dynamics of singularity and contingency in moral reflection and ethical deliberation. We need to assess not just *what* is going on. We also need to ask *how* we address situations and move forward consonant with the moral claims we are making.

Because practical wisdom is a skill, it has the potential of being learned and developed for competent use in Christian ethics. Practical wisdom is an indispensable part of transmitting moral education, according to Van der Ven.[35] By continuing to build on the insights of Ricoeur, Van der Van identifies three aspects of the development and exercise of practical wisdom. First, practical wisdom helps us find our way through complex moral mazes and plurality by helping us to "analyze the situation, select its relevant aspects, and then link them with the appropriate values and norms" or by ascertaining our structuring norms and then reasoning as to how they might work in singularity and contingency. This requires actively making moral judgments, something which if consistently and intentionally done shapes us as more and more competent in practical wisdom. Second, practical wisdom enables us to face the inevitable complexity and often tragic nature of moral reflection and ethical deliberation. Van der Ven is quick to clarify that this does not give us an excuse for moral paralysis or indifference. Instead, practical wisdom enables us to live with moral complexities, seeing these complexities as our own stories. He writes:

> At certain crucial moments we are called on to decide between life and death. At the beginning and at the end of life, for example, we make this choice for ourselves. Abortion for a daughter who has been raped, euthanasia for a mother who is in the terminal stage of a painful illness, and support for a sister who is going through deep depression because she has cancer, her marriage is ended, she has lost her job, and she wants to die: what should we do, how are we to act in these dramatic situations? Here principles, rules, and values such as respect for life and pity, integrity and authenticity,

35. See chapter 4 of *Formation of the Moral Self.*

creation and salvation, collide. Who dares to maintain the right answer? Who is not in doubt? Who is not making guesses and estimations? Who is not calculating consequences, unintended effects, or risks?[36]

While I affirm that moral reflection and ethical deliberation is directed toward the realization of what is good, I also realize that in our fallen world we are also often required to make the least awful choice out of a bunch of bad ones. We need practical wisdom to enter into ethical tragedies, and to live with complexity, because as Van der Ven reminds us, these are our stories, our daughters, sisters, parents, and friends. We are the ones asking, "What should we do?" Life is not as simple as we purport or desire it to be. We need practical wisdom, therefore, to live in complexity.

In this complexity, we need practical wisdom in order to make "considered convictions," the third aspect for the development and use of practical wisdom. When all is said and done, we must decide, we must act, we must "attest" to our convictions "after weighing all relevant aspects and carefully weighing the consequences,"[37] and be willing to live with the intended and unintended consequences of our decisions. According to Van der Ven, "considered conviction" is the result of a process of "argumentative communication,"[38] a process by which testing and deliberation with others has produced an "attestation" of our moral convictions in our exchanges with others.[39]

According to Van der Ven, practical wisdom is transmitted and is a necessary skill for negotiating the moral spaces of "singularity and contingency" and for moving us along in our potential to act according to "considered conviction." How is practical wisdom actually learned in dialogue with scripture and in Christian community? Why might evangelicals in our moral reflection and ethical deliberation need to pursue practical wisdom as an antidote to our desire for simplicity, our fear of subjectivity, and our spiritualizing tendencies of complex ethical issues?

The Formation of "Considered Conviction" in Christian Community

Johannes van der Ven equates conscience with "considered conviction." It is "considered" because it has been developed in and through sustained

36. Ibid., 171.
37. Ibid., 172.
38. Ibid. Van der Ven is putting Ricoeur and Jürgen Habermas in conversation in this section by noting how Ricoeur might dispute Habermas's conception of communicative ethics.
39. Ibid.

processes of thought, reflection, discovery, prayer, and dialogue. Van der Ven's insights again draw us to the acknowledgment of the social nature of morality and the necessity of tapping into sources for the formation and application of our "considered convictions." It is here that Allen Verhey finds the church indispensable for moral reflection and ethical deliberation. According to Verhey, the church ought to be a community of moral discourse, deliberation, and discernment.[40]

As a community of moral discourse, the church starts by actually *talking* about issues of moral importance. Verhey writes that the early Christians "talked together about what they should do or leave undone. When Christians met together in Rome—or in Corinth or Antioch or Jerusalem or elsewhere—they talked about the choices they faced. They asked each other—and instructed each other—about their personal and communal responsibilities."[41] The early church provided the pattern for us as a community of moral discourse, where issues and concerns are discussed in light of our faith commitments, a practice we ought to continue as essential for "remembering Jesus" and to save us from the dangers of an impartial or parochial perspective.[42]

To become a community of moral discourse, we must first start talking, not in sound bytes or easily digestible quips, but in sustained, intentional, and conscientious question asking and conversation. Moral discourse means that we ask, "*What* are the moral concerns here?" as a first crucial step in moral reflection. It requires the capacities to identify the various dimensions of moral issues and the will and courage to bring them out in the open. It means we acknowledge the limitations and parochialism of our particular perspectives by providing the space and respect for the points of view of others to be expressed, so that the various spectrums of concern may come out into the open. Becoming a community of moral discourse also involves fighting the fear of divisive issues or relegating certain concerns as peripheral to the Christian faith. A commitment to moral discourse may help address the temptations of reducing moral problems to "just" personal failures or finding "simple" spiritual solutions. If conscience as a "considered conviction" is to be developed, then it actually needs a considered process and a commitment to *talk* about the ethical implications of our faith commitments and the unavoidable urgency to understand our moral worlds.

40. Allen Verhey, *Remembering Jesus: Christian Community, Scripture and the Moral Life* (Grand Rapids: Eerdmans, 2002). See chapters 1 and 2.
41. Ibid., 16.
42. Ibid., 39–45.

Verhey also believes that the early church modeled what it means to be a community of moral deliberation.[43]

> They talked together not only about *what* they ought to do but also about *why* they ought to do it. They asked *why* they ought to do one thing rather than another or something rather than nothing. The concrete advice of moral discourse led inevitability in these communities to the giving and hearing of reasons. Their moral discourse was not simply the exercise of rhetorical or social power; it involved deliberation, reason giving, and reason hearing.[44]

This pattern continues and complements a commitment to actual discourse that asks "what should be done" and now in moral deliberation also "about *why* it should be done."[45] Moral deliberation requires reasoned arguments, not according to just duty, just what works, or just personal pietistic concerns. Moral deliberation takes place in light of our faith claims because "churches must also continue to test reasons by their coherence with the gospel, or defend or reject or qualify reasons by their congruity with the story of Christ."[46]

As evangelicals, we love to tell the story of Jesus. It is the foundational story of our own conversions and the impetus for our sense of mission characteristic of evangelistic activity and fervor. Yet I fear we have made the story of Jesus too familiar, too personalized, and too tame when it comes to moral deliberation. We have domesticated Jesus and made him into an action buddy. We have squeezed him into the mold of corporate life as "Jesus, CEO." We like the fact that he was "one of us," forgetting that in his humanity he was also totally different from us.[47] If Verhey is right, and moral deliberation is tested by "its congruity with the story of Christ," then it seems obvious that we must actually know the story of Christ and perhaps be reconverted by its enormous and powerful implications and, dare I say, for its "political" implications that have little to do with the power interests of American political parties. Moral deliberation takes place in light of the story of Jesus Christ, not the stories of autonomous rationality, utilitarian pragmatism, or expressive self-fulfillment. Conscience as "considered conviction" is formed when we deliberate

43. Ibid., 18.
44. Ibid.
45. Ibid., 38.
46. Ibid.
47. See Daniel Migliore, *Faith Seeking Understanding: Introduction to Christian Theology,* 2nd ed. (Grand Rapids: Eerdmans, 2004), 174–77.

together *in light of the gospel* and the kingdom of God, which challenges our assumptions, interprets us, and provides the framework for our faithful and reasoned moral deliberations.

Along with moral discourse and deliberation, the early church also provided us an example of a community of moral discernment.[48] Moral discernment aids in the development of practical wisdom, the perception to understand what it fitting in terms of attitudes and actions according to the gospel. While moral discourse starts with the important "what" of ethical reflection, complemented by the "why" of reasoned moral deliberation, moral discernment involves asking "how" we are to act "fitting to, or worthy of, *the gospel*."[49] Moral discernment, akin to practical wisdom, helps us to navigate through bumpy moral terrain, discriminating among competing claims and contingencies, positioning us for the time when we must act in ways that reflect the virtues and commitments of the gospel. Moral discernment relies on the insights of others, and often unexpected others. Whether we see discernment as a spiritual gift or as something we learn in the form of practical wisdom, it is clear that we *receive* wisdom first from sources outside of ourselves, as gifts. But crucial to this reception of wisdom is acting upon it in order to learn and grow in discernment and wisdom. We need others. We need space, time, and others for moral discourse, deliberation, and discernment if we are to develop the capacities necessary for moral reflection and ethical deliberation and to keep us from defaulting to just duty, just what works, and just personal piety.

Conclusion

I have suggested throughout this book that while deontology, teleology, and virtue are important criteria in ethics, they are not the same thing as Christian morality if we ascertain our moral obligations as just duty, just what works, and just personal piety. I have described the pitfalls of classic models of morality for evangelical ethics, whereby we miss the more formative aspects of Christian morality, particularly conscience and practical wisdom as vital ingredients of Christian moral formation. However, I also see great promise for evangelical ethics, because we value scripture, care about witness, and regularly participate in churches and small groups. We have the potential of becoming communities where discourse is valued,

48. Verhey, *Remembering Jesus*, 20.
49. Ibid.

deliberation is modeled, and discernment is shared. In conclusion of this chapter and in anticipation of the next, I must mention the importance of pastors for helping us avoid the pitfalls and for reviving evangelical ethics in promising ways.

In her book *The Pastor as Moral Guide*, Rebekah Miles identifies and explores the vital role that pastors have as moral guides of congregations.[50] Whether or not we like it or acknowledge it, pastors have enormous power and responsibility to shape the moral sensitivities and ethos of congregations and *actually do so* intentionally or unintentionally. I do not mean that pastors only have influence based on their own personal moral examples demonstrated and modeled in their own lives. Important as personal integrity and character are, pastors also have power to create environments of moral discourse, deliberation, and discernment as moral guides through the leadership they give and practices they encourage that heighten our moral sensibilities and ethical awareness. Miles writes:

> Moral guides not only respond in crisis but also train Christians before crises start. Moral guidance must begin long before a difficult ethical dilemma is confronted. Moral guidance must begin long before an accountant is asked to fudge the numbers in the company's books or before a Christian is confronted with racial slurs. Moral guidance begins in Christian communities, as we shape each other and hear stories of faith. It begins as we practice the values expressed in those stories and teach the ethical rules and goals of our traditions. Although moral guidance may find its more dramatic form in the hospital emergency room, it has its beginnings in the ordinary lessons of the Sunday school classroom and in the weekly experiences of worship. As we open ourselves to God's power in prayer and worship, we are transformed by grace. As we tell and practice the stories and virtues of our tradition, we are formed as moral persons.[51]

What are some of the practices evangelicals hold dear? It is to these practices that I turn in the conclusion by offering suggestions as to how practices of preaching, small groups, and service may be formed and re-formed for our churches to be the ethical communities of Jesus Christ.

---

50. Rebekah L. Miles, *The Pastor as Moral Guide* (Minneapolis: Fortress Press, 1999).
51. Ibid., 10–11.

Conclusion

Practices for Reviving Evangelical Ethics

Deontology, teleology, and virtue ethics are important components of moral reflection and ethical deliberation. They provide significant criteria and norms for thinking about the moral life and for giving due attention to the significance of duties, outcomes, and character. They give us some conceptual tools and help to clarify and define the types of consideration and attention necessary in ethics. Christian ethics does use and need the language of duty and obligation. It needs a conception of an end, the grand purpose and goal to which the moral life ultimately points and which it serves. Christian ethics would be pointless and even nonexistent if it weren't for the moral sensitivities, character, and capacities of humans who aspire to goodness and virtue, and who attempt to act accordingly.

I hope it has been clear throughout this book that I am not abandoning the importance of deontology, teleology, and virtue ethics in our moral discourse and consideration. I have tried to reclaim their importance and refocus them in the context of a Christian narrative so that we might take more seriously scripture, the church, and character formation in light of Christian ethics as actually Christian. Christian morality is more about who we are, what narrative we look to for our moral orientation, and how we enact these moral visions and commitments in practices as disciples of Jesus Christ as part of living out a Christian narrative. Christian morality is at the heart of what it means to be a follower of Jesus Christ, a product of the "saved life" and something that is learned and practiced as we engage with scripture, participate in Christian community, and acquire competencies in moral reflection through the formation and use of conscience and practical wisdom that are shaped and reshaped by these sources.

I end this book with some reflections and ideas about three practices evangelicals hold dear. They are preaching, small groups, and service. I want to look at these three areas as practices, "things which Christian people do together over time to address fundamental human needs in response to and in light of God's active presence for the life of the world."[1] I see our commitments to practices in preaching, small group gathering, and service as crucial for moral formation in an evangelical context and for the roles they might play in forming conscience and heightening our moral sensitivities and commitments. It's not just that we preach, gather in small groups, and serve in various areas. It matters what we preach, why we gather, and how and whom we serve.

Preaching

Evangelicals tend to be word-driven and word-centered. This is evident in the emphasis we place on preaching and teaching as central practices of the church. Pulpits are often at the center of our worship spaces. The sermon typically takes up a huge chunk of time in worship services, often placed at the end as an indication that "all roads" lead to the sermon. Its importance in worship services is hard to miss. Evangelicals purport to desire "biblically based" preaching, which means the content of sermons comes directly from the scriptures, even though sermons are themselves commentaries on the texts under investigation, often through the pastoral concerns and congregational needs of the present moment. Evangelical pastors are trained in our seminaries to attend to the text and to expository preaching that stays true to the passage under scrutiny on any given Sunday. We value the practice of preaching and fight to maintain its central place in evangelical identity and commitment.

Since we value such an important practice, how might we come to understand the morally forming dimensions of preaching, for how it can heighten our moral sensitivities and attune our consciences more to the ethical concerns of Christ?[2] First, preparation for preaching must be a practice that

1. See again Craig Dykstra and Dorothy Bass's definition of practices in *Practicing Theology: Beliefs and Practices in Christian Life,* edited by Miroslav Volf and Dorothy C. Bass (Grand Rapids: Eerdmans, 2002), 18.

2. See Marvin A. McMickle, *The Star Book on Preaching* (Valley Forge, PA: Judson Press, 2006), and *Where Have All the Prophets Gone? The Renewal of Prophetic Preaching in the American Pulpit* (Cleveland: Pilgrims Press, 2006). The Rev. Dr. McMickle is both colleague

takes seriously a continual engagement with scripture if pastors are to lead congregations in our sustained engagement with scripture as a source for moral reflection and ethical deliberation. After a theology-class discussion on scripture's authority in church life, a student asked me what I thought about topical preaching. I responded by identifying what I fear may be some unintended consequences of this practice. One might be the subtle message (or not so subtle) that we come to scripture just to find answers (on a fairly selective number of topics) for our pressing questions, a fairly reductive practice akin to the ways in which "just obedience" minimizes scripture's morally forming potential. While I do not mean to discount the necessity of this practice at certain times, I fear that it continues to reinforce that it's our concerns and questions that drive our use of scripture as opposed to allowing scripture to shape our concerns and questions in the first place. Since our questions are often related to the contexts in which we live and are constrained by our own experiences and epistemological frameworks, our questions will likely be narrow and miss the multitude of ethical and moral issues that are present *in the scriptures themselves.*

This may also have a second unintended consequence. It is the selective "cherry-picking" practice of which texts we tend to look to at the expense of the larger narrative dimensions of scripture so important for orienting our moral framework. If the scriptures are what provide the pictures of the *telos,* then it is to the entirety of scripture that we must attend in preaching, even the most difficult of passages and narratives that may take us where we do not want to go. This begs again the pastoral necessity of engaged, sustained, deliberate, and committed interaction with scripture on an ongoing basis.[3] If it is not important to us, then it will not be important for congregations. Congregants will model their use and reading of scripture on sermons. If our reading is shoddy, pithy, haphazard, and selective, so will theirs.[4]

Reading the Bible is hard work if we *actually* read it. Sermons are crucial for helping us develop a sustained practice of reading scripture in all of its complexity and richness. They do so by allowing us to linger

---

and friend at Ashland Theological Seminary as professor of homiletics. I am indebted to his insights and his own practices of an ethic of preaching, which have shaped my suggestions in this section. See also Charles Campbell, *The Word before the Powers: An Ethic of Preaching* (Louisville: Westminster/John Knox Press, 2002).

3. An acquaintance once commented to me that he had his sermon preparation time "down to one and one-half hours per week" as if this were a good thing.

4. See McMickle, *Star Book on Preaching,* chapter 2, "The Heart and Habits of the Preacher."

in texts for a prolonged period of time, by helping us "hang" with texts and keep coming back to them, asking questions, pondering meaning and attending to their various dimensions and layers. These skills are crucial for learning to read scripture, as well as for moral reflection and ethical deliberation. The ability to ask questions, the commitment to taking time and exploring angles, and the resistance to quick, tidy answers are competencies that can be developed through the practice of applying them to Bible reading. Sustained engagement with books of the Bible helps us resist the tendency to tame scripture and perhaps allows us to defend against the desire to have it all figured out by the end of the sermon. Scripture's own complexity may help us deal with the complexities of life.

Second, sermons can be a morally forming practice through the examples used in sermon illustrations. It is common to hear people talk more about the illustrations than about the actual content of a sermon. This is because sermon illustrations are used to make connections between biblical texts, messages, and the contexts of their hearers. They often resonate with one's personal experience, are sometimes funny and many times moving. Sermon illustrations are powerful for grabbing our attention and grounding significant aspects of a sermon. Yet in what ways are our sermon illustrations exclusionary and limiting to the imaginations of congregants to hear and value other voices and experiences, taking us beyond our own parochial interests? In what ways might they reinforce our particular perspectives, for the sake of connecting with *us,* an *us* that may be in sore need of a larger moral perspective and an ethical jab?

Sermon illustrations may be a way to both challenge our limited perspectives and enlarge our awareness of the world around us. In other words, *who* gets talked about and *how* may be another way to heighten our moral sensitivities and ethical concerns. Allow me to give a personal example. I spent the majority of my adult life as a single person and married for the first time when I was forty-eight years old. I was often told to accept singleness as a gift, most times ironically by married persons. I did find being single wonderfully rich in many ways and painfully lonely in others, and today accept marriage to Mike as a gift and a different kind of life that does not replace or minimize the years before June 11, 2005. In spite of the rhetoric of "singleness as a gift," the messages I received in evangelical churches were quite the opposite, and this was never clearer than in the preponderance of sermon illustrations using marriage, the nuclear family, and child rearing as the foci for grounding biblical texts and for illustrating what is perceived to be normal for evangelical Christians, especially women. I do not think this practice was intended to exclude, but it did, a larger number of congregants than imagined, simply based on the assumption of "whose" concerns matter and why.

Sermon illustrations send powerful messages as to who is important and what concerns catch the attention of white evangelicals. They often reify our own experiences and exclude the concerns of others outside and beyond the limits of our moral horizons. They tend to keep us where we are, instead of taking us beyond our own limiting experience. Sermon illustrations can be used to heighten our moral awareness. As Marvin McMickle notes, sermon illustrations ought to serve the prophetic function of our preaching not only by connecting with what we understand but also by surprising us and taking us in new directions, because this is what Jesus did as the master illustrator.[5] Even though Jesus's illustrations were in the "realm of familiarity," they also surprised his hearers because they included unlikely examples, such as widows, Samaritans, children, lepers, and the poor, to depict the kind of lives that please God.

We need examples and illustrations to surprise us and to take us beyond ourselves. We need the examples of Iraqi, Lebanese, and Palestinian Christians who are following Christ in contexts of ethnic hostility and cycles of violence and revenge. Christians who have resisted war and have taken a proactive role in working for justice and peace are illustrations of Jesus's ethic of peacemaking. We need to hear their stories and the ways in which they are examples for grounding biblical insights. Christians living in poverty can demonstrate to us the graciousness of abundance while we are consumed with prosperity, without justifying the condition of the poor *because* they teach us about gratitude. We need sermon illustrations that depict women as more than wives and mothers-in-law, the gendered stereotypes that are actually demeaning to women who are wives, mothers, aunts, nieces, sisters, mothers-in-laws, pastors, lawyers, managers, teachers, and leaders. Sermon illustrations, when approached with the possibility for expanding our ethical concerns, can be formative for taking us beyond our narrow points of view to a larger perspective that encompasses the moral concerns and lives of others as examples we need to hear, on which to reflect, and to follow. Their stories too are personal, sometimes funny, and often moving.

Third, preaching can foster moral imagination and possibility by our attention to scripture's inherent social nature and social problems reflected *in the texts themselves.* I remember my hermeneutics class in seminary and hearing repeatedly the adage, "A text without a context is a pretext."

5. Ibid., 111.

Great attention was given to the historical and social contexts of the biblical writers with an emphasis on authorial intent in order to avoid the unforgivable sin of taking a text out of its context, the practice known as proof-texting. Context does matter and all good, serious expository preachers know this. The social world of the scriptures also needs to be preached, because in many ways, this is our social world, fraught with what Charles Campbell describes as the "powers and the principalities."[6] This is an important corrective to our individualistic, personalized, and spiritualized strategies for reading and hearing the Bible that take us out of the realities scripture describes as part of *our* sacred history, as painful, as twisted, and as evil as it is. The scriptures describe a social world. The insights and contributions of biblical scholars working in the area of socio-rhetorical criticism, such as David deSilva, can help us immensely in learning how to take seriously the social contexts and worlds of the scripture in our preaching and other ministry practices.[7] It is *in* their social world that the biblical writers attempt to depict and describe God, God's interaction with the world, human possibilities and failures, the movement we make toward God's preferred future, and the ways in which this movement is sabotaged by the "powers and the principalities." Preaching is a social act and must take seriously social realities described in the Bible and paralleled in our own world as a necessary part of heightening moral awareness and ethical urgency. Preaching does so first by "exposing" the social realities of scripture as part of exposing our own and then by "envisioning" new ways of living radically and subversively against the accepted "powers and principalities."[8] Campbell writes:

> Preachers can expose the powers in numerous ways. In speaking a redemptive word that addresses ignorance, denial, and numbness, preachers will first of all need to employ clear, direct speech to name the powers and to hold up their activities for people to see. Where people are genuinely ignorant, clear naming can be important. Where denial is at work, direct speech may tap

6. Campbell, *Word before the Powers,* chapter 1.

7. I am grateful to my colleague and friend Dr. David deSilva, for his insightful and provocative work in socio-rhetorical criticism and for its contribution to thinking about scripture, ethics, preaching, and other ministry practices. See the following works by David A. deSilva: *An Introduction to the New Testament: Contexts, Methods and Ministry Formation* (Downers Grove, IL: InterVarsity Press, 2004); *Honor, Patronage, Kinship and Purity: Unlocking New Testament Culture* (Downers Grove, IL: InterVarsity Press, 2000); *Perseverance in Gratitude: A Socio-Rhetorical Commentary on the Epistle "To The Hebrews"* (Grand Rapids: Eerdmans, 2000); and *The Hope of Glory: Honor Discourse and New Testament Interpretation* (Collegeville, MN: Liturgical Press, 1999).

8. Campbell, *Word before the Powers,* 106–27.

into the deep knowledge that is already present and bring it to the surface so it can no longer be denied. Such naming may at times come close to a kind of social-issue preaching, but the goal is actually much broader and deeper. The goal is not to focus on one issue, although that may be the presenting matter, but to expose the powers of death–including their spirituality—in order to empower people to begin to live in new ways.[9]

By recognizing that preaching is a social act, an act of speaking about and against the powers and principalities described in scripture and alive in our world, the fourth way in which preaching can be a morally forming task is by attending to *what* we need to focus on in sermons. This may be intentional but is also spontaneous, given the need to address what may be happening in our social context. Some may remember when Amadou Diallo, an immigrant from Guinea, was shot nineteen times out of forty-one shots fired by police officers in the Bronx on February 4, 1999. Mr. Diallo was unarmed in the hallway of an apartment building when police officers fired, thinking the wallet he took from his back pocket was a gun. This shooting occurred three blocks from the church where a student was serving as pastor. This seminary student wondered whether or not to bring up the shooting in his sermon on the subsequent Sunday. I responded, "How could you not bring it up?" I was appreciative of his willingness to adjust what he was planning to do in order to attend to the vital need of his parishioners to name this event in their own backyard and to put it in front of them in the pulpit for the purpose of moral discourse and deliberation and possible action.[10] His desire was to help people think about this situation *from a Christian perspective* by modeling how to talk about it and why we should be concerned, and how we might be possibly called upon to act.

Attending to *what* we need to name in sermons may be an important antidote for unhinging our positions on vital social issues and current events from political ideologies that subvert, capture, and domesticate a distinctly prophetic Christian voice on these issues. Marvin McMickle notes the challenge of preaching in morally contested and politicized spaces when we delve into controversial issues. He writes:

There is literally an epic struggle under way about the place of religion in postmodern society. It is centered on such issues as the origins of the

9. Ibid., 107.

10. I refer again to Allen Verhey's proposal for the church to be a community of moral discourse, deliberation, and discernment in *Remembering Jesus: Christian Community, Scripture, and the Moral Life* (Grand Rapids: Eerdmans, 2002), chapters 1 and 2.

universe and involves such debates as evolution versus creationism and the more recent "intelligent design" theory. In addition, state after state is turning to the ballot box to determine whether the nature of the marriage union will remain one man and one woman. The question is whether our preaching is addressing the questions our people are asking and over which they may be agonizing.[11]

But delve we must, according to McMickle, because people in our congregations are asking,

> What does the Bible teach us about marriage? What is the role of women in the church? What does Jesus have to say on the topic of homosexuality? How does stem cell research infringe on God's role as creator and healer? Is it proper, after September 11, 2001, for a Christian to embrace pacifism and reject war? . . . Is Jesus Christ the only path to salvation? If so, what will happen to the souls of our devout Jewish and Muslim friends who do not confess that Christ is Lord? Is the separation of church and state in conflict with the sovereignty of God? Should a secular, democratic nation use the words "One nation under God" in its pledge of allegiance? Why are there so many different denominations and so many subgroups within almost every denomination?[12]

We must fight our fears and misconceptions that the church is not about prophetic social ministry in our contemporary context, somehow believing that our greatest tasks are "spiritual" and "just saving souls." If Christians are to follow Christ in our complex and pluralistic context, then we must be empowered and equipped to recognize the moral dimensions of our world *through the eyes of Christian faith and commitment*. We must resist the habit of allowing political leaders, elected and nonelected, to shape our moral awareness and to set the rules by which morality is discussed for Christians. This is the task for the church, and the most powerful means by which this can occur is through the practicing of prophetic preaching. McMickle calls for this recovery of prophetic preaching as crucial for increasing our moral capacities and fostering ethical urgency. He writes:

> Prophetic preaching shifts the focus of a congregation from what is happening to them as a local church to what is happening to us as a society. Prophetic preaching then asks the questions, "What is the role or the appropriate response of our congregation, our association and our denomination to the events that are occurring within our society and throughout the world?" Prophetic preaching points out those false gods of comfort and of

11. McMickle, *Star Book of Preaching,* 71.
12. Ibid., 143.

lack of concern and acquiescence in the face of evil that can so easily replace the God of scripture who calls true believers to the active pursuit of justice and righteousness for every member of society. Prophetic preaching never allows the community of faith to believe that participation in the rituals of religious life can ever be an adequate substitute for that form of ministry that is designed to uplift the "least of these" in our world.[13]

Preaching is a treasured practice in churches that are "evangelical," who believe that the gospel is good news to be preached, one that can actually make a difference and be made real in people's lives. It can be a formidable force for Christian ethics if we attend to its morally forming dimensions such as engaged interaction with scripture, and sermon illustrations that tell the unexpected stories that expand our horizons and take us beyond ourselves to others. Preaching that shapes our moral sensibilities places us in social contexts where the "powers and principalities" are operating at death-defying speed. We need help in naming these social realities, which are also named in scripture, and in learning how to live in, contest, and resist in these moral spaces *as Christians*. Prophetic preaching calls us to respond in the spirit and power of the prophets and Jesus, bringing hope and healing, justice and righteousness to an alienated and broken world.

Small Groups

Evangelicals have discovered small groups, as have many Americans.[14] Even though small groups were likely the shape of the early church meeting in homes, and were at the center of Wesleyan spirituality and ethics as class meetings, evangelicals have capitalized on these recent trends toward small groups by actively promoting them as important for spiritual growth and establishing relationships in a place "where everyone knows my name," particularly in larger or megachurches. Many evangelical churches have small-group pastors to oversee this burgeoning aspect of ministry. Our appetite is whetted for small groups by an appeal to our various desires, needs, and life situations. There are small groups for the young married, for singles, for empty-nesters, for people in recovery from trauma and addiction, for working professionals, for men, and for women. In other words, small groups are formed and fashioned around

13. McMickle, *Where Have All The Prophets Gone?* 2–3.
14. See *"I Come Away Stronger": How Small Groups Are Shaping American Religion*, edited by Robert Wuthnow (Grand Rapids: Eerdmans, 1994).

all sorts of personal needs and considerations, reflective of what Robert Bellah refers to as "lifestyle enclaves" as a primary conception of community in American life.[15]

Most evangelicals are fairly familiar with Dr. Martin Luther King's observation that 11:00 a.m. on Sunday morning is the most segregated hour of the week.[16] This ought not to be surprising, given the demographic realities of the social location of white evangelicals and the racial segregation of American life in general. It was true then and it is sadly true now. I fear that the ways in which small groups are formed in many evangelical churches continues the racial segregation of American culture, given the white suburban contexts where many large evangelical churches are located, and also fosters segregation along generational and lifestyle lines. The practice tends to reinforce the desire for comfort and security found in contexts of likeminded souls who share many of the same interests and perspectives and who may see small groups as a way to have needs met and to receive support needed for living the Christian life.

Small groups can be valuable contexts for stretching our moral perspectives. If morality is inherently social, as I have argued, then we need places to learn from others, to test our ideas, to seek advice, and to practice our skills in ethical reflection and moral deliberation. We need places to talk, to deliberate, and to discern. We need places to engage with scripture and with the perspectives of others, particularly perspectives that are not shared or birthed from the same sociocultural context and sets of experiences. While I see preaching as a crucial pastoral task for the moral formation of congregations, I also see small groups as intentional community holding imaginative possibilities for developing skills in moral reflection and ethical deliberation. How might this happen?

First, small groups ought to cut across generational, class, lifestyle, and gender boundaries. This was part of the witness of the early church. Theirs was a powerful, radical, and subversive witness to a culture that was socially stratified, ethnically divided, gendered, and class-conscious, not unlike ours. The power of the gospel was made concrete as the diverse members of the early church began to be together with their differences,

15. See Robert Bellah, Richard Madsen, William Sullivan, Ann Swidler, and Steven Tipton, *Habits of the Heart: Individualism and Commitment in American Life* (Berkeley: University of California Press, 1985), 71–75.

16. See Martin Luther King, "The Role of the Church in Facing the Nation's Chief Moral Dilemma," in *The Papers of Martin Luther King, Jr., Volume 4: Symbol of the Movement, January 1957–December 1958,* edited by Clayborne Carson, Susan Carson, Adrienne Clay, Virginia Shadron, and Kieran Taylor (Berkeley: University of California Press, 2000).

talking about them and working through them *for the sake of one another and for the sake of the gospel.* Small groups that cut across the lines that divide us can be a powerful witness. Small groups ought to cut across generational, class, lifestyle, and gender boundaries because we need wisdom from others who have experience and insights to share. As I mentioned earlier, perhaps the last thing I need is another person "like me." We need others not like ourselves. We need sages and people just starting out on their Christian way. We need the voices of the lonely and those who have lost children. We need the voices of victims and those struggling with their power and privilege. We need men actually listening to women, and women talking out of their own voices across these boundaries. We need those overwhelmed with the pressures of raising children, taking care of parents, and failing in their own bodies and health. We need those who have lost jobs and those making life-changing vocational choices that actually matter for the transformation of our world as opposed to jobs that ensure degrees of success and monetary security. We need them *and* they need us. Together we grow in our capacities to think of others and their concerns, taking them on as our own and allowing their experiences to shape and challenge our own moral perspectives and commitments. This closeness in relational commitments brings others into my space and me into theirs and in doing so builds our capacities for empathy and compassion, virtues crucial for moral reflection and ethical deliberation.

Second, small groups provide opportunities to put into practice the virtues of the Christian life, such as empathy and compassion and so many more. I can see myself as a forgiving, loving, and generous person, but this is not the same as actually being forgiving, loving, and generous. I really do not need to exercise these virtues unless I'm in communities and relationships where I learn to forgive and to experience the bittersweetness of being forgiven of the myriad ways in which I hurt and offend others. Or where I am required to share possessions, or to love those who get under my skin, and I under theirs. I am not the one able to provide the best estimate for how I am learning the virtues of the Christian life. This is the task of others who are helping and observing me in the practices of patience, hope, love, kindness, gentleness, and self-control. Virtues are learned. The context and closeness of small groups may be one way to acquire and practice virtues that are crucial for the formation of Christian character that attempts to model the life of Christ. Small groups can be an important venue for taking us beyond our immediate needs to a grander vision of where we need to go as followers of Christ. Others help us get there by their presence and wisdom and in their differences from us, which can expand the range of our moral capacities and ethical concerns.

Service

My experience in forming and participating in small groups in evangelical contexts has left me with the impression that many see small groups as existing to meet one's needs, whether they be spiritual or some kind of psycho-spiritual or existential needs, shared by the "people like me," to whom I can relate. I also perceive that participants in small groups see growth in Christian maturity as occurring through the amassing of more information, particularly biblical data, through Bible study, popular reading, or various workbooks. There tends to be a linear approach to this perspective that indicates that once one becomes mature, whole, or ready, *then* one can reach out to others in service. I proposed in the previous section that small groups can be a context for learning virtue from and in relationships with others. I also see service, through small groups, as a powerful way for learning the Christian life by following Christ in service to others *as part of* becoming a mature, whole, and responsible Christian.

I worked closely as the Director of Outreach with the Director of Small Groups at an evangelical church. In our time of thinking and reflecting about the meaning and purpose of small groups, we decided to encourage any new group being formed to identify a ministry commitment and service focus as part of their identity. We started this at Christmas time, an easier time for people to think about generosity and service to others. Some of the small groups formed prior to this commitment grimaced at what they perceived to be a legalistic requirement and something that would damage the integrity and closeness of *their* small group. Others jumped right in and, much to their amazement, realized how much this commitment to service actually enhanced the quality of their small communities because they started talking about different things as result of their shared, new experience and their engagement with others beyond their group. They were stretched together in their capacities to think about others, to find balance and perspective about their own problems, and to reach beyond themselves, which broadened their horizons by involvement with various avenues of service.

Imagine the possibilities for moral formation and heightening our ethical sensitivities if a commitment to serving others is placed right in the center of our communities *as a means* for being transformed into the image of Christ instead of being an addendum after we think we have it all together. This builds into the very fabric of our commitments that loving and serving others is loving and serving God. What are some possibilities for us to consider? I offer these suggestions for consideration.

First, a small group can commit to being a community of hospitality, one that is not closed out of fear and safety, but one that is open to others, indicative of our openness to God and willingness to be transformed by others. Christine Pohl provides us with rich biblical, theological, and historical resources for the role of hospitality as a Christian practice in our traditions and communities.[17] She observes that "Christian hospitality was to be remedial, counteracting the social stratification of the larger society by providing a model and equal welcome to everyone."[18] According to Pohl, hospitality is not only remedial, but "central to Christian practice."[19] We have been welcomed into the trinitarian love and community of God. How can we not extend this welcome to others in practices of hospitality, since it is so central to our own identity as Christians and members of Christian communities, once strangers to God who have been welcomed by Christ through the Holy Spirit? Pohl writes:

> Our contemporary situation is surprisingly similar to the early Christian context in which the normative understandings and practices of hospitality were developed. We, like the early church, find ourselves in a fragmented and multicultural society that yearns for relationships, identity, and meaning. Our mobile and self-oriented society is characterized by disturbing levels of loneliness, alienation, and estrangement. In a culture that appears at times to be overtly hostile to life itself, those who reject violence and embrace life bear a powerful witness.[20]

Our ability to welcome others is crucial to the practicing of hospitality as a Christian witness and moral exercise. Small groups can be a way to "recover hospitality" as a concrete manifestation of the welcome and reconciliation of Christ, which gives people a new "home" and new start.

Second, small groups can be avenues not just for charity but for seeking justice by taking on moral concerns as their own. In charity, we give out of our abundance to others in need. This is an important virtue, one that

17. Christine D. Pohl, *Making Room: Recovering Hospitality as Christian Tradition* (Grand Rapids: Eerdmans, 1999).
18. Ibid., 19.
19. Ibid., 31.
20. Ibid., 33.

is able to see the pressing needs of others and respond accordingly. Justice, however, is the means by which we address the causes of deprivation and want. Shalom seeking justice and righteousness works to make things right so that persons might live in justice and peace. Small groups can be grassroots beginnings for taking on particular issues that have created the conditions of injustice. It is easier to become involved in these issues *as a community* than with our individual efforts, as valuable as they may be. Small groups may consider partnering with such groups as Bread for the World, Call to Renewal, and Habitat for Humanity. There is a myriad of local community groups, such as the Ashland Christian Health Center, Pump House Ministries, and the Ohio Association of Free Clinics in my "neighborhood," seeking to provide quality health care to under- and uninsured adults. Organizations and ministries that attempt to transform social structures and the material realities of people's lives, realities that thwart God's intentions for reconciliation, justice, and peace, are wonderful ways to see service *as a means* of heightening moral awareness and developing skills in working for change. *We* need to be involved, and *we* need to be changed and reconverted to the cries of our world for justice and peace.

Final Thoughts

The title of this book, *Reviving Evangelical Ethics: The Promises and Pitfalls of Classic Models of Morality*, encapsulates the concerns, passions, and ideas I have expressed in these chapters. Christian faith and commitment take us beyond classic ideas to ones that are true and transforming. They do so because they are nourished by scripture, which makes the vision of the Christian moral life far richer, more imaginative, and more compelling than anything offered to us by Kant, Mill, and Aristotle. Because of this, our duties as Christians are far more rigorous, and the virtues required are far more Christian. The Christian moral life is offered to us by Jesus Christ and nourished in communities following the kingdom way. This takes us "beyond the classics" and into the imaginative possibilities of how it could be, as we really obey the scriptures, really follow Jesus, and really learn how to live as Christians in the world.

Index